Tax Revolt

Other books by Martin A. Larson

Milton and Servetus
The Theory of Logical Expression
The Modernity of Milton
The Plaster Saint
The Religion of the Occident
Wanton Sinner
Church Wealth and Business Income
The Essene Heritage
The Great Tax Fraud
The Churches: Their Riches, Revenues, and Immunities
Praise the Lord for Tax Exemption
Tax Rebellion: USA
The Federal Reserve and Our Manipulated Dollar
When Parochial Schools Close
The Religious Empire
The Story of Christian Origins
How to Protect Yourself Against the IRS
The Essence of Jefferson
How to Establish a Trust and Reduce Taxation
The IRS vs. the Middle Class
How You Can Save Money on Your Taxes
Jefferson: Magnificent Populist
The Essene-Christian Faith
New Thought: The Religion of
Health, Happiness, and Prosperity

TAX REVOLT

The Battle for the Constitution

Martin A. Larson

Devin-Adair, Publishers
Greenwich, Connecticut

DEDICATION

To all those American patriots working to restore constitutional government in the United States.

Manufactured in the United States of America.

First Edition

Library of Congress Cataloging in Publication Data

Larson, Martin Alfred, 1897-
Tax revolt.

Includes index.
1. Income tax—United States. 2. United States.
Internal Revenue Service. I. Title.
HJ4652.L328 1985 343.7305'2 84-14219
ISBN 0-8159-6922-8 347.30352

Contents

Devin-Adair is America's foremost publisher of quality conservative books. Founded in 1911, the company has championed the cause of the Thinking Right and historically has published the work of major conservative writers. In recent years, Devin-Adair has increased its emphasis in this area and today is considered the leading publishing firm of the Right.

The company also has a long-standing reputation for works of significance in the fields of ecology, Irish literature, health, nutrition and the environment, and Americana. It publishes superbly illustrated nature and travel books on the Eastern Seaboard through its Chatham Press subsidiary.

Devin-Adair's newest emphasis is in the area of books, programs, and software relating to the personal computer.

Devin-Adair operates the Veritas Book Club for conservative readers, the Ecological Book Club for nature and health audiences, and the Irish-American Book Society.

Publisher: Claudine de la Belle Issue
Managing Director: Roger H. Lourie
Book Design and Production: Arthur Hamparian
Jacket Design: Michael Spizzirri
Typesetting: Coghill Book Typesetting Co.
Printing: Fairfield Graphics

Devin-Adair, Publishers
6 North Water Street
Greenwich, Connecticut 06830

EXCELLENCE, SINCE 1911

Introduction

This book deals with a multitude of complaints, but there is no situation or problem discussed herein that could not be resolved simply by a return to constitutional government in the United States. So that is what this work is about: the battle to restore the constitution, waged by American patriots who are struggling to reinstate the Supreme Law of the Land as left us by our Founding Fathers.

The individuals, publications, and organizations criticizing or resisting income taxation and other federal procedures are indeed numerous and increasing; and those who are now rebelling—in one way or another—total in the tens of millions. Most are merely intent upon retaining more of their own earnings or savings; but all agree that the restoration of constitutional government is their grand objective.

Those who oppose government policies, for the most part, focus their attention upon the Internal Revenue Service and the Federal Reserve System, both of which are in violation of the Constitution, either in their structure, their operation, or both.

Let us then summarize some of the positions taken by spokesmen for a movement which included only a handful of patriots ten or fifteen years ago, but which has now proliferated to a point where it involves a considerable portion of our entire population.

There are those who say that the Constitution is now outworn, that it was the product of a horse-and-buggy age, and that modern developments require centralization and increased functions and powers for government. But consider this: All the current abuses from which our producers suffer so bitterly are similar or identical to those against which our Founding Fathers rebelled; for the nature of tyranny is basically the same in all social forms; and the Constitution which the Founders left to us—especially the Bill of Rights—was devised specifically to prevent for all time a recurrence of depredations by the government against its citizens. No: The Constitution is not outworn or passé; it is the bastion and the beacon-light of liberty and self-reliance, of political and economic justice, the ideal of those who now speak for the burgeoning rebellion.

In passing the Federal Reserve Act, the Congress conferred upon a consortium of private financiers, operating on a global scale, one of the most important functions mandated to it by the Constitution, that is, the power to coin (or issue) money and regulate the value thereof, which means the control of the nation's monetary system and policies. Our national legislature had no more constitutional authority to do this than it has to confer upon a private corporation the power to lay and collect taxes or to raise armies and wage war at its discretion, regardless of the sophistry used to justify this action.

In violation of the Fourth Amendment, the Internal Revenue Service is empowered by its statute to examine the private records of individuals and corporations; to obtain other private documents of third parties that pertain to the taxpayer; and to punish any refusal to accede to such demands with fines, imprisonment, and the confiscation of property.

In flagrant violation of the Fifth Amendment, the IRS

1. forces everyone to make complete disclosure of his most personal affairs and is able to use this information, not only to assess more taxes, but for criminal indictments and prosecution, in spite of the fact that no one shall be compelled to be a witness against himself;
2. seizes bank accounts, real estate, and other property without due process of law or even establishing that any tax liability exists;
3. compels taxpayers to prove their innocence on pain of property confiscation;
4. often arrests and tries citizens without a grand jury indictment.

In violation of the Seventh Amendment, the IRS denies the taxpayer the right to a jury trial, no matter how great a sum may be in dispute.

When the Service uses information obtained from secret informers to indict taxpayers and/or seize their property, and when judges at the trials of tax patriots refuse them the right to subpoena government witnesses for examination, they are all in violation of the Sixth Amendment.

Since the IRS arrogates to itself the legislative, judicial, and executive functions of government, it violates the constitutional principle of separation of powers and is, therefore, guilty of what James Madison called the perfect definition of tyranny.

By conferring Sovereign Immunity—that holdover from the Divine Right of Kings—upon its agents, the Internal Revenue Code violates the spirit of the Constitution.

By establishing its Tax Court—which it pretends is independent of the Service, but which is actually an integral part of it—it is in violation of ART. III, Section 1, of the Constitution, which provides for the establishment of tribunals inferior to the Supreme Court, but which must observe constitutional procedures.

When federal judges at trials of tax patriots deny them the right to quote provisions of the Constitution, they violate their oaths of office. When such judges show bias against the defendants, they are no longer objective referees, but have become a part of the prosecution. When judges prevent defendants or defense lawyers from advising a jury that it has the right of nullification, or punishes them for doing so or attempting to do so, they are in violation of constitutional law.

Those who oppose the operation of the Internal Revenue Service agree unanimously that they do so on the basis of the Constitution, because:

1. It employs deceit, misrepresentation, threats, and actual lies in order to collect taxes not due.

2. It conceals the rights of the taxpayer and distorts the meaning of provisions in its own statute in order to collect taxes not due.

3. If it does not actually pay bonuses to agents who are unusually successful in seizing property or obtaining quick consent agreements, there is no doubt that agents who compile outstanding records in such work are in line for important promotions and eventually, perhaps, even judgeships in the Tax Court.

4. It illegally seizes not only property owned by taxpayers, but any asset held by others and due the taxpayer, including equities in insurance policies.

5. It pays spies, informers, and betrayers to give information to the IRS.

6. Its code is filled with esoteric, even contradictory provisions, in language so obscure that no one can understand it, which serves a twofold purpose: (a) it enables IRS agents to collect taxes not due from ordinary taxpayers; and (b) it enables clever lawyers, representing rich clients, to defeat the IRS even when it files a valid deficiency judgment.

7. The entire Code is a fraud which violates the principle of equality before the law because while it purports to impose progressive taxation, it is filled with loopholes, exclusions, and deductions by which the rich and favored can escape most or all taxation, and at the same time contains traps and snares to destroy the honest, self-reliant middle-class taxpayer, unable to defend himself in this swamp of obscure statutory law.

8. The IRS is known to audit certain taxpayers year after year and to invent some excuse for making a deficiency levy, which is usually paid, since it seems easier and cheaper to do so than to hire competent and reliable counsel for defense.

9. The IRS sometimes forces taxpayers to spend thousands of dollars to prove that no additional tax is due.

10. Whenever it is successful in convicting an individual, the in-

formation is made available throughout the news media; however, when the IRS loses or commits an atrocity, it says nothing or refuses to comment, based on the provisions of the Privacy Act.

11. One of the particularly detestable practices of the IRS is to seize property belonging to third parties who owe nothing to the delinquent taxpayer and who have no dispute with the Agency, for example, a warehouse rented by a person who has some dispute with the Service. Such action is in direct violation of its own law, as stated in Section 6331(b) of the Code.

12. Although the Sixteenth Amendment authorizes only levies on revenue, the IRS Code taxes various transactions that do not produce any income; these levies are therefore illegal under its own law. For example, it will tax a person who owns shares in a corporation if it purchases stock by going into debt, calling it a constructive dividend (Sections 544(a)(1) and 1,239(c)), even though the corporation is no richer than before and even though the stockholder neither receives any income nor owns any asset with an increased worth. It also taxes as capital gain the value of stock received by the owner or owners of a corporation when it is dissolved if the assets of the corporation are greater than when the stock was first issued.

There are other situations in which the IRS taxes transactions that produce no income for anyone.

The Federal Reserve and the Internal Revenue Service work together to harass and impoverish the members of the middle class, and, as a result, an enmity has developed between them which can only become more intense. An IRS *Supplement*, dated January 10, 1979, warned its agents against calling at the homes of suspected tax resisters without an armed escort; agents have sometimes been subjecte to abuse and harassment, even beatings. The Gordon Kahl case, which has received wide publicity, is undoubtedly only one example.

The roots of all these problems lie in the unconstitutionality of the Fed, the IRS Code, and their operation and implementation. The solution, therefore, is quite simple: a return to the principles so clearly enunciated in the Constitution.

However, the violations committed by the Internal Revenue Service in its administration and by the Federal Reserve in its operation, are not the only ones of which the federal government is guilty. Is it not ironic that the Congress should confer one of its principal powers and functions upon a private corporation, while arrogating to itself an untold number of activities that are specifically prohibited? These include the Social Security system and a multitude of other programs which, under the Ninth and Tenth Amendments, are left to the states or to the people.

Another example of federal violation of the Constitution consists in retaining and owning about 25 percent of the entire land area of the United States in direct violation of ART. I, Sect. 8, Clause 17. In the western states, this ratio exceeds 40 percent. Even worse, perhaps, is the fact that the government operates an enormous and very costly power grid in competition with private enterprise, which, even though it pays no taxes of any kind, or any interest, dividends, or other costs imposed on private enterprise, still operates at heavy deficits—as do all government-owned enterprises.

Thus we find that the federal government has become an almost total subversion of the Constitution. The movement we describe in this volume is dedicated simply and totally to a restoration of the ideals that were the passionate convictions of our Founding Fathers.

In this work, I make no secret of my beliefs or sympathies. I am unalterably committed to the repeal of the Federal Reserve Act and to the abolition of federal income taxation. In my estimation, therefore, those who have been crushed, destroyed, or imprisoned by the Internal Revenue Service are martyrs to a great cause; and those who have won court victories over the IRS or defeated it in other ways are nothing less than heroes.

Martin A. Larson

Prolegomenon

I am sometimes asked why I am so deeply involved in the problem of income taxation and the inequities in IRS laws and administration; I reply that my primary concern is not with any financial considerations, but rather with the injustice and the discrimination inseparable from them. They are a cancer on our body politic; and until they are eliminated, there will be no peace, freedom, or constitutional government in the United States. It is as simple and as basic as that.

I should also state that my concern began many years ago as the result of personal experiences which, I am certain, were no worse than those suffered by millions of other Americans.

So here is the historical background for my involvement.

The time was 1945–46, shortly after WW II; for ten years, I had worked an average of twelve hours every day, six days a week, in my Detroit paint store; I had never had a vacation; I lived in a room I had constructed in the upper back of the shop; my personal expenses, including food, were about a dollar a day; and, against almost overwhelming odds, I had made a success of the business. By this time, I owned two apartment houses, with 58 rental units, that cost $142,000; my gross income was about $65,000 a year, and my after-tax net about $25,000, at a time when the average pay for all federal employees was less than $3,000.

I had survived the onslaughts of the federal Office of Price Administration (OPA), which destroyed about seven million small landlords in the United States; I had obtained paint for my customers when almost all other dealers lost their sources of supply because they had entered into exclusive contracts with the federal government. I was on my way to financial independence.

Then I discovered for the first time that the true purpose of the Internal Revenue Service is not primarily to collect taxes, but to regiment and control the people; to make some fabulously wealthy, while destroying those whom it resents or fears. Since I was guilty of succeeding in a small and highly competitive business—a crime for which an arrogant bureaucracy had no tolerance—I was targeted for destruction. I discovered that those who think for themselves and cannot be closely policed are the true enemies of the super-state.

Also to my "discredit," was the fact that I had made myself highly visible and obnoxious by writing a great number of letters, printed in the Detroit *News* and *Free Press*, in which I condemned the operations of the federal government in general and of the OPA in particular. I was also the president of a taxpayer's association that made its influence felt in local politics. Finally, I was guilty of far too much strident criticism of federal rent control; every year, I testified before congressional committees about its iniquities.

When I was ordered to appear at the IRS office, however, I had no fear; after all, I had made complete disclosure of my finances and, to the best of my belief and knowledge, had paid every penny of taxes due. In fact, most years I had paid enough to support at least two full-time bureaucrats.

For several years, I had been doing income tax work during the slow season preceding March 15; I sometimes had from 50 to 75 clients a day, and I never had a single complaint from anyone about my work.

I therefore slept well. But I was due for a rude awakening. When I appeared at IRS headquarters, an arrogant bureaucrat informed me brusquely that they *knew* that I had *evaded* $45,000 in taxes, and that before they were through with me, they would not only confiscate everything I owned, but would also see me behind bars! "Over my dead body, you will," was my retort.

I was then ordered to surrender all records pertaining to my paint business and apartment houses, including all bank statements, deposit slips, checkbook stubs, invoices, rental journals, receipt books—everything! They kept all this material for eighteen months. In addition, I was ordered to prepare a Ten-Year-Net-Worth Statement, listing my total assets ten years previously, all personal expenditures, total income, and my net worth at the close of that year; and then make the same computation for each succeeding year. Outraged by this demand, I asked a prominent attorney-friend whether I could be forced to comply. His answer was: "No, but if you don't the IRS will, without previous notice, come to your store, seize and carry away everything in it that is movable; they will also take any money you have in bank accounts; and they will go to your apartment buildings and force the tenants to pay *them* their rentals and leave you with the obligation of paying all taxes, utilities, repairs, and other operational expenses; and if you fail to do so, your buildings will also be seized—all without the slightest process of law."

I therefore prepared the notorious Ten-Year-Net-Worth Statement—largely from memory. And since I never heard any more about it, I concluded that the IRS had been unable to find any serious flaw therein.

The battle continued for about a year and a half. Since this was the period in which almost every IRS auditing agent—including the Commissioner and eight Regional Commissioners—were enriching themselves by soliciting bribes in return for giving evaders clean bills of health, a lawyer-friend slyly suggested that I take my auditor—a woman—to lunch, and, just before leaving, place twenty twenty-dollar Federal Reserve notes under her plate, so that she could see the corners of them. My reply was that I would rather cut off my arm than bribe a stinking bureaucrat.

When the IRS found that their original threats against me could not be sustained, they attempted to add more than $10,000 to my tax liability by disallowing a multitude of perfectly valid business deductions; in all these attempts, however, I was able to defeat them, and I thought I would emerge virtually unscathed. Then it was that a smart snoop discovered that I had purchased one of my apartments in a February and that an obscure provision in the Code provided that, in such event, *only the seller could deduct property taxes as a business expense during the following eighteen months!* It was an incredible fact; I simply could not believe that so absurd and ridiculous a law was actually on the books—but it was, and it cost me about $2,000. This provision was deleted when the Code was revised in 1954.

Finally, the agent called me and stated that they were sure I had underreported my income by several thousand dollars, but that they could not prove it; to which I responded: "Now, isn't that just too, too bad!" My documents were then returned; I paid the assessment based on the trap in which I had been caught, and was left undisturbed for fifteen years.

But as the outrage I had suffered sank deep and deeper into my consciousness, I made a vow that if ever I could do anything to compel this monster to operate with some semblance of decency and legality, it would become a principal objective of my life. However, I had to wait many years; it was only about 1967 that I could begin doing something to fulfill that vow—when I wrote a book called *The Great Tax Fraud*.

We should note that we have come a long way since that day I was summoned to appear at IRS headquarters: The Agency can no longer force anyone to submit the outrageous Ten-Year-Net-Worth Statement; it cannot compel anyone to bring in and leave records at an IRS office; it is not empowered or permitted to copy them or remove them from the taxpayer's home or office; threats against taxpayers can now bring dismissals from the Service; the Privacy Act and the Freedom of Information Act—unknown in 1945–46—can now be used for the taxpayer's protection; the IRS may no longer examine the records of any year more than once; if an audit results in no additional tax, but requires expenditures by the taxpayer to prove his innocence, the IRS can be forced to reimburse him. It cannot examine records held by a third party, including a bank, without lengthy hearings and litigation. In various other ways also the talons of the Service have been clipped.

Then, in 1961, during the presidency of John Kennedy—whom I had opposed in several published articles—my next confrontation with the IRS occurred. Three years before, I had traded a debt-free apartment building for another which was mortgaged; at the exchange, I received a check which I used at once to pay off the encumbrance. Now, the IRS declared that this money was taxable "boot" and that, as a result, I owed $24,000 in capital gains taxes, interest, and penalties. A tax "expert" wanted $2,000 in advance to do the necessary research for my defense and added that he would expect a goodly portion of any amount he might save me by "negotiation." I decided to do my own research and write my own brief in carrying the case to the Appellate Division. However, when I asked the leading tax lawyer with the most prestigious law firm in Arizona (where I had moved) to accompany me to the meeting with the Appellate judge, he agreed that the money was due; but that, since the three-year statute of limitations had expired, the IRS case rested on shaky ground. Therefore, he offered to settle at thirty percent. The judge said that he had intended to offer a seventy-five percent settlement, but later he accepted the thirty percent compromise.

However, in due course I discovered, without the help of any lawyer, that because I had sold a commercial project in Phoenix at a loss, I was entitled to a refund of $45,000—the amount I had paid in 1960 after dissolving my corporation. I also discovered that I had overpaid my taxes in 1959 by an amount equal to the sum called for in the agreement with the Appellate judge. Instead of paying the IRS so much as one penny, and without the aid of a CPA or a lawyer, I collected $38,500 from them; even so, they cheated me out of $7,000, as they should have refunded me the full $45,000.

Some years later, my research revealed that not only the IRS but also the high-priced lawyer—to whom I paid $350 for about three hours of his time—was completely in error; I did not owe anything under IRS law, since the exchange of the apartments did not result in a gain. The whole procedure was based on sheer bluff and deceit, and the ghastly part was that the lawyer agreed to it. Under Section 1031(b), because there was no gain in the transaction, only the assumption of a debt which cancelled the money received, no tax was due. It was admitted on all sides that had the owner of the apartment building I received in the trade paid off the mortgage previous to the consummation of the trade, I would not have been charged with any tax liability.

After I was convinced that the levy was illegal, I wrote IRS headquarters describing the transaction and asking whether a tax levy could be due as a result. I received several lengthy letters, but never a definite answer. The IRS continued its policy of bluff and tergiversation.

As a result of my own experiences and my observation of what has happened to others, I have been forced to conclude that the Internal Revenue Service is a criminal operation, guilty of deceit and misinterpretation. It capitalizes on the fears and ignorance of the ordinary taxpayer; it utilizes the ambiguities and complexities of the IR Code to collect money not due under its own law.

An additional example from my own experience is illustrative: Some years ago, I owned a warehouse in which a tenant was delinquent in his taxes. The IRS went to the premises in the middle of the night, removed *my* locks, substituted its own, and posted the building as government property. Since Section 6331(b) states specifically that the IRS may levy only against the assets of the delinquent or upon obligations due him, it cannot, under its own law, commandeer the property of a third party with whom it has no current dispute and who owes nothing to the person who does. I demanded that the IRS cite authority for seizing my building in order to impound the personal property of my tenant. After a great deal of correspondence, *their* defense was that they had not seized *my* property at all—only its contents. When I asked what they would call such action, posting my building as government property, they replied that further argument would be useless.

I then asked them if they had authority to enter another building, eject an owner or tenant, and use it for the storage of the seized personal property; and if not, how was that different from what they had done in my case. To this, I received no reply at all. They did offer to pay the actual rent of the building for the days they had it under seizure, provided I could prove that the tenant had paid nothing for these days. So, at least I had a reply of sorts.

I should add here that after receiving the refund of $38,500 and paying nothing on the IRS demand for $24,000 in 1961–62, the Agency has left me strictly alone. My observation has been that if a taxpayer gives them a good whipping, they will avoid him in the future as if he had an infectious plague that might be transmitted to any IRS agent attempting to audit him again.

Tax Revolt

1

The Pioneer Constitutionalists

Austin Flett: Agitator and Lecturer

Austin Flett of Chicago was one of the earliest and best known among modern American tax resisters. As a lecturer, pamphleteer, propagandist, and constitutionalist, he was without peer.

His interest in tax discrimination began in 1942 when he found that tax-exempt underwriters could undersell the protection he offered as an insurance broker. He spent several years studying cooperatives and other tax-exempts and in 1954 he embarked on a public career to obtain basic reforms in the federal tax structure. After he lost his job, he began appearing on radio and TV programs and earned considerable sums by lecturing throughout the country. In 1956, he paid a tax of $277.07 under protest; in 1957, he paid $903.13 under the same conditions. Thereafter, and for the remainder of his life, he not only filed in blank, but billed the government for progressively increasing sums due him for information by which the IRS might collect vast sums from such tax dodgers as co-ops, credit unions, mutual banks, churches, foundations, etc. In 1959, he demanded $5 million; in 1961, $25 million; and in 1966, $50 million.

On April 15, 1960, he wrote Douglas Dillon, Secretary of the Treasury: "I will complete the information demanded on this form and pay whatever income tax may be due . . . after I have . . . been indicted by a federal grand jury so that I may state and prove the fact that known and unknown officials of the Treasury Department are guilty of violating many Federal laws that relate to the collection and disbursement of public funds."

He declared that these officials were using taxpayer funds to finance outright subversion of the Constitution. On March 30, 1963, he wrote again, asking that he be indicted and tried by a jury so that he might expose the fact that "certain officials of the United States Treasury are guilty of violating Section[s] 241, 371, 1,001, 2,381, 2,382, 2,383, 2,384 and 2,385 of Title 18, U.S. Criminal Code, and the Constitution. . . . I am prepared to resume assisting officials of the Treasury Department to prove their case and collect unpaid taxes from organizations that have been guilty of defrauding the government."

On April 5, 1966, he had his wish: A criminal information was issued against him for filing in blank. When the Service tried to effect a compromise settlement, he scornfully refused. The IRS seemed completely powerless.

We should note that Flett never challenged the constitutionality of the Sixteenth Amendment itself—only its administration. He was, nevertheless, no small thorn in the side of the IRS. Since he kept no bank or checking account, since he owned no property (not even the furniture in his office), and since whatever income he received was in the form of cash and not subject to SS or income tax withholding, the IRS could neither determine what he earned nor seize any assets. He declared repeatedly that if you want to fight the IRS, you should divest yourself of all visible assets and have no traceable income.

However, even though there was nothing for the IRS to seize, they continued to harass him. They assessed deficiencies, which remained unpaid; they sent letters to organizations that sponsored his lectures, demanding detailed information concerning fees, expenses, manner of payment, photostats of checks, number of people attending meetings, etc. On July 20, 1965, the La Salle National Safe Deposit Corporation was forced to permit the IRS to break into Flett's safe deposit box, where, to the Service's chagrin, they found nothing but material denouncing IRS officials as "communist conspirators."

According to a headline in the New York *Daily News* of April 15, 1967, he had recently fired his "9th Blank at the Tax Man." On January 6, 1969, he wrote that, ". . . there is nothing in the Constitution of the U.S. Criminal Code that states that taxpayers shall, under threat of prison sentences, be forced via . . . audits, liens, levies, seizure notices, summons for production of records . . . to pay the Federal income taxes of approximately 1,200,000 tax-exempt, non-audited and non-supervised politically favored . . . organizations . . . that, as political 'sacred cows' unlawfully escape each year, the payment of many billions of dollars of Federal income taxes."

Mr. Flett declared that as a result of IRS harassment, he had been forced to spend $200,000 and had been involved in nine court cases, in all of which he acted as his own counsel. (By declaring he had spent such sums, he must also, by implication, have admitted earning them; nevertheless, the IRS was unable to prosecute because it could not document such income.)

On August 28, 1969, the government made a last desperate effort to silence Mr. Flett. Chief Judge William J. Campbell of the U.S. District Court of Northern Illinois ordered Flett to report to a government hospital for psychiatric evaluation. Instead, he went to Washington where he had a series of conferences with officials in the Justice and Treasury Departments and with various members of Congress. He did not undergo any mental examination; instead, on January 4, 1970, at the age of 77, he filed his return for 1969 in blank for the twelfth consecutive time. The story made headlines everywhere. In a June release, he urged citizens to organize in local groups, publicize the illegal acts of the government, and protest the extortion of taxes for criminal subversion.

On March 18, 1969, Flett took a bold and unprecedented step: Acting for himself in his own proper person, he filed suit in the Northern United States District Court of Illinois against Judge William J. Campbell, United States Attorney Thomas Foran, and IRS District Director Eugene C. Doyle, Jr., charging them with violations of the Constitution by proceeding against citizens in income tax cases via the Administrative Procedures Act of 1946 and by collaborating in criminal acts in violation of Title 18, USC, Sections 241, 242,371, and 1,001. He also declared that in depriving him of a trial by jury, the IRS had violated not only the Civil Rights Act but also the Sixth and Seventh Amendments to the Constitution. He demanded damages in the sum of $2,000,000 for "unlawful harassment, intimidation, threats, obstruction of justice, deprivation of rights of citizenship, character assassination, and premeditated criminal libel."

On June 26, 1970, the case was "Dismissed for lack of jurisdiction."

Austin Flett did not pay one penny of income tax during the last thirteen years of his life. He would not compromise. The government did not give him a jury trial, but instead attempted to railroad him into an institution for the criminally insane. But he was not intimidated. He never handed over any records. No one ever laid a hand on him.

On June 21, 1971, he delivered an address at the Breakfast Club of Phoenix, Arizona. As he finished, the audience gave him a standing ovation. He was, however, hardly aware of the applause, for in that instant he was struck down with a massive coronary occlusion and he died instantly—with his boots on.

He could have been only dimly aware of the immense crop growing from the seeds he had sown. If all those who now file in blank or do not file at all got newspaper headlines such as his, there would be no room for any other material in the newspapers.

Vivien Kellems: Embattled Warrior

For many years, the redoubtable Vivien Kellems of Connecticut had operated the Cable Grip Company, which she sold in 1962. She first gained national publicity in 1948 when she refused to collect and transmit income and Social Security taxes to the IRS. Although her 100 employees had paid these levies themselves, the government seized $8,000 from her bank account; she then sued for a refund, which she obtained after a jury trial. However, the bureaucrats harassed her, causing her great expense, untold anguish, and much loss of time; and finally they were able to avoid a Supreme Court test on the constitutionality of the 1942 law that requires all employers to be unpaid tax collectors, by inserting Section 3402(d) into the Code, which provides that if employees make all of their own payments directly, the employer will not be liable for them; however, if they do not, the latter must pay the entire levy. Thus, the IRS won by evading the issue, for few employees will make their own reports with double contributions to Social Security, nor are the employers likely to take the same risk.

In 1952, Miss Kellems published *Toil, Taxes, and Trouble*, describing in detail her confrontation with the IRS.

It was not until about 1970 that she became a tax rebel in the larger sense, rather than merely a critic of certain features of the system. On March 17, 1971, she published an Open Letter to the Secretary of the Treasury, John B. Connally, in the Washington *Post*, describing her latest battle. She stated that on October 7, 1970, two IRS "cogs"—as she called them—intruded upon her privacy to examine her personal records, which she refused to surrender, quoting the Fourth and Fifth Amendments of the Constitution. The Sixteenth Amendment, she declared,

> did not nullify my rights under the 4th Amendment, nor is it possible for Congress to pass any law which takes these rights away from me. The only way to get these documents is to get a Court Order. In that case, I wish you to explain in detail exactly what documents you wish. If you want cancelled checks, I want the dates, the amounts and the persons to whom issued. Every single document must be described in detail, because you have no power whatsoever to take these documents from me. They're my personal property and the Constitution says my right to personal property shall not be violated.

She also cited the Fifth Amendment against the possibility of self-incrimination and added: "You are accusing me of being a thief and a liar. You are demanding my property to make me incriminate myself and to prove that I am dishonest. I refuse. . . ."

On December 16, 1969, Judge Canella in the United States District Court ordered her to surrender her records. But when she ignored this ruling, she was hauled before Judge Zampano on February 25, 1970, in the U.S. District Court in New Haven, where she appeared *pro se*. The IRS sent several high-ranking "cogs," who attempted to trick her into stating under oath that her tax returns were fraudulent, but she reminded them tartly that no one has to convict himself of perjury in order to plead the Fifth Amendment, and she added: "A tax proceeding of this kind is the only one in our whole legal process where a person is dragged into court as guilty and must prove his own innocence. Everywhere else, a person is innocent and it is up to the Petitioner to prove he is guilty. I come here accused and guilty before I even open my mouth."

It soon became apparent that the prestigious bureaucrats were on their way to defeat. The judge gave both parties two weeks to prepare supporting briefs which Miss Kellems did; however, the Assistant Attorney General, Tax Division, Johnnie M. Walters—later Commissioner of Internal Revenue—wrote that ". . . it is the wish of this Office, having studied the transcript of the hearing, to withdraw our request for enforcement of the three summonses at issue. We are of the opinion that Miss Kellems has properly pleaded the Fifth Amendment privilege against self-incrimination as to her payment records."

Thus, the IRS officially admitted that it has no right or power to commandeer personal records in the face of a Fifth Amendment plea *even when the taxpayer denies any danger of self-incrimination*. By implication, it also admitted that many provisions in the IR Code are unconstitutional and therefore null and void.

Again, the IRS evaded the real issue. However, on December 27, 1970, the Agency placed assessments against Miss Kellems of $43,346.10 for 1966 and $6,507.95 for 1967. They simply disallowed all deductions which had been reported and assumed that property she sold was without basis or book value. "I wouldn't demean myself," she retorted tersely, even "by discussing such ridiculous figures."

After this confrontation, Miss Kellems not only refused to show any records but also stopped making any returns or paying any taxes at all. She defied the IRS to do its worst, and it did nothing in regard to her. They made no attempt even to collect the assessment levied in 1970 on the returns for 1966 and 1967.

Hers had, in fact, became the kind of highly sensitive case that must not be prosecuted and which is described in the documents the IRS was eventually forced to make public and which were published by the Church of Scientology as *The IRS Papers*.

Miss Kellems died in January 1975 at the age of 78, after nearly thirty years of constant warfare over government taxing policies. As noted above, she made no reports and paid no taxes during the last seven or eight years of her life, although the IRS was well aware that she had a substantial personal income. Shortly after her death, I received a letter from the firm of attorneys that handled her $1.8 million estate, stating that only $265,000 had been paid to the government in full settlement. Thus, we know that no income taxes were paid even after her death.

J. Bracken Lee: American Statesman

Among elected officials, the great majority are mere time-serving politicians who could scarcely care less about the future welfare of their cities, states, or nation, but who are principally, if not wholly, concerned with the outcome of the next election. There are, however, exceptions; among these, the Honorable J. Bracken Lee, former governor of Utah and mayor of Salt Lake City, is perhaps America's most brilliant and praiseworthy example.

Mr. Lee began his public career in Price, Utah, where he served as mayor from 1936 to 1947; he was governor of his state from 1949 to 1957; and mayor of Salt Lake City from 1960 to 1972.

Early in his career, he focused attention on himself by opposing an almost all-powerful federal government and as an exponent of free enterprise. And, since he directed his attacks especially against the Internal Revenue Service and served as Director of the National Committee to Repeal the Sixteenth Amendment, he became the target for IRS retaliation. Beginning in 1935 and until 1968, he was audited every year; and every year the Service found something on which to hang a deficiency—usually a few hundred dollars, which he paid because it was easier than doing the research necessary to defend himself and cheaper than hiring competent counsel for defense. However, since he was convinced that the constant extortions were unjustified, illegal, and actually the result of bureaucractic venom against him, he began to feel intense hostility toward the federal octopus, which found expression in various ways. On one occasion he said that IRS agents should be required to wear red uniforms so that taxpayers could take a bead on them.

About 1952–53, he decided to test the validity of federal grants and loans to nations, some socialist or communist, who were enemies of the American people. He therefore withheld and placed in trust a portion of his income tax, saying that he would release this if the Supreme Court finally upheld the constitutionality of such giveaways. The IRS promptly—albeit illegally—invoked the jeopardy assessment, under which it impounded all his assets so that he had no money to pay personal expenses. In due course, all were freed, except some seized from the bank without a hearing or any due process of law. After the United States District Court and the

Circuit Court of Appeals ruled against him, the Supreme Court denied certiorari; thus, the IRS again avoided a legal adjudication.

This experience created even greater resentment in Mr. Lee. Why should the IRS invoke the Jeopardy Assessment against the governor of a sovereign state, since the purpose of this law was only to prevent delinquent tax-evaders from fleeing the country with their assets? Was the IRS afraid that the Governor would abscond to South America? Not so! It wished merely to squelch an outstanding patriot and to terrorize anyone else who might question the authority of the Internal Revenue Service.

In 1969 and 1970, there was a new development; as a result of his wife's illness, Mr. Lee submitted returns showing heavy medical deductions. When he was ordered to bring his records to the IRS headquarters to verify the deductions, he declined, saying it was a trap to enmesh him further; that the IRS could easily determine his expenses by calling the hospital where his wife had been treated and the doctors who had attended her. This, of course, the IRS refused to do, and simply disallowed all deductions and levied a deficiency of more than $28,000.

Now, finally, Mr. Lee was forced to mount a defense; he obtained an honest, competent, and fearless counsel who proved to the IRS that the mayor had overpaid and that a refund of $13.90 was due him, which was paid.

After that, Mr. Lee was left alone—no more telephone calls, no more letters, no more audits from the IRS.

In a letter dated March 1, 1972, Mr. Lee wrote:

> I agree with you concerning the tax burden and its ultimate destruction of this country. . . .
>
> I did not run for re-election as Mayor of Salt Lake City because of the feeling that Washington is slowly but surely taking over the operation of the states through the so-called furnishing of tax-dollars from Washington. I retired as Mayor of Salt Lake City on January 3, 1972, and do not again intend to seek public office.

So declared one of the finest and greatest of the patriot-statesmen and constitutionalists ever to walk on American soil since the days of Thomas Jefferson.

Arthur Julius Porth: Father of the Movement

Arthur J. Porth, a former Wichita, Kansas, contractor, became, and for some time remained, America's best-known and most active tax rebel. He was well in advance of Flett in techiques of resistance, and the first to utilize the full panoply of the Constitution in defense.

His first battle occurred in 1952, when, having transmitted $125 withheld from the pay of his employees, he sued the IRS for a refund, contending that as an unpaid tax collector, he was subjected to involuntary servitude, outlawed by the Thirteenth Amendment.

In 1957, having seized Mr. Porth's records, the IRS assessed a deficiency of $4,000; when he refused to pay, a lien was placed on his house. The result was a compromise settlement of $3,000.

Persuaded that this was barefaced extortion, Mr. Porth transferred full ownership of the property to his wife, who then submitted her own separate income tax returns. From that day on, he had nothing of value for the IRS to seize. And when he read the 1927 Supreme Court decision in *U.S.* vs. *Sullivan* (which states that a taxpayer need not divulge privileged or incriminating information), he decided to become a full-fledged tax resister.

Thus fortified, he began his crusade. For 1961, 1962, and 1963, he submitted his 1040s in blank, with the statement "I plead the V Amendment to the Constitution of America." On December 27, 1962, Mr. T. Peltzer, IRS agent, sent Mr. Porth a summons demanding that he surrender all records relating to his income and expenses for the calendar year 1961. Mr. Porth ignored the summons.

During 1963, the IRS continued to harass him; after suffering a heart attack and spending a great deal of money in what seemed a futile crusade, he turned over his 1963 records to the IRS in Wichita on April 15, 1964. Since there was only a small net income, he was under the impression that this would be the best way to solve his difficulties. In so doing, however, he committed his greatest error; for, having voluntarily surrendered his documents, he was at last open to prosecution on a criminal charge. The IRS computed his personal federal tax at $438.51 and his self-employment tax at $134.75—a total of $573.24.

With material to indict on a criminal charge, the IRS lost no time in preparation. In the meantime, unaware of the IRS plans to entrap him, Mr. Porth continued to study the Constitution, the Federal Reserve System, the Internal Revenue Code, and various other laws and documents; as a result, his resistance assumed a more elaborate and sophisticated form, which he proclaimed to all who would listen. On his 1963 return, he cited 26 specific violations of the Constitution which, he declared, occurred regularly under the administrative law known as USC Title 26.

During this period, Mr. Porth became inspired with truly evangelical zeal and determination. In 1966 he published *Manual for Those Who Think That They Must Pay An Income Tax,* in which he declared that no one need "become fearful of an agent or officer of the Internal Revenue Service. They cannot put you in jail for refusing to file what they call a proper income-tax form. . . . Mr. Austin Flett . . . and myself have not filed a proper return or paid a tax for many years. (We are not in jail.) We had no experience. Nobody supplied us with books, charts, and counsel. . . . What was rough, has now been made smooth for you."

Mr. Porth distributed his writings to every corner of the land; he lectured wherever he could find anyone who would listen; and, more important, he organized small cells of tax rebels in cities from Florida to Michigan to Utah to Oregon and California. In state after state, tax rebels attributed their original inspiration to him.

But now, at last, the IRS was ready to strike; on October 21, 1965, it brought a three-count grand-jury indictment against him in the U.S. District Court in Topeka, charging that in 1963 (1) he had failed to collect from his employees and transmit to the IRS $242.77 in FICA taxes; (2) that he had gross earnings of $10,318.32, for which he had made no accounting; and (3) that he failed to collect and turn over to the government withholding taxes on approximately $1,391 of income received by his employees.

Also, at long last, Mr. Porth had his oft-expressed wish: a trial by jury, which began on June 27, 1967, which lasted three days, and which filled 765 pages of testimony. The jury found that Mr. Porth had income exceeding $600 in 1963 and that he had transmitted no FICA or employee income taxes to the government, nor had the employees done so.

In a spirit of revenge, Judge Templar sentenced Mr. Porth on July 18, 1967, to 13 years in prison and a fine of $50,000. However, he later modified this by canceling the fine and permitting the prison terms to run concurrently, thus reducing the period to five years.

The importance of the case may be gauged from the fact that the government threw six leading lawyers into the fray, including Johnnie M. Walters.

After all appeals had been exhausted, Mr. Porth was transported to the U.S. Medical Center at Springfield, Missouri, on November 13, 1970, where he was to be kept under observation for 180 days. When this became known, however, there was an unprecedented reaction from thousands of citizens. If Porth could be committed to a prison for the criminally insane, as are dissidents in Russia, what protection is there for any American? When various multi-millionaires pay no taxes at all, can a patriot who protests against injustice be made to rot among diseased felons over a dispute over an insignificant sum of money? Protest meetings were organized; mail for Mr. Porth—which was *not* delivered—poured into the prison; and a campaign was soon under way in which the warden received hundreds of telephone calls from protesters.

Mr. Porth was released on probation after 77 days. Hundreds of individuals who had never resisted taxation refused to file 1040s. The movement grew by leaps and bounds.

A very interesting development occurred in 1973 when the IRS admitted officially that it had made a ghastly error in computing Mr. Porth's 1963 tax liability at $573.24 instead of $100.36, the correct amount. Since the agent had at his disposal all the necessary papers, it appeared that he committed a felony under Section 7214, which provides that for such an error an agent is subject to dismissal from the Service, a fine of $10,000, imprisonment for five years, and that summary restitution be made.

We have no doubt that the IRS spent at least $100,000 in its attempt to silence Mr. Porth and thus terrify others who might be tempted to emulate his actions. But he has not been silenced; and the rebellion he helped to instigate, instead of diminishing, has been increasing on all hands. He has established his own tax-consultant service and helped innumerable clients in their battles with the IRS. He appears frequently at seminars and conventions, where he presents his novel techniques for defeating the monster that incarcerated him for two months and sixteen days.

In one of his many publications, *Truthful Income Tax Reporting*, 1974, he says that since only specie, or notes redeemable in gold or silver, can legally be called dollars, the fiat Federal Reserve notes do not qualify as such. In another document, issued in March 1976, entitled *Sovereign Citizens Are Not Subject to the So-Called Income Tax: Only Corporations Are Subject to the Special Excise Tax*, he maintains that the income tax is actually an excise tax which can be levied only against corporations or other activities permitted to exist or operate under special licenses granted by the state. Since every citizen is a sovereign individual and the right to work, contract, or earn a living cannot be denied or restricted, wages or salaries cannot be classified as income subject to taxation. He quotes extensively from the *Congressional Record* and cites various Supreme Court decisions and opinions in support of his position. He also wrote a series of letters to Donald Alexander and Jerome Kurtz, Commissioners of Internal Revenue, which, so far as we know, were never answered.

In the meantime, Porth continues with unabated energy his battle on different fronts. He remains a physical and moral giant; and he is truly the Patriarch of the Tax Resistance Movement to Restore the Constitution. Even if he has made some errors, millions have learned much from him; and tax rebels are becoming more and more sophisticated. Porth was not defeated; and while his persecutors have dwindled into pygmies, he has emerged a hero. In 1983, he and his wife moved to Velma, Oklahoma, where he continues his consulting and research, and where he works closely with a library known as The Heritage Foundation.

Jerome Daly and the Basic Bible Church

Perhaps the toughest of all American constitutionalists is Jerome Daly of Minnesota, who once told this writer that, having been born in a corn-crib, there was no hardship too difficult for him to endure and survive.

He first made history as a result of a $14,000 loan he received from the First National Bank of Montgomery in his state and on which he was $476 in arrears in 1967. The bank, having purchased the property at a sheriff's sale, brought action to obtain possession in the court of *Martin* v. *Mahoney*, Justice of the Peace in Credit River Township. At a two-day trial December 7–8, 1968, Daly contended that since only gold and silver can be legal tender under the United States Constitution, the current Federal Reserve currency is purely fiat money and represents nothing of value. Furthermore, in making a loan to him, the bank simply out of thin air created debt-money on its books; therefore, since he had received nothing of value, Daly maintained that the bank was not entitled to seize his real estate.

In a stunning decision, the jury found in favor of Daly, who thereby not only retained the property but did so without encumbrance.

But this was not Daly's principal battle. Beginning for the year 1965, he filed what came to be known as improper Porth-Daly Returns, which included his name, address, and occupation, and only such income as consisted of gold or silver coins, and an attachment called *The Daly Eagle*, dealing with taxation and the monetary question. The portion of the 1040 below line 25, including the signature and the perjury lines, he simply cut off.

With the zeal of a missionary, he traveled across the country giving seminars, organizing groups of tax rebels and defending them in court battles. He proclaimed that he had discovered a *modus operandi* by which to defeat the IRS. He found many followers and sold thousands of his tax forms and of *The Daly Eagle*, which fed the growing tax rebellion.

On April 8, 1966, Daly filed his first "improper" return, to which he attached a 10-page memorandum dealing with constitutional issues. The IRS quickly served a 7602 summons, charging him with willful violation of the IR Code and listing 14 categories of records he must produce. He appeared on September 30, but refused to be sworn, recognize the jurisdiction of the Service, produce any records, or answer any questions. On December 29, Judge Miles Lord ordered him to appear at the IRS office on January 6, 1967; however, when he did so, he again refused to divulge any information except his name, address, and Social Security number. In response to each question, he took the Fifth Amendment.

For almost a year, the matter hung in abeyance. Daly must produce his records, or go to prison, or win a landmark decision. Then, on April 11, 1968, a panel of three judges in the U.S. Court of Appeals for the Eighth Circuit determined in an opinion filed April 22, that his reliance on the Fifth Amendment privilege against self-incrimination was valid, and the case was remanded for plenary trial.

On July 17, 1968, an epoch-making event occurred in the court of the same judge who had previously sentenced Daly to prison. In addition to leading administrators, the government tossed three of its most important lawyers into the battle to determine once and for all whether a taxpayer can stand on his Fifth Amendment rights. Daly, who defended himself, won a complete victory. It was established that when a taxpayer is ordered to appear, he must do so, and must give a response to all specific questions; however, he is completely within his rights in refusing to surrender records if he takes the Fifth Amendment in response to every question. As a result of this and similar, subsequent decisions—such as that involving Vivien Kellems—several provisions of the Internal Revenue Code—especially Section 7203—although they are still in print—are actually null and void.

The State Board of Examiners then moved to disbar Daly, and so decreed on September 17, 1968. Daly was never charged with any real offense; he was punished simply because he had become a thorn in the side of the establishment.

However, the IRS was not yet through with Daly. Four years later, on July 28, 1972, he was arrested under Section 7203, fingerprinted, and indicted for willful failure to file proper returns for 1967 and 1968. Judge Miles Lord ordered him held for trial and declared that he would "get" Daly even if it cost the taxpayers $2 million.

After a trial from October 12–14, for which the government spent years in preparation, Daly was convicted in the court of Judge Edward J. Devitt. The government's evidence included a large number of canceled checks, proof of payment to Daly for legal services rendered.

After 90 days at the Springfield Medical Center in Missouri for psychiatric evaluation, Daly was placed on probation with the provision that he must not leave Minnesota without permission. This he disregarded and was arrested in another state. He was committed to the Federal penitentiary at Sandstone, Minnesota, where he was held from April to October 1974. Upon his release, he at once resumed his activities in aid of those in conflict with the IRS.

After studying the tax laws and the immunities and privileges of churches and their organizations, Daly decided "to go religious," not primarily for his own advantage and protection, but to expose the inequities in the tax laws and to take advantage of some of them. He therefore took over an existing organization known as the Basic Bible Church of America. As President and Archbishop, he chartered eight or nine hundred member congregations during the following years. He was also the Leader in The Order of Almighty God.

The Preamble to the Bylaws of the Basic Bible Church declares that it is a religious organization dedicated to a belief in the Bible, the Declaration of Independence, and the Constitution of the United States, and to the furthering of a universal acceptance of the laws, principles, morals, ethics, and works of the Creator. The document emphasizes that the Church and its members believe in the Common Law and in state constitutions established to guarantee the security of life, liberty, and property, as well as the happiness of the individual and his religious freedom. It further proclaims a firm belief in free enterprise.

As President and Archbishop of the Basic Bible Church and Leader of The Order of Almighty God, Jerome Daly ordained individuals as ministers, bishops, and doctors of divinity. Those who took the Vow of Poverty in the Order considered themselves entitled to all the benefits conferred by the IR Code upon members of long-established apostolic organizations—such as the Jesuits—as they are called in USC Title 26.

To those who applied and qualified for it, the President issued a Certificate of Ordination; once an individual attained this status, he incorporated under state law, and his congregation—consisting of himself as a Sole—became an integral but separate community in the Basic Bible Church, entitled to all the perquisites conferred upon churches in the IR Code.

In addition to this Certificate, the new ordinate received a huge packet of materials that described in detail how the new church should operate in every particular and what to do if the IRS challenged its operation. It outlined all the provisions of the IRS Code relating to ministers and churches. It also included releases from the IRS and transcripts of various court decisions relevant to religious entities and operations.

Thus, Daly now believed that he was beyond the jurisdiction of the Internal Revenue Service. However, the Agency promptly labeled the Basic Bible Church a Tax-Protester Entity.

Those ordained in this Church deeded their homes to their church organizations, transforming them into parsonages and sanctuaries, to qualify for exemption from local property taxation. They gave half of their outside earnings to their churches as tax-exempt donations; they insisted not only upon immunity to Social Security taxation on taxable income from their own churches, but also substantial allocations as housing allowances; they also sought other tax-free emoluments so that, as ministers, they could receive incomes of $20,000 or $30,000 without incurring any income taxation.

Those who took the Vow of Poverty simply conveyed their entire income to the Church and paid no income or Social Security tax at all.

The IRS, as well as the older denominations viewed this proliferation of "illegitimate" churches with deep concern, and did everything in their power to prevent their further development.

Daly continued on a course that brought him into confrontation with the government again and again. He was once arrested for carrying a load of marijuana, which he declared could be used as a kind of soothing sacrament for the members of his Church. On another occasion, he defeated the IRS soundly when it demanded a list of all his ministers and churches.

One of his members, Lou Kegeler, an airline pilot who paid no taxes because he had taken the Vow of Poverty in the Order of Almighty God, was tried in 1980 and convicted in a Texas court. Actually, he had not violated any statutory provision in the IR Code, but only a regulation issued *after* the alleged violation first occurred.

However, the ultimate target was Daly himself who, over a period of nearly twenty years, probably caused the government more trouble than any other single individual. In 1981, the IRS spent about a million dollars in an attempt to convict nine Texas airline pilots who were members of the Basic Bible Church who had taken the Vow of Poverty. Desperate to crush this rebellion, the government went to extraordinary lengths to obtain convictions.

In his *Newsletter* of January 26, 1982, Daly described the methods used to obtain grand-jury indictments. James Rolfe was the U.S. attorney in charge of prosecution; however, while in private practice, he had represented some of the pilots and had betrayed them by inducing them to incriminate themselves in testimony before a grand jury. Because of this and other perversions of law and justice, all indictments were dismissed on January 21, 1982, but without prejudice—the charges could be reinstated.

Determined to put Daly away forever, new indictments were secured against him and eight pilots; they all went on trial on a multitude of charges in the U.S. District Court of Fort Worth. After a five-month trial, the judge delivered instructions to the jury comprising 83 pages; verdicts of guilty were returned on March 12, 1983. Daly was at once ordered to report to the local Federal prison, where he was placed in solitary confinement; shortly afterward, *he was sentenced to 16 years in prison and a fine of $100,000!* The pilots received sentences ranging from two to two-and-one-half years and fines of from $5,000 to $75,000.

In his *Newsletter* of April 1983, written in prison, Daly states that the government spent more than $3 million on this case; that the investigation began in 1977 and the grand-jury probe in 1980. He declares that constitutional rights are gradually being destroyed by the federal government and the courts; in his case, for example, agents entered his Church headquarters twice with nothing but General Search Warrants and took evidence in violation of the Fourth Amendment, which was then offered and accepted at his trial. The Supreme Court is now trying to devise a means by which to eliminate the exclusionary rule concerning evidence obtained by illegal warrants or no warrants at all. They have abolished the rights of citizens to due process of law; they have eliminated jury trials in tax cases; they have abrogated the rights against self-incrimination and the right to remain silent.

In this case, the IRS never asked the pilots for information, never called them in for an audit, never sent a demand for a tax payment. Since the full income of each was disclosed on returns, the IRS needed merely to disallow deductions, recompute the tax, and demand payment. If this were then not remitted, the Ninety-Day Letter of Deficiency could and should have been sent, which would have routed the dispute into the Tax Court in a civil proceeding instead of criminal, since no willful act was involved and there was no attempt whatever either to conceal income or to deceive the government.

But the IRS, desperate to crush all opposition, never made the slightest attempt to collect any taxes; the sole objective was obviously to end forever even the mere thought of making a return based on a vow of poverty. The pilots undoubtedly would have fared better had they made no returns at all, for such omission is only a misdemeanor, not a felony. Furthermore, the members of apostolic orders in the Roman Catholic Church certainly do not make any returns.

Mr. Daly declares that the procedures used in his trial prove that no matter what basis you may have in law or in fact for making a claim of any kind, the IRS can bring a criminal charge and obtain an indictment and a conviction based on any statement made in a 1040 form.

Daly remains in the federal prison at Lompoc, California, where he was incarcerated in 1983.

Vaughn Ellsworth: Pro Se Litigant

One of the first and most outstanding patriots to challenge the unconstitutional administration of the IR Code was Vaughn Ellsworth, who, beginning for the year 1969, filed his returns in blank, giving only his name, address, and certain other items of information, but no data from which an income tax could be determined. The catalyst that sparked his resistance was the demand by the IRS that he surrender the records of the defunct Sonel Corporation; the court proceedings in this case, which began on July 6, 1970, ended in the court of Judge Carl Muecke on September 20, 1972, with a complete victory for the defendant.

Among other defenses, Ellsworth maintained that because fiat Federal Reserve notes are not redeemable in specie, as required by the Constitution, he had no dollar income. He sometimes pasted a pre-1965 25-cent coin to the upper right-hand corner of his 1040, with the suggestion that it be used to pay the national debt. For years, he issued leaflets, pamphlets, and Civil Rights and Court-Fight Packets, advising tax resisters on how to defeat the IRS. He published numerous articles in such periodicals as *The Tax Strike News* (now *The Justice Times*) and the *Utah Independent*. He lectured all over the country in the tradition of Austin Flett and Arthur Porth.

Because of Ellsworth's outspoken defiance of the IRS and his continual activities, it is curious why the Agency waited so long to institute proceedings against him. During the battle over the Sonel records, he declared in one of his brochures:

> Either the Constitution of the United States is the Law of the Land and the Internal Revenue Code is null and void, or the Internal Revenue is supreme and the Constitution has been junked as a ridiculous scrap of paper. . . . American tradition has always held that citizens are innocent until proved guilty. The Internal Revenue Code reverses this and insists that all are guilty until they prove themselves innocent. . . . The only possible way to make the Internal Revenue Code legal and lawful is to pass another Constitutional Amendment cancelling our sacred and basic rights and immunities under the Constitution.

In 1974, the Intelligence Division of the IRS finally called Mr. Ellsworth into its office, read him the Miranda Warning, and declared that he was under criminal investigation, not only for filing "improper" returns for 1969, 1970, and 1971, but also for fraud in his conventional return for 1968. At the time, it was doubtful that any of the charges could be substantiated at a jury trial, as the IRS could not properly document income for the last three years, and there was no basis for the charge of fraud in the 1968 return.

Between September 28 and October 2, 1975, Vaughn Ellsworth underwent what can only be described as a kangaroo trial. To a large extent, Judge Muecke took over the role of prosecutor, and conducted the proceedings with unparalleled venom. The jury, which may have included two undercover agents, consisted largely of women living on Social Security, which they were persuaded would be lost if the defendant were acquitted. Even though the charge was patently defective, the judge reinforced the government's position in every possible way. Thus, in the face of overwhelming contradictory evidence, a conviction was obtained largely as a result of the judge's instructions to the jury.

When Vaughn appeared for sentencing on November 24, the judge offered probation if he would agree to file "proper" returns in the future and desist from his crusade against the IRS and the Federal Reserve System; he even read a letter from the president of Vaughn's church, which declared that the income tax was constitutional; he gave the defendant 48 hours to consider the offer. On the following Wednesday, Vaughn declared that he was no criminal, that he could not change his position, and that he must obey the dictates of his conscience. He was thereupon sentenced to prison.

After all appeals were exhausted, he became an inmate at Terminal Island, California, on July 25, 1977, whence he issued a constant stream of letters, brochures, and comments on his situation and the battle for constitutional taxation. In one release, he declared: "I turned down a suspended sentence and took, instead, a three-year prison term rather than abandon my opposition to the income tax, based on constitutional issues. . . . After my six-day trial, in which the judge denied me assistance of counsel [Jerome Daly], apparently he was partially ashamed of his role in which he acted as 'prosecutor' before a courtroom packed daily with Defendant's friends."

Vaughn, who had no attorney, may have made some errors, but he was not guilty of concealment or dishonesty. He was prosecuted not because of his failure to pay taxes, but because of his outspoken criticism of the government. In several instances during the trial, the judge conducted hostile cross-examination of defense witnesses; he sneered at them in the sight of the jury; he refused to permit a monetary expert to testify for the defense, although he permitted the prosecution to cross-examine him!

In one of his many releases during his confinement, Vaughn declared: "A few, perhaps many, persons are going to jail for standing up for the interests and inalienable rights for which our forefathers risked their liberty and their blood. . . . Again, my only regret is that I did not learn earlier so that I could have fought more successfully—with court procedures, etc. I know that my constitutional arguments are sound—and they must be maintained."

Exactly one year after entering Terminal Island in July 1977, Vaughn was released. He had paid no income taxes since 1968, and he intends never to do so in the future.

He is now a consultant in various areas of taxation, trust formation, etc. He remains a great patriot, and will undoubtedly continue to be a thorn in the side of the IRS as long as he lives.

2

IRS Atrocities

In 1967 and 1968, John Barron published three articles in *Reader's Digest*, describing in detail the harrowing experiences that a number of innocent taxpayers had suffered at the hands of the Internal Revenue Service. Doubtless, thousands, even hundreds of thousands of similar cases could be documented. What follows are just some tragic examples.

The Case of Senator Arthur E. Wood

I observed firsthand the tragedy of a close friend, State Senator Arthur E. Wood of Michigan. During the 1920s, real estate developers had subdivided and sold hundreds of thousands of homesites around Detroit. The promotional gimmick was that those who bought land at the edge of a growing and wealthy city would enjoy comfortable retirement.

When the Great Depression struck, however, almost all of these lots, even those fully paid for, were taken over by the government for unpaid taxes. In 1935–36, Wood began buying the choicest lots at $25 or $30 each until he had acquired more than a thousand. He was not a realtor, had no broker's license, had never handled a deal for anyone else.

He kept the properties until 1946–47, when he sold them at a profit exceeding $1 million—and paid the capital-gains tax of 25 percent. With about $750,000—the result of foresight and expertise—he looked forward to years of creative retirement.

A conservative Republican, he was an opponent of the liberals and the corrupt Truman administration, which may or may not have had anything to do with subsequent events. When the IRS audited Wood, they told him that he had never been an actual investor at all, but was, instead, simply a broker and that his lots belonged in the category of a store inventory and could not, therefore, qualify as capital assets, as defined in Section 1221. Consequently, he must pay a tax rising to 91 percent and would be subject to an additional levy of 6 percent per year since the tax became due.

Since the definition of a capital asset excludes "stock in trade of the taxpayer or other property of the kind which could properly be included in the inventory of a taxpayer . . . or property held by the taxpayer primarily for sale to customers in the ordinary course of business," Wood could not understand how his homesites fell under this classification. The IRS, however, declared that if a taxpayer sells only one or two pieces of vacant land, regardless of size or value, during one year, he may take capital gains; but if he sells more than three, he is regarded as a broker.

This ruling seemed so irrational to Wood that he could not believe it to be the law or that the courts would uphold it, even if it were specifically in the Code, which it was not. After all, he could buy and sell any number of shares of stock or any number of corporations, and no more than a capital-gains tax would be due.

Why should vacant land be any different?

He was, however, in for a tragic disappointment; after he spent about $200,000 in litigation, the Supreme Court ruled against him. In addition to the tax, he was forced to pay a huge amount in interest and penalties, which came to more than his total profit.

Not long thereafter, the ex-senator died, a broken man and a virtual pauper. The IRS had performed its deadly work with precision.

The Case of Edson McCanse

In July 1964, Edson McCanse and his two daughters sold their Oregon ranch for $980,000, taking less than 30 percent down so that the capital gains tax would be due only after the basis was recovered. The IRS claimed they received more than this, demanded an additional $119,000 to be paid immediately in a lump sum, and placed the jeopardy assessment against all the McCanse assets on December 23, 1965, making it impossible for him to raise any funds at all. The IRS demanded that McCanse pay within ten days or everything that had been seized would be sold at sacrifice prices, including his 50 percent interest in a mill, which alone was worth at least half a million dollars. McCanse pleaded for a two-day extension, but this was curtly refused. He then borrowed the $119,000 from his partner in the mill, using his stock as collateral, and paid the IRS what it demanded.

The Service then informed McCanse that he had not borrowed the money, but had sold his half interest in the mill and therefore owed an additional $11,000 in capital-gains taxes. The partner gleefully agreed to this interpretation, since he thus obtained an asset worth $500,000 for less than one-fourth of its value.

After several years, McCanse was able to prove that he did not owe the $119,000 in the first place; and this sum, together with interest, was refunded by the IRS. He also finally proved that he did not sell his half interest in the mill to his partner, but borrowed the $119,000.

However, the nine years of legal battles, which cost the McCanses $500,000, bore some good fruit; for it was partly as a result of his testimony before a congressional committee that Section 7429—which restricts IRS power in making jeopardy assessments—was added to the Code. And more than that: Under the Tax Equity and Fiscal Responsibility Act of 1982, the IRS could, under circumstances similar to the McCanse case, now be forced to reimburse the taxpayer for the entire expense incurred in the litigation.

The Case of Dr. James A. Owen

Dr. James Owen of Portland, Oregon, a chiropractor and member of the Church of Jesus Christ of Latter-Day Saints, was for years involved in a unique dispute with the IRS, described in detail in his compendium, *We Dare Be Free*.

Dr. Owen initiated his confrontation with the IRS when he filed conventional returns for 1969 and 1970 with a complete statement of income, expenses, deductions, and allowances; since rent and other business disbursements were substantial and since he had nine children, the IRS publicly agreed that there was no income-tax liability. However, since he was determined to provide for his own old-age retirement, he did not transmit any contributions for Social Security, which, for two years, including interest—according to IRS computations—amounted to $1,360.67. On November 5, 1971, without previous warning (the Notice of Seizure arrived in the mail ten days later) the IRS took $249.83 from his bank account, and, on the same day, two agents appeared at his home—which was also his place of business—to seize a 1967 station wagon and a 1963 travel trailer. A memorable scene ensued. At about 1 P.M., the agents placed a Notice of Seizure upon the vehicles. Dr. Owen removed it. Mrs. Owen telephoned a friend who alerted others, and soon 14 or 15 autos arrived to block the driveway and prevent the removal of the vehicles. As other IRS reinforcements arrived, people gathered, including representatives of radio, TV, and the newspapers; it was 4:30 before the IRS left—without their booty.

On January 14, 1972, Dr. Owen filed his 26-page Motion to Dismiss, resting his case on "whether the Constitution of the United States is the Supreme Law of the Land or whether Title 26, Internal Revenue Code, Section 6331, is superior to the Constitution. . . ."

Fourteen other individuals filed affidavits declaring that they were equally guilty with Dr. Owen and demanding that they be prosecuted in the same manner. However, the IRS ignored them completely. The IRS offered to dismiss all charges against Dr. Owen if he would settle with them, which he flatly refused to do. His trial, on December 6 and 7, 1972, is a classic illustration of how the federal judiciary is being used to subvert the Constitution. When Dr. Owen stated that he relied on the Constitution as his principal witness, Mr. Hammersly, chief government prosecutor, objected. "Sustained," declared the judge. Again and again, the Doctor appealed to the Fifth Amendment, which states that no one shall be deprived of life, liberty, or property within due process of law. Each time, the prosecutor sprang to his feet, objecting on the ground of irrelevancy, and each time the Court upheld him. Although Dr. Owen was only quoting the Constitution, he was accused of "interpreting" it!

Finally, in desperation, Dr. Owen cried out that if he could not cite the Supreme Law of the Land, he had no case. In his final summation, he again began to quote the Constitution, but the judge cut him short: "Doctor," he declared brusquely, "I've told you not to make that argument. I do not intend to repeat the admonition."

Mr. Hammersly then told the jury that it had taken an oath to try the case "according to the law as you are instructed by the court." The judge then warned the jury: "It will be a violation of your sworn duty to base a verdict upon any other view of the law than that given you by the instructions of the Court. . . ." which were simply that Sections 6331 and 7212 of the IR Code constituted the applicable law in this case and that the only question for the jury to decide was whether Dr. Owen had or had not attempted to impede the IRS in its attempts to seize his property.

Under such circumstances, the jury had little choice other than to find the Doctor guilty. He could have been fined $5,000 and imprisoned for three years or he could have been turned over to the U.S. Attorney General for "psychiatric evaluation." The judge, however, perhaps aware of the public mood, merely ordered him to spend ninety days as a medical assistant in a county hospital, an order never carried out.

Nevertheless, as a result of the terrible cost, personal drain, and harassment involved, Dr. Owen was unable to continue his flourishing practice. He and his family moved to another state, and he ceased his efforts to restore the Constitution.

The Case of Charles Steen, Bankrupt Millionaire

Charles Steen, known as the Uranium King, had mineral holdings in several western states—mostly in Nevada—and, according to news items in *The Arizona Republic* on November 19, 1972, and

June 9, 1973, owned properties worth about $17.5 million before the IRS struck him with a jeopardy assessment of $2.8 million, which reduced him to living on charity from his friends. Since such an assessment should be invoked only when there is imminent danger that a tax evader might conceal his assets or remove them to a foreign country, the procedure in this case was obviously illegal under IRS statutes.

The courts finally ruled that Steen owed only $480,817—including all interest and penalties—which he could easily have paid had this been the original levy and had his properties not been sequestered. Since the assessment could not possibly be paid under the jeopardy procedure and since many months elapsed before any disposition could be made in the dispute, this multi-millionaire was reduced to pauperism by an agency of the government which operates not only in total violation of the Constitution, but even of its own laws.

The Case of Victor L. Cain

On October 18, 1973, Victor L. Cain, in a state of desperation, phoned from Bryson City, North Carolina, to tell me that after eight years as a used-car dealer, he had been ordered by the IRS to change his method of accounting from cash to accrual for purposes of taxation; and that, as a result, an assessment of $38,545.92 plus a 50 percent penalty of $19,872.96—a total of $57,818.88—had been placed against him, a sum he could not possibly pay. He explained further that he handled only older cars, sold them with very small down payments, required no insurance, and carried his own interest-free contracts.

I told him that under Section 446(a) and 453(a) of the Code, he had an unquestionable right to continue to do business on a cash basis provided he had done so previously, and that notes received from sales on an installment plan are not treated as income until cash exceeding the investment is received. The following day I wrote to him explaining that hundreds of court decisions, summarized in *West's Annotated U.S. Code, Title 26*, guarantee this right and that in making the determination it had in this case, the IRS was in complete violation of its own law.

Cain had written to various politicians, pointing out that he had always paid his taxes promptly. His receipts from sales increased from $19,935.50 in 1966 to $188,341.93 in 1972. For seven years, he had never heard from the IRS. But then, on December 13, 1972, an agent strode into his office to make a "routine audit." The next day, he produced a little book containing an IRS Regulation that stated—

so the agent said—that all used-car dealers must be on accrual, which meant that Cain's notes, or accounts receivable, totalling $115,000 in 1970–71, were taxable just as if cash had been received in full at the time of sale.

However, Cain's method of accounting was the only one that could possibly reflect his taxable income. Furthermore, Section 481 completely negates the position taken by the IRS, for it states that as long as the taxpayer himself does not initiate a change in the method of accounting, he may continue to use it; and the law specifically prohibits the IRS from changing it in order to levy an assessment.

On August 27, 1973, Cain appeared at the IRS District Office, where he was told that: a) Accounts receivable are income and must be taxed; b) if Cain did not pay, everything he owned would be seized and sold; and c) he could get his case before a jury only by first paying the entire assessment and then suing for a refund in the U.S. District Court.

Desperate, Cain then sought the advice of a lawyer, who informed him that the IRS has power to force a used-car dealer to switch from cash to accrual—and do so retroactively.

Cain found that he could not continue his battle and also conduct his business. He therefore sold some real estate for cash; and by offering to discount his car contracts up to 50 percent, he was able to obtain cash for most of them.

On November 21, he drove to Greensboro, North Carolina, where he told Appellate Judge Scoggin that Section 453(a) of the Code should prevent the IRS from enforcing its rulings against him. The Judge offered to accept the previous returns as filed, provided Mr. Cain would report future contract obligations as cash received. When the IRS learned that there was now no property to seize, they offered a compromise. However, it was too late; Cain was already ruined and out of business.

Again, the IRS succeeded in destroying a thriving business which was paying goodly sums in taxes, and in reducing a hard-working family man to complete penury.

Cain wrote me that in his opinion, the IRS set out to ruin him because by carrying his own accounts receivable, the banks could not profit by financing sales at 24 percent or more of interest; furthermore, since he did not require insurance, the underwriters were unable to make huge profits in their business. Finally, he was gradually putting other used-car dealers out of business. Because he was giving the ordinary citizen a better deal, thereby depriving parasites of their lush emoluments, the IRS was used to remove him from the business scene.

The Case of the *American Mercury*

The *American Mercury* was established by Henry L. Mencken in 1924; under various subsequent owners, it continued as a national voice of conservatism. In due course, it came under the aegis of the Legion for the Survival of Freedom, a Texas-based (501(c)(4)), tax-exempt entity with headquarters in Torrance, California, which was a staunch exponent of limited federal government and free enterprise and which consistently criticized the Internal Revenue Service and the Federal Reserve System.

In 1971, an IRS agent appeared at the *Mercury*'s offices and spent nine days going over all its documents. The editor then spent five more days at the IRS district office undergoing intensive interrogation. During all this time, no representative of the publication was permitted to present any material, ask any question relating to the information sought, the nature of the investigation, or to discover what proposals or disallowances the IRS might be contemplating. Eventually, without giving any reason or explanation, the Agency revoked the magazine's exempt status and assessed a deficiency of $38,500.

A lawyer, entrusted with power-of-attorney, charged $500 for writing a brief note, without even consulting the publishers, in which he agreed to the revocation of exemption.

The publishers then fired the lawyer and tried, as best they could, to defend themselves against the vague, unspecified, and unexplained assessments. The IRS later confirmed the revocation of exemption; years went by, without any action or word from the Agency, while potential charges for interest and penalties mounted into the stratosphere.

The Service failed, or refused, during all this time to furnish a Bill of Particulars explaining their assessments and disallowances; nor would they answer any questions concerning the legality of the actions taken.

There was, in fact, absolutely no basis for revoking the exempt status, and *even if the income had been $45,000 greater than it was, even if the organization were a private corporation for profit, it would still not have owed any income taxes.*

Finally, in 1975, the IRS issued its Ninety-Day Letter, which meant (1) that the execution of its edicts would take place at the end of this (90-day) period unless they were disputed in the Tax Court; (2) that if this were done, the IRS would finally be forced to supply a Bill of Particulars; and (3) that the publishers were now compelled to hire an expensive attorney to defend themselves.

When the Bill of Particulars was issued, the IRS case collapsed—it was utterly without foundation. As the moment of truth approached, the IRS offered a compromise: If the publishers would agree to the revocation of exempt status, the Agency would admit that no taxes were due. When this offer was rejected, the government, at the last moment, dismissed the case and permitted the magazine to continue as it had before the litigation began.

However, the six-year ordeal had cost an enormous amount of money and was a dreadful strain upon the publishers—in fact, it virtually destroyed an extremely successful and potent voice of dissent. Shortly thereafter, the magazine was sold to a man who did not continue publication or make payments on his contractual agreement.

And so the IRS was used to destroy the freedom of the press by means of its devious powers to accomplish this objective.

The Case of Robert William Smiley

The known facts are as follows: On March 4, 1976, two IRS agents—Clyde H. Allisan and Ralph W. Foster—entered the truck-camper that Robert Smiley used as a business office in Salem, Virginia. Ten minutes later, Smiley was dead of a bullet wound in his head; the IRS men had departed; the corpse was seated upright in a desk chair; there was the mark of a bullet—which could not be found—in a wall; a gun, with no finger prints, was found in a corner at the other end of the camper; $2,000, which Smiley had in his pockets, was gone; the two agents were whisked into concealment by the government and shielded from any interview or interrogation; there was no autopsy or hearing on the strange death or the circumstances accompanying it; the only IRS official permitted to discuss the matter declared that he knew nothing about the incident; the local police reported the death as a suicide; and the media hushed up the whole affair.

A week following Smiley's death, five IRS agents seized all the vehicles comprising his business inventory and sold them to competitors at prices far below their value. In the meantime, Smiley's close friends declared that the suicide theory was absolutely contradictory to the known facts and completely at variance with the character of this jovial and good-natured man.

The Spotlight was the only publication to cover the Smiley tragedy—in the May 24, June 14, August 9, November 8 and 15, 1976, and May 30, 1977, issues. The Treasury Department adamantly refused to answer any questions or permit an interview with the two agents who were with Smiley when he died. Meanwhile, the

IRS continued to harass the broken-hearted widow to the point where, despondent, destitute, and ill, she attempted suicide on October 23, 1976, which, nevertheless, did not stop the IRS harassment.

The Case of Jasper and Lucille Gates

The story of Mr. and Mrs. Jasper Gates of Denver, Colorado, was told in the *Rocky Mountain News* of May 3, 1979. Whether they owed any taxes or not was never established. They were never even audited.

When this husband and wife in their sixties were ousted from their home in August 1978, they had been engaged in a fruitless battle with the IRS for nearly seven years. It began with a letter stating that they had overpaid their 1972 tax by $1,197; however, the refund never arrived. Instead, in June 1974 they were notified that they owed $4,451—with no explanation. Soon another letter arrived, stating that the deficiency was $4,206.

In October, a notice arrived stating that they owed $13,700; in November, it was $15,000; in October 1975, it was $16,000—and still there was no explanation.

The IRS then seized their savings accounts and other assets, totaling $10,000. Next, it seized their debt-free home, worth about $100,000, but which the IRS sold for $16,000. Mrs. Gates, in a wheel chair because of a broken leg, was evicted; then, with the help of sheriff's deputies, the man who purchased the house at such a bargain threw all the personal property found therein into the street.

When the news media contacted the IRS for an explanation, officials explained that the Privacy Act prevented them from making any statement.

Mr. and Mrs. Gates had to keep watch over their belongings for days before they could find a place to store them. They had nowhere to go; their life became a complete nightmare.

Editorially, the newspaper remarked: "Forget about Dracula. . . . Lucille Gates has a more terrifying story. It concerns the IRS" which "is so frequently heavy-handed and arrogant. . . . It seems to us that the Gates' congressional representative should raise a little hell with the IRS. . . ." And so should twenty million other citizens!

The Case of Addicks and Turel

One of the most bizarre and frightening cases to come to our attention is that of Jim Turel, Roderick Addicks, and Floyd C. Forsberg in Oregon.

During the 1960s, Turel and Addicks worked as tax preparers in the employ of H. R. Block & Co., which, many believe, works hand in hand with the IRS. However, these two enterprising young men were helping their middle-class clients utilize legal tax shelters to reduce their taxes substantially; and because their employers did not approve, they established their own Columbia Bookkeeping Service about 1970. In due course, they had three offices and thousands of clients whom, it was estimated, they helped to legally avoid about five million dollars in taxes annually. Furthermore, Addicks and Turel always made sure their clients overpaid slightly so that, should they be audited, they would receive refunds instead of having to pay additional taxes. In short, Turel and Addicks were teaching middle-class citizens how to profit by the esoteric loopholes planted in the Code for the benefit of the favored.

This, however, was a practice that could not be tolerated; should it spread throughout the nation, the income of the federal government might be reduced by $50 billion a year.

The Turel-Addicks business ended abruptly in August 1974, with the murder of Jim Turel and the arrest, trial, and conviction of Addicks for the crime. The FBI, the IRS, certain detectives, the prosecutors, and the courts all seem to have entered into a conspiracy to tamper with evidence and to offer perjured testimony by which a conviction was secured. Although the accused could prove that he was fifty miles away from the scene when the crime was committed, he was not permitted to present this evidence to the jury on the grounds that he was mentally incompetent. He was sentenced to life, without the possibility of parole.

Then, Floyd C. Forsberg, an FBI informer, general criminal, bank robber, murderer, and prison inmate entered the scenario by relating an extraordinary tale. It seems that while in prison, he had been converted to a belief in Jesus Christ by a Salvation Army missionary and thereupon became obsessed with a desire to clear his conscience by confessing all his felonies—including the murder of Turel. His story, in part, is as follows:

For years, he had worked as an informer for the FBI, and, under orders from this agency in cooperation with another man, had murdered an undercover drug-runner suspected of double-crossing his employers. Then, to get another murderer off the hook, the Agency double-crossed Forsberg so that he was convicted and given a thirty-year sentence, from which, in due course, he was paroled.

In 1966, he was arrested by the FBI fifteen minutes after he committed a bank robbery arranged by the Agency. Again, he was sent to prison; but this time, when he emerged, he was so angry at the FBI that he refused to continue as an informer; instead, he vowed revenge. He started to tail the Agency's operatives and sometimes drove them off the road. In the meantime, they pressured and harassed him; once they even tried to kill him.

In July 1974, a long-time criminal associate, Dennis Cartright, approached Forsberg with an offer of $5,000 to kill Jim Turel, a proposition Forsberg rejected. The next month, the man returned with an offer to reveal the names and addresses of all FBI agents in the area as well as a promise that all harassment would stop if Forsberg would agree to kill Turel. This time he accepted and with the help of Cartright murdered Jim Turel.

Although Addicks and Forsberg compiled impressive documentation to prove the innocence of the former and the guilt of the latter, no legal authority has shown the slightest interest. Neither man is permitted to tell his story in court.

Forsberg stated (in *Freedom*, July 1979, published by the Church of Scientology): "I know that I am responsible for my own actions. But it's ironic that the FBI's attempt to again make me their informer so they could catch another of their informers, involved me in the murder of an innocent man who was convicted for a crime that I performed. . . .

"I feel like I've gone insane and am in a mental hospital. What has this country come to? I thought it was people like myself who were the real threat to it, but I honestly feel I am no worse than Agent Renning, who has committed many crimes and continues to cover it all up. I don't want out at fifty. I don't honestly care if I ever get out, and I really don't feel that I should. I am asking for nothing for myself. My only interest in pushing this is so that the proper people are brought to justice and that Addicks is cleared of the murder which I committed. If this entails another life-sentence for me, I don't care."

According to reports (which I cannot verify), the authorities offered Forsberg parole and a good job as an FBI informer again, if he would sign an affidavit declaring that he lied when he confessed to the murder of Turel; but he has refused the offer, preferring to remain in prison with a clear conscience.

The Case of Walter M. Froembgen

In 1972 or 1973, Walter Froembgen's employer (a public school official in Lake Stevens, Washington) refused to honor the allowances listed on his W-4 form. And when the IRS recomputed his tax liability and assessed deficiencies which varied widely, he began a battle that eventually gained national recognition.

As he delved deeper and further into the law, the IR Code and Regulations, and particularly a mass of court decisions and opinions, Froembgen became convinced that the federal judiciary at the District level was totally corrupt. He prepared a document that explained and summarized more than 350 Supreme Court decisions that taxpayers can use to defend themselves against the incursions of federal bureaucrats who negate the rights and freedoms guaranteed by the Bill of Rights.

The more he studied, the more determined and militant he became. He was certain that the judges in the U.S. district courts are committing treason by upholding dozens of blatantly unconstitutional provisions in the IR Code; that they are urging and abetting IRS agents in the commission of theft and oppression; that they should be punished severely, including imprisonment. He made these declarations in letters; he repeated them in the seminars he conducted; he even made similar statements in courtrooms; and he stated that if IRS agents "stole" a citizen's property in violation of the Constitution, they should expect to be beaten.

In addition, he filed a multitude of suits against officials and helped others do the same. He became a major thorn in the flesh of the Establishment.

When one judge issued an injunction forbidding Froembgen to file any more suits, he promptly filed one against the judge, charging violation of his civil rights.

Three times he was ordered to appear for psychiatric evaluation so that he could be sent to a prison for the criminally insane. Twice he frustrated his enemies. However, when he was ordered to either appear or be seized by United States marshals and forcibly transported to the federal Medical Center in Springfield, Missouri, he submitted to an examination by Dr. Manfred Joeres on February 21, 1979. He passed with flying colors. One hundred and fifty-five friends wrote letters testifying to his sanity.

Judge Donald Voorhees brought Froembgen in for trial on April 4, on the charge of violating Section 7212(a) of the IR Code by threatening Agency personnel with bodily injury while they were engaged in the performance of their duties. This was, however, a distortion, for he had only said that *if* agents "stole" property in violation of the Fifth Amendment, they could *expect* taxpayers to react by giving them a beating. The trial, at which 52 defense motions were denied, and conducted the way tax resisters have learned to expect in U.S. District Courts, resulted in a conviction. The judge told the jury that all IRS laws are constitutional and that his instructions must be obeyed. Froembgen wrote: "I unglued him with the Constitution, finally trapped him, discredited the IRS witnesses completely, and then watched him deny the Constitution and American jurisprudence."

Although the jury found the defendant guilty, the spectators and the news media were sympathetic. Two radio stations favorably featured his battle; and the Seattle *Post-Intelligencer* published a long article, complete with pictures, that portrayed him as a constitutional patriot.

His sentence, on May 4, 1979, could have been a fine of $3,000 and three years in prison; however, he was given only six months at a half-way house, suspended, and five years probation, with the stipulation that he write no more letters threatening violence to IRS personnel.

In spite of this stipulation, Froembgen continued his verbal assaults on the judges, the prosecutors, the attorneys, and other federal personnel; and as his language became more bitter and the volume of his literary output increased, the judges apparently determined that he must be silenced for good. It seems that the pretext for revoking his probation was a letter which came to the attention of the trial judge, who then issued an order incarcerating Froembgen indefinitely. He languished for some time in the Snohomish County jail in Everett, Washington, where he was denied the use of a typewriter. In spite of this, however, he wrote a spate of letters in longhand, which his daughter typed and reproduced. In the meantime, his wife was in straightened circumstances, because the IRS had seized the pension payments due him as a retired veteran of the Air Force.

During his incarceration, Froembgen was subjected to various kinds of degrading treatment. His mail was opened and his privacy violated in every possible manner. Not long after his release, he developed cancer which eventually rendered him almost helpless. However, he continued his battle even though bedridden, and he was able to have his case docketed for hearing by the Supreme Court. His elation, however, ended abruptly when it denied certiorari. When he was no longer able to write, he dictated cassettes from the bed where he lay dying.

Was Walter Froembgen injected with cancer cells or germs or with some virus that could create them, during the period of his imprisonment? Such things have been done to others. At any rate, the bureaucrats, the judges, and the prosecutors were finally able to get rid of the most uncompromising and articulate rebel-voice yet to appear in the tax resistance movement in the United States; he died on December 11, 1980.

Walter Froembgen was obviously made of the same kind of stuff as the Founding Fathers of this country who laid down their lives, their fortunes, and their sacred honor to bequeath to us the greatest nation ever known on this earth.

The Case of Charles Cadwell

Charles Cadwell, a carpenter of Phoenix, Arizona, who earned more than $15,000 in take-home pay, had a wife and mother-in-law who embezzled $80,000 from their employer over a two-year period. He knew nothing whatever of this theft at the time it was committed. As a condition of probation, the two felons agreed to make restitution; and in order to keep them out of jail, Cadwell signed a second mortgage on their home in favor of their employer. The house was then foreclosed and seized in partial payment. Thereupon, the wife moved taking everything moveable with her.

At the ensuing divorce, the judge declared that since the husband might have benefited from the wife's theft, he was liable for half of the repayments to the employer. This seems strange, in view of the fact that far from receiving any benefit, Cadwell lost his entire equity in his house and all the personal property therein. This, however, was only the beginning of his nightmare: the IRS declared that since he had signed a joint income tax return with his wife, he owed taxes on the theft, from which he never received one penny. The assessment against him originally was $26,634, plus $13,317 for fraud, and even this did not include the interest, which continued to increase rapidly.

Section 6013(d)(3) of the IR code provides that an innocent spouse is not liable for unknown income exceeding 25 percent of the total received by either. "In such case, the innocent spouse will be relieved of the liability attributable to the omission" (1979 *Master Tax Guide*, Section 141).

When Cadwell took his case into the Tax Court at a cost of $8,000 in attorney's fees, he found that the judge had a somewhat different interpretation of the law. He declared that under the above provision, the innocent spouse would be held liable for taxes on any income obtained feloniously by the guilty partner if (1) the amount involved exceeded 25 percent of reported income, (2) he/she benefited in any way from the theft, (3) he/she had any knowledge concerning it, or (4) he/she had any reason whatever to suspect that the theft had occurred.

This made it virtually impossible for the innocent spouse to escape; how could he prove he had no possible reason for suspicion?

At any rate, while the criminals went free, the Tax Court heard the case in the fall of 1980 and declared in a lengthy determination issued eighteen months later that Cadwell could have had some reason to suspect that his wife had received unreported and stolen income and that therefore *he* must pay the tax thereon. Since by this time he was completely penniless, he could neither hire lawyers nor furnish the bond necessary to make an appeal to the Circuit Court.

This deficiency will hang over Mr. Cadwell indefinitely, and the IRS stands ready at all times to seize every dollar he may earn. His prospects are bleak indeed.

The Case of Dan Pilla

The experience of Dan Pilla of St. Paul, Minnesota, an articulate critic of the Internal Revenue Service, illustrates a common technique used by the Agency. In July 1974, the IRS seized Pilla's prosperous printing plant without a court order and without even establishing that he owed any taxes whatever. By the time the Agency took this action, the original assessment of $5,000 had increased to $10,500 because of penalties and interest. The IRS then sold $500,000 worth of equipment for $3,100, and charged $2,200 for conducting the sale, leaving only $900 against the alleged tax liability.

(Such procedures, however, routine for many years, are now prohibited under provisions of the so-called Tax Equity and Fiscal Responsibility Act of 1982, which requires the IRS, when seizing and selling property, to credit the citizen's account with an amount equal to the fair market value of the property at the time of seizure.)

Although during the years following this confiscation, Pilla had no substantial income, the IRS continued to increase his alleged liability. It arbitrarily assessed a deficiency of $194,126, plus a penalty of $50,000—for what we have no idea—together with interest of $78 a day. How the original $5,000 deficiency, alleged but unsubstantiated, could grow to nearly $250,000 without substantial interim income, is one of those mysteries that exists only in the Internal Revenue Service.

In order to collect a portion of this sum, the IRS seized Pilla's home, and on January 14, 1983, conducted an auction for its sale. More than 80 friends accompanied Mr. Pilla and his wife to the Federal building in St. Paul where the auction was held. There was no judge to supervise the proceedings or any court reporter to record them; no motions or appeals were permitted; bidders were told that they would have to pay down 25 percent of their bids either in cash or certified check, with the balance due in ten days. The federal auctioneer declared that the minimum bid was $20,000. An attorney in the Tax Division of the United States then bid $20,000 in the name of the government. So the authority conducting the sale of the property was also purchasing it—although a private attorney stated that a valid deed could not be conveyed by the government.

Then someone bid $20,050—and was forced to produce $5,012 from his pocket to prove that he was a qualified purchaser. The government attorney then raised his bid to $22,000, upon which the private individual bid $22,050. This went on until the private individual bid $30,050, after which there were no more offers. When the government officials were told that the sale was illegal because they could not provide an acceptable deed, the U.S. attorney declared that the buyer would receive a Bill of Sale, for which "a Torens Title could be obtained" at the court house.

On January 25, the buyer paid the remaining $22,538 and received a Bill of Sale. However, when he presented this to the Register of Deeds at the courthouse, he was told that it was defective and that no valid deed could be issued.

Pilla believes that the federal government perpetrated an act of colossal fraud and theft; his friends are in complete agreement.

3

Profiles of Freedom Fighters

Following are vignettes of some leading Freedom Fighters who have been, or are now, battling to restore the Constitution in the United States. Because there are so many of them, we present a representative cross-section, reflecting the motivations that impel them to action—sometimes at great cost to themselves. These are people who offer their lives, their fortunes, and their sacred honor upon the altars of liberty and justice.

Mike Tecton: An Architect with a Conscience

Mike Tecton of McLeod, Virginia, was one of the most controversial and outspoken critics of the federal government in general and of the Internal Revenue Service in particular.

For many years, he was a successful architect; the designer of 1,000 townhouses and 4,000 single-family units, some costing $200,000. He holds 35 patents and has invented many products used in the commercial and industrial fields. However, during the '50s, he became convinced that the entire federal system of taxation was not only unjust, but also completely unconstitutional; thus, for 15 years, he simply made no reports to the IRS. Strangely enough, even though he occasionally received form letters and personal visits from the IRS, and though he was earning from $25,000 to $40,000 a year, nothing was ever done to enforce payment of income taxes. He is sure that had he simply gone on as he did, beginning in 1958, he could have continued for the remainder of his life earning large amounts of money and retaining it all for himself.

However, in 1973 he underwent a profound emotional and intellectual experience: He became obsessed with the conviction that it was his patriotic duty to proclaim his conclusions to the world. He began writing pamphlets and distributing them everywhere; he prepared news releases; he went on the lecture circuit; he appeared on radio and TV programs throughout the country.

Soon after he embarked on this course, two IRS agents offered him immunity from taxation and prosecution if he would cease and desist from his crusade. When he spurned the offer, he was arraigned in the U.S. District Court in Alexandria, Virginia, on June 16, 1974, on a charge of failing to file returns for 1971, 1972, and 1973. The next day he appeared on the steps of the Capitol in Washington and while newsmen took notes and cameras cranked, he burned the 1040 "Slave-Confession" form as his gesture of opposition and contempt.

His first trial was on September 9–10, 1974. Since his attorney had failed to prepare the case or subpoena any witnesses, he went before the jury *pro se* to present his constitutional defense. The government presented 17 witnesses and put into evidence one of the pamphlets in which he stated that he had paid no income tax for fifteen years. Tecton declared that he was perfectly willing to pay an equal or constitutional tax, but not one that created elite, privileged, and slave classes in society.

After eight hours of deliberation, the jury was hopelessly deadlocked, and the judge declared a mistrial. He scheduled the second trial for October 22, 1974. Since Tecton had sued all the judges in Virginia, one had to be imported, who conducted the proceedings in a disgraceful manner. In spite of objections, the jury consisted almost entirely of federal employees; Tecton was denied the right to present witnesses; he was told that if he mentioned the previous trial to the jury or cited the Constitution, he would be held in contempt; the judge even suggested that Tecton should be committed for a 90-day psychiatric evaluation. However, no such motion was made, perhaps because of a possible suit.

Although the jury found Tecton guilty, his sentence was mild. He was fined $100 (never paid) and given six months of unsupervised probation. He could have been fined $30,000 and imprisoned for three years. He attributed the light punishment to the fact that he had sued a great many people and that the majority who had witnessed his actions and heard or read what he had to say agreed and sympathized with him.

Although the IRS spent an estimated $200,000 in its futile attempt to silence Tecton, it did not succeed, nor did he ever send any money to the Agency. However, he was caused great personal injury; checks from his employers were seized, he lost his employment, his bank accounts were confiscated, and he was reduced to such economic straits that at times he could hardly pay his utilities or rent.

All this, however, did not deter him from continuing his crusade. He organized the Thomas Jefferson Equal Tax Society, which distributed a newsletter called *The Emancipator*, a tabloid, *U.S.A.*, a series of cartoons, and documents such as *101 Reasons Why Unequal Taxation Is Illegal, Class Tax Is a Crime*, and *How to Stop Illegal Taxation*.

Tecton objected to the federal income tax chiefly because it is discriminatory, creates social classes, is unconstitutional because it violates the principle of equal protection under the law, and establishes an elite nobility on the one hand and a great mass of tax slaves on the other. The income tax, he declared, can never be constitutional until it lays the same burden on everyone; in 1974, he estimated that such a levy might be $400 per capita, regardless of economic position or personal income.

In *The U.S. Income Tax is Illegal,* he described in detail the classes the income tax creates: first, the Elite Tax-Subsidized Class, which actually obtains its operating and business capital from the federal Treasury. This class not only pays no taxes, but is enriched by the tax slaves.

Second: the Tax-Free Class, which consists of welfare recipients, favored individuals, corporations, foundations, churches, and other "charitable" entities, etc., which pay no taxes on commercial incomes.

Third: the Tax-Slave Class, which consists of wage and salaried workers, small, struggling business people, farmers, etc., who are forced to pay not only their own tax burden, but also the cost of financing the Elite Master Class and the share that should fall on the Exempts.

In order to continue this system of robbery, extortion, and slavery, the Congress, the courts, the federal bureaucracy, as well as those who profit by the system, are united in a vast conspiracy to bring down, oppress, exploit, deceive, and rob the producers who create the wealth of the nation.

In *101 Reasons,* Tecton exposes the inquisitorial 1040 form, the wage-withholding tax, the Social Security fraud, and, in general, the unconstitutional procedures of the federal government. Slavery, he declares in *Class Tax Is a Crime,* is taking money from producers and giving it to others who have not earned it.

Tecton blames the people themselves for electing and re-electing the congressional traitors who have created a system in which the American producing classes are reduced to subservience.

Tecton's experiences did not prevent him from continuing his crusade. In one issue of *The Emancipator,* he listed 51 reasons why the 1040 tax return is unconstitutional. Among these is that Congress has no power to lay or collect an unequal tax upon constitutional equals. The income tax is a crime because it is based on extortion, and creates a forced-informer type of government; it violates the common law and common rights; it is an instrument that destroys honesty, safety, property, freedom, and honor in American citizens. Because the income tax both confers and withholds various privileges or immunities, it denies equal protection under the law. It constitutes a Bill of Attainder, outlawed by the Constitution. It takes property without due process of law from some citizens for non-public use and thus creates a caste of nobility through forced discrimination. It destroys the incentive to work and produce among formerly free and independent citizens. It forces citizens to use an illegal currency.

Elsewhere, Tecton declares that when a person files a 1040, he is guilty of aiding and abetting in the commission of a felony because: (1) The Constitution permits only an equal tax on all citizens; (2) the Constitution forbids any Bill of Attainder law; (3) the Thirteenth Amendment prohibits the establishment by law of favored classes of citizens; (4) the Fourteenth Amendment forbids unequal taxation; (5) the withholding tax is illegal because it is an indirect tax; (6) the 1040 form violates the Fourth Amendment because it is actually a search warrant that pries illegally into the private and business lives of all individuals.

The foregoing is merely a sample of the material Mike Tecton has distributed far and wide.

George L. Kindred: Layman Versed in the Law

Through contact with Arthur Porth, George Kindred and his friend James Freed became the sparkplugs of tax rebellion in Michigan in 1968. To both the state and federal governments they made Porth-Daly type returns; they conducted rallies and distributed literature attacking the Internal Revenue Service and the Federal Reserve System.

However, it seems that the IRS ignored them during confrontations with the State; and, since the charge against them was not failure to pay a tax, their refusal to produce records, their arrest and subsequent imprisonment by the State were of singular significance.

The rebels asserted their immunity to such surrender under the Fourteenth Amendment, which extends the protection of the Fourth and Fifth Amendments to all the States and declares that: "No State shall make or enforce any law which shall abridge the privileges and immunities of citizens of the United States; nor shall any State deprive any person of life, liberty, or property without due process of law; nor deny to any person within its jurisdiction the equal protection of the laws."

Since no one may be sent to prison by a federal court for asserting rights conferred by the Fourth and Fifth Amendments, neither could a state court legally do so. They believe that records are inviolable under the Fourth, and, under the Fifth, no one can be forced to supply testimony which could lead to prosecution. Furthermore, under the Sixth and Seventh Amendments, no one can be sent to prison except by due process of law, which would include a trial by jury.

On March 16, 1970, Kindred and Freed both received letters from the State Treasurer stating that their returns were improper and demanding corrected ones. Instead of complying, the men requested jury trials to test the constitutionality of the State income tax. On December 7, the State subpoenaed their books and records; since the subpoena had no court seal, it was ignored. After new subpoenas were issued and ignored, Judge Roy Hotchkiss ordered the two men to appear in court with their records on June 4.

However, instead of making an appearance there and pleading the Fifth Amendment privilege—which legally they could have done—they stood on a corner near the courthouse, handing out their literature.

The Attorney General then petitioned the Ingham County Court for a contempt citation and arrest. Without a trial, the two were each fined $150 and sentenced to six months confinement in the county jail for contempt.

Now deep in the study of law, Kindred either issued a release or took some kind of action almost every day for months. Although friends did their best to effect the men's release—which the Michigan authorities promised in return for a surrender of their records—they refused such a compromise with scorn.

They were finally set free on November 22, after 148 days of incarceration. Shortly thereafter, they issued a 36-page report on *A Chronological Synopsis of Legal Events Concerning the Battle of Patriots George L. Kindred and James A. Freed*, the first in a long series of publications released by these men during the coming years. Kindred soon emerged as one of the most outstanding American crusaders advocating the abolition of the income tax.

A group of people in Cedar Rapids, Iowa, had been induced to make a declaration under oath—in return for a promise of clemency—accusing George Kindred and two others of "aiding and abetting" in the preparation and filing of false W4-E forms. They agreed to swear to this before a grand jury and to repeat the testimony in a United States District Court.

On March 22, 1972, at least a dozen vehicles, occupied by more than two dozen heavily armed officers, surrounded the home of George Kindred. There was no warrant for his arrest—only a teletype message from Iowa stating that there was a bench warrant for the arrest of Mr. Kindred. He was whisked 70 miles from Pinckney to Detroit, where he was fingerprinted and treated as if he were a major criminal.

However, as he had never seen or spoken to the Cedar Rapids group, he wrote U.S. Attorney Van Doren that the indictment "was false, erroneous, and spurious, and that if he did not move immediately to quash and annul, he [Kindred] would have no alternative but to initiate both criminal and civil actions against all those involved in the false and malicious charges. . . ." Thereupon, the witnesses repudiated the statements they had made before the grand jury, since Kindred could prove that he was hundreds of miles distant at the time when the alleged statements were made. The prosecution dismissed the indictment and all proceedings were *nol prossed.*

In 1974, Kindred founded his Patriot's Committee, which disseminated a great deal of information about the tax rebellion and the Federal Reserve System. On December 4, 1975, he wrote that because "[A]ction without knowledge of basic law is foolhardy at best," he had given birth "to the Layman Educational Guild of Law, including *Legal Law Course for the Active Patriot,*" a textbook with this introductory inscription: ". . . this text is gratefully dedicated to . . . every brother and sister in Christ who has the character and courage to stand up and fight to preserve our Christian and American heritage. . . ."

There is no doubt that Mr. Kindred has learned a great deal and become far more sophisticated in techniques of defense than he was when he handed out leaflets on the Capitol steps in Lansing in 1971. In April 1977, he began publishing a newsletter called *The Daily Eagle,* of which we have a complete file.

It was indeed remarkable that the IRS took no action against Kindred following 1967–70, for which he filed Porth-Daly type returns; or later, when he filed nothing at all. However, on June 29, 1976, Internal Revenue advised him that if he did not promptly file a proper return, the Service would seek information from third parties and levy taxes on the basis of that information.

Kindred made no response so the Agency sought information regarding commissions paid to him by real estate firms in 1967–70 inclusive; and, since no information was available for the following years, they assessed taxes on presumed income. On November 12, they sent a 35-page document explaining their levies.

We know of no other case in which the IRS went back more than six years and assessed taxes against five of these years without the slightest information on which to base such assessments.

The taxes and penalties assessed for 1967–70 totalled $9,734.55. Then, for the five subsequent years, a tax of $5,795.19 was assessed, for a total of $15,529.73. Of course, before settlement would be accepted, heavy interest charges would be added and perhaps a penalty fraud of 50 percent.

Instead of signing the "Waiver of Restrictions on Assessments," Kindred countered with a letter, dated December 6, 1976, asking that a number of IRS documents be sent him and that all letters, memoranda, reports, and other material in any way dealing with his case be made available under the Freedom of Information Act. On January 1, 1977, he wrote that: "since it is beyond comprehension how the IRS can 'lawfully' concoct and fabricate 'income' data out of thin air, I must respectfully reserve all rights, immunities, and protections mandated by the Constitution of the United States of America and all laws pursuant thereto, including . . . Amendment[s] I, IV, V, VI, VII, VIII, IX, X, and XIV, and attach copy of the same as an integral part thereof."

On March 14, the IRS advised Kindred that certain documents would be available for inspection and copying at the IR office in Ann Arbor. But the 374 pages he found there did not include everything; some documents were withheld for unspecified reasons. Mr. Kindred noted that his case was marked "Special Handling," which meant it had become highly sensitive.

The government case was built on shifting sands: Why did they wait nine years to take action on his 1967–70 reports? Why did they file only a civil action? How could they maintain that Kindred had received taxable income when there was absolutely no data whatever available to them for the years 1971–75 inclusive?

In October 1977, Kindred filed a formal Petition with the Tax Court for a redetermination of the assessments placed against him on November 12, 1976. On February 28, 1978, the Appellate Appeals Officer wrote that "Kindred's case file had been transmitted to 'Office of Regional Counsel . . . for defense in the United States Tax Court'."

Three years after the IRS began its intensive investigation through third parties it set June 25–26, 1979, for a hearing in the Tax Court. On February 28, 1980, the Court handed down a decision supporting the IRS. Kindred then filed a motion to vacate the decision, but this was denied.

He then prepared briefs that reflect the expertise and masterly style which he had developed over the years and in which he soundly refuted the legality of an assessment based on pure speculation. The fact that he and his family continued to occupy a house and consume food, did not, he declared, constitute evidence that he had taxable income. In its brief, the government admitted that gifts for Kindred's personal support might be non-taxable, but it contended that any sum received to underwrite travel or other expenses incurred in his tax work would be taxable as if it were income paid for services rendered.

In the spring of 1982, the IRS ordered Kindred to produce his records for 1976–70; he appeared, but pleaded the Fifth Amendment, after which nothing more was heard from the Agency. Kindred believes that any one of several reasons may account for its failure to take any further action: Perhaps the Agency is uncertain of its position; possibly the courts are so clogged that it would be years before the case could be resolved; and that perhaps the IRS is afraid of defeat!

In the course of his battles in the Tax Court, Kindred discovered that many of its judges and other functionaries are not only former employees of the IRS or the Treasury Department, some may even be nominated by the Commissioner of Internal Revenue. Contrary to its own claims, the Tax Court is actually an integral element of the IRS itself. These judges, therefore, cannot be without bias and prejudice; in fact, they are a part of the prosecution.

After uncovering these facts, Kindred demanded a congressional investigation into a situation in which IRS officials, having retired with very good pensions, can become Tax Court judges with large salaries, operating in complete contempt for the Constitution and the most basic rights it guarantees. Kindred's charges and revelations shook the whole system from top to bottom and resulted in the demotion and resignation of several U. S. attorneys and agents; the reverbations echoed even into the offices of the Commissioner of Internal Revenue in Washington.

In due course, the Sixth Circuit Court denied Kindred's appeal by confirming the decision of the Tax Court, but he has not heard from the Agency since. He was never charged with tax evasion until the statute of limitations for criminal prosecution had expired; the IRS brought only a civil proceeding for *nine* years, an unprecedented action; and it is now attempting to collect taxes on income totally unsubstantiated by the slightest evidence.

Kindred has concluded that the IRS—uncertain of its position—is egging on the State authorities to do their dirty work for them. Meanwhile, the IRS has placed liens on "George L. Kindred's real and personal property" at the court house without any specifications; since no such assets exist, this is understandable. He believes that the Agency is now ready to declare his tax liability at something like "40,000 frauds." However, the State bills him every month for ever-increasing amounts—which he ignores and which, by January 31, 1983, had grown to $6,304.05, according to the fabricated information supplied by the IRS.

However, neither the State nor the federal tax collector can document the existence of any income—much less, any taxable income—for many years past; and Mr. Kindred owns no real estate or even any personal property, except the clothes on his back and perhaps some writing paper and equipment.

In the meantime, Mr. Kindred travels from one end of the country to the other; he speaks at seminars, conducts classes, and teaches patriots everywhere how to defend themselves against arrogant bureaucracies. In the Special Edition of the *Legal Eagle* of May 1983, he reports meetings attended by 650 patriots in Alaska. He deals not only with disputes involving taxes, but with every species of legal confrontation—even traffic fines; in this endeavor, he offers a massive document setting forth the legal techniques which serve a similar purpose.

He has letters from countless people whom he has helped; probably George Kindred is now better qualified in court procedures than are many members of bar associations. He tells of one man whom the IRS had billed for $100,000, but who ended by receiving a refund instead, as a result of his help.

The reader can obtain full information concerning Mr. Kindred's law course for Active Patriots by writing him at 9600 Cedar Lake Road, Pinckney, Michigan, 48169. For anyone needing help in any legal matter, especially in the field of income taxation, he can be relied on as a reasonable and dependable source of help and information.

Lucille Moran: Woman Invincible

Lucille Moran of Tavernier, Florida, and her Independent Bar Association of Massachusetts have distributed such publications as *How to Refuse Income Taxes Legally* and *Taxation Depends on Confession*. It has been said that she has caused the IRS more trouble and headaches than anyone else and that her method of resistance may eventually compel the Congress to abolish or drastically reform the present federal system of taxation.

She first became a rebel in the early 1960s in Massachusetts, fighting the courts, lawyers, and probate judges and other officials who were fleecing her father's estate. When she discovered that they were in collusion with the IRS, she declared that she would never again pay any income taxes. When the IRS moved against her in March 1967, she immediately closed her checking account and began to do all business on strictly a cash basis.

In *How to Refuse*, which is principally an argument based on the

Constitution and the Common Law, she maintains that: No one can be forced to file a 1040, and that almost every indictment or assessment against a taxpayer is based on information supplied by himself.

She points out that by filing the "Confession Sheet"—the 1040—the taxpayer waives all his constitutional rights; if he is guilty of an omission or misstatement therein, this is treated as a felony, while failure to file or submit something is only a misdemeanor. Section 7203, which provides that a fine of $10,000 and imprisonment for one year—in addition to costs of prosecution—may be imposed for a refusal to answer questions, failure to surrender records, or declining to file a return, is therefore totally unconstitutional, null and void, *ultra vires, ab initio*, and of no effect, as if it had never been enacted.

Since no criminal sanctions can legally be enforced against a taxpayer for failure to file, surrender records, or submit to interrogation, the only crime punishable under the Code is perjury, which can be invoked for filing a 1040 containing false or incomplete data.

Ms. Moran has consistently taken a strong stand against those who advocate filing a so-called Fifth-Amendment return, or any other, involving any species of protest; for, she maintains, this simply exposes those who do so to the full wrath of the IRS. The only effective method of protest, she believes, is to drop out completely, to supply no information.

With utter disregard for the Bill of Rights, declared Ms. Moran, the IRS forces citizens to make full confession without informing them of their constitutional rights or their immunities under the Miranda Decision. The Agency declares that compliance with Title 26 is voluntary; yet it threatens a prison term and confiscation of property for non-compliance. While professing the highest moral principles in its Code of Ethics, it violates every rule of honest and decent conduct.

In a personal letter Ms. Moran wrote: "I laugh out loud when I hear talk about Terrorist organizations and such Terrorists taking people hostage. The biggest and most notorious Terrorist organization in the world is Internal Revenue. Thus, in Section 7203 and elsewhere it threatens fines and prison terms for failure to fill out a form properly. The Agency warns you of your right under Miranda and the Bill of Rights only *after* you have filed your *Confession Sheet*, when it already has your sworn testimony of self-incrimination." However, she declared,

> You are under no constitutional compulsion to help the Revenuers or any other opponents score against you, before or after that first step is taken. . . . The income-tax stratagem begins with Sec. 6012, which states that a return must be filed, but says

nothing about taxes; by obeying this, the filer waives his rights under the Fourth Amendment against search and seizure; those under the Fifth against self-incrimination; and those under the Seventh to a right of trial by jury. Thus, the unwary are trapped into surrendering all their constitutional rights; and this leads directly to Sec. 7203, which provides that anyone who fails to report all of the information required by 6012 is subject to criminal penalties.

The whole sequence and procedure is therefore based on fraud, lies, cajolery, and entrapment. Signing a return which is incomplete or which contains false information is "the cardinal sin, indeed the only sin in the revenuer's credo." And without "a signed (but unsworn) return on which to draft a case for prosecuting you for fraud and criminal evasion, in bona fide courts, Internal Revenue attorneys are hamstrung because they're chained to the limits of their bogus procedures in their make-believe 'Tax Court'."

Commenting further on Sec. 7203—which makes non-filing of the Confession Sheet a crime—Ms. Moran observed that one good informer is worth 50 FBI agents:

> If crooks and hoods would only cooperate enough to give a yearly accounting of themselves to their friendly neighborhood FBI office, on or before a designated day of holy obligation, Federal agents could enjoy the fun of busting them for crimes against the state. This would be a much easier task than trying to nail them for crimes against Natural Law. . . . Then shady characters could be prosecuted for willful failure to file annual confessions, supply information. . . . Then the culprit could be convicted, locked up, and federal coffers could ring merrily. He'd have to ante up the costs of his own prosecution, as well as a disobedience tax or not more than $10,000.

The point is that the IRS punishes all the decent, self-reliant taxpayers precisely as felons could be treated under the procedures outlined above. But criminals who know their rights do not fall into any such trap. If they give evidence at all, it is only after they are paid heavy informers' fees or if they are guaranteed immunity from prosecution.

Law-abiding citizens, however, are rarely versed in their own rights.

Thus, the basic tenet of the Moran System is that: No citizen should file any return at all; and there is no valid reason for executing a signed or unsigned return under protest. The citizen should have no written or verbal communication whatever with the "revenuers."

After Ms. Moran began receiving requests for help from people in trouble, she prepared and distributed her *Complete Guide* nationally. In a two-page letter, she set forth the conditions under which she would accept fees from clients:

1. fee must be remitted by postal money order or cashier's check before April 15 (this is so that neither will leave a paper trail);
2. client must have had no previous difficulty with the IRS;
3. clients must submit summaries of their tax situation;
4. clients must not call attention to their dropping out from the revenue system;
5. client must agree to never again file any tax return; and
6. failure to abide by these conditions will put an end to the relationship.

Filing nothing whatever and then disappearing from sight, declares Ms. Moran, is the technique by which the IRS computers can be defeated; give them no data, and they will have nothing with which to work. Millions of people die; other millions move, leaving no address. When the taxpayer simply vanishes, the IRS sends three form letters demanding a prompt reply and an income tax return, each more threatening than the last. Sometimes such letters contain bait in the form of a promise to make a refund, if it is due, to people from whose pay taxes have been withheld.

When no response is elicited, the computer in due course concludes that the taxpayer is dead or out of reach. According to Ms. Moran, this usually ends all attempts on the part of the IRS to locate at least 75 percent of its vanished victims. It does not have the manpower to track down millions of people, nor would it pay if it could. Without the voluntary cooperation of their victims, the IRS is virtually powerless.

As a result, we can expect selective criminal prosecutions to become more vicious and frequent. Genghis Khan burned one or two villages every now and then in order to keep the remainder of his victims in line. Now, the IRS sends people to jail, destroys their businesses, breaks up their families, and bankrupts them, in order to terrify others into abject submission; this is the method used by every tyrannical government. Thus it is that Fifth-Amendment protesters—as if they were waving a red flag at a bull—invite the most severe reprisals; for they not only declare their positions, they dare the government to come and "get" them.

Ms. Moran notes that in 1977, the IRS admitted that in Florida alone, 300,000 taxpayers did not file any returns. Extrapolate that number for the whole country, and you have a total of at least ten million; the actual number is probably much higher than that.

How, asks Ms. Moran, can the IRS contend with all of these when it cannot even audit more than a very small fraction of the people who file various types of protest returns and highly questionable conventional reports?

In a release I received from Ms. Moran in October 1980, she declared that: "The quiet stop-filing approach is an attack on the revenuers' jugular—their computers. . . . Any notion that the income tax scheme is unbeatable is not supported by what happened in the 1970 decade. . . . To date, the names of 25 or 30 million non-filers have been slipped off the Internal Revenue computers. These individuals successfully availed themselves of the way these business machines are programmed automatically to release identification stencils when no return—with matching information—is filed."

Ms. Moran described the service she offered in her Newsletter *Fine Points*, for Nov/Dec 1979. "Our primary function is to provide . . . expert advice and strategy—assistance to fit your particular situation and to counsel you on what to do—and what NOT to do under various circumstances. Should documents or other material become necessary to back up your First Amendment non-filing—as occasionally happens—we write the letters for you."

In a personal letter, Ms. Moran stated: "The Revenuers have been generally UNSUCCESSFUL in identifying our subscribers because our approach begins with basic training to prepare the individual on how to become a NON-FILING Protester. This course also includes instructions on how to elude detection. This is NOT to say that NONE of our people have ever been discovered. When the Adversary obtained copies of the checks I had cashed at . . . a local bank back in 1974, they DID identify a small handful of our associates. These individuals were eventually subjected to the Revenuers' Inquisitorial Prosecution Ordeals. . . . Our strategy of NON-FILERS elude [sic] detection is geared to the awareness of the tricks, ruses, and subterfuges the Junta uses to DEFEAT the cause of justice and equal protection of the law in the courts and other forms they now control. The most rewarding effects of our Silent QUIT-FILING approach are that there are now, at least, thirty million NON-FILERS who have quietly slipped through the Adversary's computer net—and that the Junta is blaming us for the so-called 'Underground Economy' which they admit they have no way of measuring."

That her technique has been successful is an established fact. The *Wall Street Journal* noted in an article published March 20, 1980, that "Lucille Moran's clients have been traced to virtually every state in the country and Puerto Rico," and, according to an IRS memo, she is "one of the most significant cases in the tax-protest movement."

However, in 1980 Ms. Moran was indicted by a grand jury for "aiding and abetting" in the filing of false income tax returns, which is a felony under Section 7206.

I do not know all the details of what happened, but the Service must have felt that its case was rather fragile; quite probably it did not relish the prospect of facing this highly articulate and persuasive woman in court, for on August 27, 1980, the government in the U.S. District Court for the Southern District of Florida moved to dismiss the indictment against her "in the interests of justice."

However, in preparing the prosecution, the Department of Justice conducted a full-scale investigation in 15 states, employed 47 Special Agents to gather information, issued a great many subpoenas, and spent perhaps more than a quarter of a million dollars.

And so Lucille Moran remained triumphant to the end. She died on July 5, 1983.

Armen Moths: Dedicated Scholar and Organizer

As a result of a confrontation between the IRS and the owner of a warehouse in San Diego, Armen Moths was to emerge as a national figure in the movement to restore the Constitution. On May 9, 1972, John R. Heck, accused of failure to pay taxes totalling $8,255.62, rescued property which had been seized, sealed, and padlocked by the IRS without court order or semblance of due process.

The chronology of events was as follows: On the morning of that day, accompanied by friends and supporters, Mr. Heck appeared at IRS headquarters demanding that his property be returned to him until any alleged tax liability be determined by a court; otherwise, he would re-occupy his premises according to his "guaranteed constitutional rights." The protesters then went to the site of the warehouse and rescued the property by forcible entry. There was a scuffle outside the building; after throwing a stone through the glass on the front door, Mr. Heck entered his building, where he was arrested and handcuffed.

Seven individuals, including Armen Moths, then a candidate for Congress on the American Independent Party ticket, were arrested for "conspiring and attempting to rescue property seized by the IRS" and for assault upon a federal officer. The entire procedure was unique; for whereas in other cases—such as with Dr. James Owen in Portland, Oregon—the IRS refused to prosecute individuals who obstructed government agents, here it sought to involve as many as possible. Present at the scene were not only Treasury personnel, but also heavily armed FBI agents and others who, according to eyewitnesses, herded several demonstrators together, pushed them inside the building, and then arrested them for trespassing on government property.

Then, not satisfied with arresting six people in addition to Mr.

Heck, warrants were issued for four others, including Henry Hohenstein, who had driven from Los Angeles simply to gather information for a book he was writing on IRS procedures. To his amazement, although he took no part in the action, he too was charged with conspiracy to rescue government property.

After charges against one individual were dropped, the trial of the San Diego Ten, as they were known, began on December 5; on the 22nd, the jury brought in verdicts of guilty on one to four counts against all defendants. The handpicked jury included a number of government employees, who received full pay from their jobs, plus the regular jury compensation; Judge Leland C. Neilsen barred from jury duty anyone who doubted the constitutionality of the IR Code or who had ever had any trouble with the Service; he overruled all constitutional motions and made it a contempt-of-court offense to quote from or even refer to the Constitution. He also prohibited any mention of the fact that no lien had been placed on the warehouse—as required by law—before the property was seized.

Since no one had attempted to prevent the original seizure and since nothing had been disturbed inside the building, the defendants could only be charged with some vague sort of conspiracy. It also turned out that even the Notice of Seizure was not completed until the day after the demonstration. Furthermore, the government appraised the personal property impounded at only $91, whereas Section 6334(c)(3) states that books and tools of a trade, business, or profession not valued at more than $250, are exempt.

Although the IRS did its best to prevent publicity in the conventional press, the case attracted national attention. Nicholas von Hoffman wrote in a syndicated article published February 22, 1973:

> Hank Hohenstein is not your ordinary garden-variety fellow. Still, on March 5, he's going to drive down to San Diego and get himself sentenced by a federal judge for conspiracy, and it doesn't matter that he's a major in the Marine Corps Reserve . . . or that he writes poetry. . . . Hank's crime was to publicly protest the way the IRS treated another businessman, a stranger Hank didn't even know until last May 9, the day of the "overt act," as the prosecutors put it when they come at you under the Conspiracy statute.

Shortly thereafter, the judge reversed Hohenstein's conviction and ordered a new trial for him; and, after exactly one year, all charges were dismissed.

The remaining defendants received sentences ranging from fines of $50 to $1,000 and probation varying from six months to three years, all of which were appealed to the Ninth Circuit Court in San

Francisco. In a 22-page Opinion rendered on June 3, 1974, the Court reversed all charges based on conspiracy but upheld some of the convictions for assault. This was an important, if only partial, victory. The judge in San Diego then ordered certain fines to be paid within hours; and two of the defendants, who were paraded in public view in chains, actually spent a few hours in jail while awaiting the arrival of their funds.

Out of all this emerged Armen Moths, Harvard graduate and military pilot in the Korean War, to become one of the principal leaders in the movement to restore the Constitution. In 1974, he organized the United States Taxpayers Union (USTU), which issued pamphlets, news releases, and other material useful for tax resisters. The Union held meetings and conventions from time to time in different parts of the country; it was constantly active. It published articles advising its members how to conduct themselves during an audit and what protections are available under existing law; and it reprinted voluminous excerpts from Supreme Court and other decisions that taxpayers could use in their confrontations with the IRS. The organization also offered help to any dues-paying member who found himself challenged by, or in trouble with, the Service.

At a meeting in Washington, D.C., in July 1978, shortly after the overwhelming approval of Proposition 13 in California, the USTU launched its campaign "Yes on 23," the congressional proposal to repeal the Sixteenth Amendment. The specific goal at that time was to obtain 23 million signatures on petitions in support thereof; although this total was not attained before the elections of that year, several million signatures were gathered, and the movement to abolish the personal federal income tax gained greater momentum than ever.

Moths is now the principal collaborator with Willis Stone in a campaign, begun several years ago, to bring pressure upon State legislatures to repeal the Sixteenth Amendment. The story of this endeavor is detailed in Chapter 5.

Marvin Cooley: Silver-Tongued Orator

Perhaps no name in the resistance movement is better known than that of Marvin Cooley, a quondam farmer in Mesa, Arizona, who, without much formal education, began to study law and economics in the mid-1960s. He concluded that in order to regain personal freedom and reestablish constitutional government, we must get the federal government off our backs.

He was one of the first to hold seminars in which he instructed his auditors in techniques of tax avoidance; he declared that he had no objection to constitutional taxation, but was strongly opposed to the methods used by the IRS to collect its money. At his seminars, in public addresses, and in interviews on radio and TV, he maintained:

1. that IRS procedures are illegal;
2. that threats, lies, bluff, and intimidation are its normal *modus operandi;*
3. that its vest-pocket summons (Form 2039A) is illegal;
4. that the Agency routinely fabricates charges against innocent citizens;
5. that its operatives are unlawfully protected by sovereign immunity when they commit criminal acts;
6. that the withholding tax is illegal;
7. that the Agency violates every protection to which citizens are entitled under due process of law;
8. that many of its statutes violate the Constitution;
9. that tax monies are used for illegal purposes;
10. that it cannot legally force a citizen to answer questions, produce records, or obey its summonses;
11. that its illegal acts should be challenged in court and otherwise;
12. that it is the right and duty of all patriots to do so;
13. that sworn testimony before congressional committees proves that the procedures, methods, and rules employed by the IRS are arbitrary, dictatorial, and illegal; and
14. that the Agency constantly uses its threat of punishment under statutes that have been declared illegal and void in prior court decisions.

For 1968 to 1970, Cooley filed "improper" returns, that is, he did not supply the financial data from which a tax could be computed. In January 1972, he published *The Big Bluff*, a book consisting largely of the transcript of Vaughn Ellsworth's confrontation with the courts because of his failure to produce the records of his defunct Sonel Corporation. The book includes a number of legal documents to be used in litigation, letters from and to tax resisters, citations from Supreme Court opinions, and other pertinent documents. It also reproduces Cooley's amended 1040 returns, which reveal only his name, the names of his children, and objections to the form of the return as an invasion of privacy, the possibility of self-incrimination, and the fact that no valid or constitutionally legal dollars had been received. In answer to some of the questions, he simply wrote "Unknown." On his 1971 return, he included only his name, address and the statement that he was a private citizen with an estimated income in real specie of about fifteen dollars. But he also declared: "I will no longer pay for the destruction of my country, family, and self. Damn tyranny! Damn the Federal Reserve liars and thieves! Damn all the pettifogging, oath-breaking U.S. attorneys and judges, who will not uphold the clear and unambiguous language of the Constitution!"

After the IRS obtained an indictment under Sections 6012 and 7203, it arrested Cooley on June 27, 1972. At his trial, which began April 26, 1973, he was charged, not with non-payment of taxes—which he did not owe—but with failure to file "proper" returns—a misdemeanor.

The jury was hand-picked; the defense was not permitted to mention the Constitution, or even the provisions in the IR Code that relate to it. The jury was told that it had no function except to determine whether or not the defendant had gross income in the form of Federal Reserve dollars sufficient to require the filing of a return, whether he had filed a "proper" one, and whether or not he understood what he was doing, i.e., whether or not his action was intentional and therefore "willful." The judge told the jury that he and he alone would instruct them as to the law, and that they had taken an oath to accept the law as explained by the Court.

Thus sworn and instructed, the jury had little choice except to find the defendant guilty. On October 28, 1973, Judge Walter Craig "threw the book" at Cooley. He was given just 24 hours to post bail bond of $6,500, which would be returned only if he won a reversal, and he was given the maximum prison sentence of three years.

After all appeals were exhausted, Cooley began his incarceration early in 1975; most of his time was served at the minimum security facility located near Safford, Arizona. When he was released in March 1977, a great banquet was held in his honor, attended by hundreds of admirers.

Others who have served time are quelled by the experience: not so with Marvin Cooley. If he had been an outspoken propagandist before, he now became a leader for tax resistance. Even while free on bail bond, he conducted seminars. And while he was in prison, he began work on his book, *Tea Party 1976*, in which he reproduced his 1040 form filed for the year 1974 and on which, in several indicated spaces, he wrote "Object: Self-Incrimination." Although he continued to maintain that Federal Reserve notes are neither "dollars" nor real money, he gradually moved from the monetary defense to one based entirely on the Fifth Amendment privilege against self-incrimination.

In using this defense, he warns over and over that any other approach is likely to result in punishment. He stresses that if a tax resister adds material dealing with the monetary issue to his 1040, it is irrelevant; if such material is added to a Fifth-Amendment return, it indicates that his objection is not made in good faith, that the filer has motives other than simply guarding himself against the danger of self-incrimination.

In support of this position, he cites *Grosso*, *Marchetti*, and especially *Garner*, which, although they dealt with income from illicit sources, constitute also, he declares, a valid defense for any citizen.

Since Cooley has become a symbol of the tax rebellion, he is at last treated seriously and objectively by the media. In a long interview in the *Arizona Republic* on January 20, 1979, he admits that he made several errors before and during the 1973 trial that resulted in his conviction. Since then, he stated, he learned to object on grounds of self-incrimination, which has prevented the IRS from prosecuting him.

He emphasizes that taking the Fifth on an income tax return carries no implication of guilt, whereas giving complete information on a 1040 can often lead to indictments for various crimes. There's not a return in the world, he declares, in which IRS agents cannot find something wrong if orders are given to "get" the taxpayer. He adds that he does not advocate a refusal to cooperate with the authorities, but he does insist on his right to privacy and individual free enterprise as guaranteed by the Bill of Rights.

He maintains that he would always respond to a summons, but he would not answer any questions or produce any records. Instead, he would make a good-faith Fifth Amendment challenge, about which the IRS could do nothing. Although Section 7203 requires the citizen to file a return, that is all he has to do; he can take the Fifth thereon. However, if an individual includes irrelevant material, even though he writes Fifth Amendment somewhere on his return, it constitutes a bad-faith claim.

He compares those who refuse to pay tax because they did not receive money in the form of gold or silver to himself, "seven or eight years ago, but I found out . . . it's suicide to bring up that as a defense. . . . The Supreme Court has ruled that this paper money is valid dollars and the judge instructs the jury that the Federal Reserve note is a dollar for tax purposes." It is a mistake to assume that you are not required to file because you are a sovereign citizen, unlike a corporation, which must pay an excise tax.

Since 1977, Marvin Cooley has devoted much of his time conducting seminars in various parts of the country, some of which have been attended by several hundred people.

On his own 1040, he writes only his name, address, and Social Security number; he also signs it under penalties of perjury. He does not make a blanket Fifth-Amendment claim, but writes None or Object on almost all the lines. On his 1979 return, he wrote None 21 times and Object 8, and reported a capital gain of $1,500 on the sale of a boat. In the January 1981 issue of his newsletter *Tax Facts*, he stated:

> If anyone is incredulous about all this [the efficacy of his technique] let me say this: I have done this for 10 years now and have not been challenged; and I have not been assessed any income tax for these last ten years. I file a return each year, but I refuse to answer specific questions relating to my income on grounds of self-incrimination. I would estimate there are at least two or three thousand others, at a minimum, doing the same thing, and doing it validly and successfully.

As a matter of course, a Fifth-Amendment return will bring a letter from the IRS stating that the return is unacceptable, because it contains no information upon which a tax liability can be determined. If the IRS then issues a 2039A Summons demanding that you bring in all bank records and other documents, you may disregard it, or make a Fifth-Amendment challenge; if the Service then obtains a show-cause order from a U.S. District Court, you file a Motion to Dismiss, together with arguments explaining all the legal protections available against self-incrimination. According to Cooley, no one has ever been held in contempt for refusal to testify or produce records when this technique is followed. His Fifth-Amendment Packet contains specific instructions on how this defense is to be used, an example of the letter the IRS sends to "delinquent" taxpayers and the response they should make, the form used in Show-Cause Orders, an 11-page argument which can be used in a Fifth-Amendment plea and defense, and a sample Motion to Dismiss, to be filed in the court.

However, he warns that although many of the actions of the IRS and various sections of its Code are unconstitutional, and are, therefore, illegal, taxpayers cannot use this as a defense, because the courts and the judges deny it. The only valid defense the courts recognize and the IRS observes, is a good-faith plea against self-incrimination.

Cooley's newsletter is now called *Tough Talk*. It gives less attention to the Fifth Amendment defense and more to the legal protections available to the taxpayer.

"Red" Beckman's Message

An extremely provocative book, *Born Again Republic*, was published in 1981 by M. J. "Red" Beckman, a Montana rancher and businessman. In his dedication he explains that after the IRS audited his books and records, in 1976, he became active in the tax protest movement. And, after some research, he became convinced that confiscatory taxation is merely the symptom of a disease that threatens to destroy our constitutional republic.

In his book, Beckman attacks the welfare state, or what he calls the "free-lunch syndrome." Mr. Beckman declares that our Congress, our legislatures, our courts, and all their agencies have become hopelessly corrupt. There is nothing to be hoped for from them as long as the free-lunch syndrome continues. However, like Thomas Jefferson, he points out that the people still have one rock of refuge, the pillar of defense, which is stronger than all the other elements of government combined: the jury of peers, who possess the power of nullification and can, therefore, stop the criminals cold in their tracks. When a tax protester is tried by this criminal government, we need only one well-informed person on the jury to prevent conviction.

Beckman declares that Montana is the first state to regain its freedom; there, "the government doesn't get many rubber-stamp juries anymore, and IRS agents are now afraid of the taxpayer. The people are refusing to give their consent to a government that wastes our tax money because they now know the truth."

Thus, in Montana the juries determine not only the facts in a case, but also the validity of the law under which it is charged; and therefore it has become extremely difficult to assemble a jury without including people who are prepared to use their power of nullification. The government—the IRS—is powerless, and subject to the informed will of the people.

Beckman now devotes full time and all his energy to the restoration of constitutional government in the United States. Early in 1983, he published the book *Do Unto the IRS As They Would Do Unto You*, in which he states:

> Independent Grand Juries will use their power to investigate the activities of tax-consuming public servants. They will investigate the Federal Reserve and the Internal Revenue Service. Indictment of I.R.S. agents by Grand Juries will result in convictions by independent Trial Juries. U.S. Attorneys and Judges who have participated in prosecutions of tax protesters should be investigated and indicted by Grand Juries. They should then be tried and convicted by Juries. Sentencing of these convicted tax-consuming public servants should be very cut and dried. 'We the People' owe a debt to the victims of the crimes of the IRS and the cover-up. Every U.S. Attorney and Federal Judge who has been involved in the cover-up should be sentenced to one day in jail for every day in jail served by their victims. That would be justice! All of the assets of convicted U.S. Attorneys

and Judges should be seized and the proceeds distributed to the victims of the greatest cover-up in history.

Thus would the people be doing to the IRS as They Would Do Unto You.

If the IRS calls you for an audit, Beckman suggests the following procedures:

1. Never do any business with the IRS by phone; demand that all business be conducted in writing.
2. When notified of any audit, demand that the IRS state specifically what data it wants.
3. Notify the IRS that you will use a tape recorder.
4. Tell them that you will have at least two witnesses.
5. Ask for the bond numbers of all agents—they do not have any.
6. Inform the IRS that you signed the 1040 under duress.
7. Demand that witness fees be paid.

When the conference begins, behave with self-confidence; act as if you were in complete control, and then follow this procedure:

8. Demand to see the identification of each agent.
9. Start your tape recorder.
10. Ask about witness fees. If they refuse, you will have their refusal on tape.
11. Determine whether the information being sought will be made available to other government agencies.
12. Ask if any information obtained could be used in any future proceeding—either civil or criminal.
13. When they admit that it can be so used, ask for a written grant of immunity, under the Fourth and Fifth Amendments to the Constitution.
14. When this is denied, you are ready to terminate the conference.

If these suggestions are followed, the IRS will often drop any further demands. If the taxpayer must go to the Appellate level or to the Tax Court, he will understand his defenses, described elsewhere.

In a personal letter, Beckman wrote that his books are doing very well, but he adds that, "Our number one priority is still TV programming. . . . Educational TV programs are a must if we hope to accomplish a restoration of our constitutional republic." Beckman has produced five television specials: *People and Taxes*, 1979; *People Controlled Government*, 1980; *The Consent of the People*, 1981; *The Taxpayer Fights Back*, and *Tax Revolt and the Scriptures*.

Beckman reports:

> We have now shown our programs in over 25 states and should be into the other 25 in the near future. . . .
>
> The exciting thing about TV and the meetings that follow is

> the exposure we get to the people. Also, the quality of these people. We also go into the living rooms of judges, lawyers, politicians, bureaucrats, etc. The judges, prosecutors, and I.R.S. are hard put to identify the people who have watched the programs. . . .
>
> Every tax rebel should produce a TV special on jury nullification. The judges would go through all kinds of contortions to keep those tapes out of the court room. I doubt if anyone who concentrates on educating the jury will ever be indicted and tried. I keep hoping for the chance to teach my seminar to a jury in a court room.

Beckman's recently published books, *The Church Deceived* and *The Black-Robed Cover-Up*, as well as *Born Again Republic* and *Do Unto the IRS as They Would Do Unto You*, may be obtained for $6.00 each from Common Sense Press, P.O. Box 1544, Billings, Montana 59101.

In collaboration with Bill Benson of Illinois, Beckman has written a new book entitled *The Law That Never Was*, in which the research done by Benson in all the States and the District of Columbia clearly reveals that only four States ever ratified the Sixteenth Amendment exactly as proposed by Congress. The other 33 did so only after making changes in capitalization, punctuation, or actual wording. The authors contend, therefore, that this addition to the Constitution is null and void: In short, it is the Law That Never Was.

Floyd Wright: The Man Who Beat the IRS

Floyd Wright has published a very interesting book entitled *Beat the I.R.S.? I Did!!*, available for $7.00, postpaid, P.O. Box 323, Grass Valley, Calif., 95945.

Soon after Wright's graduation from college, he went into the real estate business, where he soon discovered to what extent the socialist cancer had been spreading in the American body-politic. While the government cannot as yet actually seize or nationalize private property, it accomplishes the same objective to a considerable degree by extensive control. The debasement of our currency is one of the means the government uses to destroy our republic; another is the income tax, which is used to control the people rather than to obtain revenue.

Wright began delving into law books, case law, and court histories. "[For] three-plus years," he declares, "after a snooping Special Agent came to my office, I spent hundreds of hours in the State Law Library in Sacramento. . . . My studies convinced me that the government was legally incapable of carrying on a criminal suit pertaining to an income-tax matter. Furthermore, I was convinced that a 'crime' had to be so designated, have a penalty affixed for the commission, and have it listed in the Criminal Code (Title 18). But I looked in the Criminal Code, and found no mention of income tax crimes."

This, he concluded, was the Achilles heel of the entire system. Under its own law, therefore, the government can legally bring only a civil proceeding against a citizen for non-payment of income taxes; it has no legal power to conduct an investigation of a criminal nature.

However, Wright had problems finding a lawyer who would challenge the jurisdictional power of U.S. District Courts to conduct criminal trials in tax cases. After paying his lawyer 1,500 Federal Reserve "dollars," he fired him and found one with whom he could act as co-counsel in any proceeding.

The government made an egregious blunder when it ordered Wright to appear in court: One of its agents had testified before a grand jury in order to obtain an indictment that Wright had committed a felony by making false statements under penalties of perjury. However, Mr. Wright had covered the perjury line on his return with a strip of paper and made copies which he used in filing. *Thus, there was no perjury line, without which no criminal prosecution can be conducted!*

On April 24, 1980, he filed a Motion to Dismiss on the ground that the Court had no criminal jurisdiction. On May 9, after a warrant was issued for his arrest, he made a special appearance, but refused to plead, thus denying the Court's jurisdiction; on July 29, his Motion to Dismiss was denied.

Wright then prepared a 20-page brief and appeal to the United States Court of Appeals for the Ninth District, demanding that the decision of the District Court be reversed. As the litigation dragged on into the next year, the government spent hundreds of man-hours preparing for the trial, which took place on June 9, 1981. Thomas T. Couris of the U.S. Department of Justice wrote that it was declining any further prosecution in the case. Wright believes the lack of the perjury line may have been instrumental in the Justice Department's decision; but he is convinced that the most likely reason is that the Department *knows the U.S. District Courts have no power or jurisdiction to treat income tax cases as crimes, and therefore does not dare bring this matter to a decision in the higher courts.* In the meantime, the IRS will of course disregard the Floyd Wright case as non-precedential, and, until the matter is settled by the Supreme Court, will continue to try others on criminal charges for failure to file proper returns.

However, Wright advises that a number of people have successfully challenged the jurisdictional power of the IRS to prosecute criminal cases. One example was Gail Sonocki, against whom the IRS obtained a 12-count indictment from a grand jury for violation of Section 7201 of the IR Code, as well as Section 7203 (failure to file). On December 29, 1981, the Department of Justice refused to handle the case in the U.S. District Court for the Central District of California. This was a tremendous victory; and in this case there was no deletion of the perjury line. However, as noted, the IRS accords no precedent to adverse decisions at any level below the Supreme Court, although it will cite as ultimate authority any court decision or opinion in its favor.

James Walter Scott: An Early Rebel

In 1973 James W. Scott was tried and convicted in Fresno, California, for failure to report his income or pay taxes thereon. He was then president of the National Tax-Rebellion Committee, dedicated to drastic reforms in the tax system, and was, perhaps, at the time, the most articulate tax rebel in the United States. He minced no words in declaring what he thought of the bureaucrats and the tax collectors; and he stated publicly that he could travel first-class because he did not pay seven kinds of taxes. He had, for some years, earned substantial commissions; his great crime, however, was not that he failed to pay taxes, but that he proclaimed the fact from the housetops, organized a nation-wide tax resistance movement, and persuaded others to follow his example.

The federal government obviously considered him very dangerous; it spared no effort or expenses in indicting and convicting him. His trial lasted several days; Scott did not deny that he had received unreported income; he seemed to enjoy stating in open court what he thought of the entire system and the methods used by the government to extort collections.

There were at least 35 armed federal agents in the court room. An undercover government agent had penetrated the defense by posing as a tax protester; he supplied the prosecution with concise reports of Scott's activities.

During the trial, the government managed to surreptitiously place one of their documents with those of the defense; as a result, four people who had come to assist Scott were arrested for tampering with evidence, although they knew nothing about the matter. They were released only after posting bonds of $5,000 each; but eventually the government dismissed all charges as pure fabrications.

Scott was found guilty of tax evasion and sentenced to prison; it was claimed that he owed something like $50,000 in income taxes.

Free on bail, he went underground and traveled through the midwest, using various aliases. He was finally apprehended and served about a year at the Lompoc Penitentiary in California.

Far worse than the prison term, however, was the tax deficiency charged against him, which kept increasing by leaps and bounds. The sum is now so huge that there is no possibility of paying it. For a time, Scott tried to earn a living selling kitchenware door to door; but the IRS caught up with him and simply seized whatever he earned, making it impossible for him to continue in any honest endeavor.

Thus, he was reduced to a position in which many others find themselves; no matter how capable they are or how willing to work, they cannot, because the government will simply confiscate whatever they earn. When a person finds himself in this position, the alternatives are bleak indeed: He may go on Skid Row, become a beggar, or turn to crime.

And this is what James Walter Scott finally did. A friend of mine in Fresno, who knew Scott well, recently sent me a newspaper clipping, stating that Scott had been indicted for counterfeiting and that thousands of dollars in bogus Federal Reserve notes had been found in his possession. According to the article, he had declared in court that he did not expect anything except a prison sentence.

Irwin Schiff: A Different Gospel

One of the best known tax rebels is the author of *The Biggest Con*, Irwin Schiff, a former insurance agent. He has been widely publicized in the newspapers and he has appeared on countless radio and TV programs. He has paid no income taxes since 1974 and made no returns of any kind since 1977. His books, cassettes, and other materials have probably outsold those of any other tax resister.

He was twice tried for failing to file "proper" income tax returns; his first conviction was reversed by the Court of Appeals because the prosecution had introduced irrelevant testimony; after the second trial, in June 1980, he served about four months in prison. His best seller, *How Anyone Can Stop Paying Income Taxes*, published in 1982, contains information which is unusual and intriguing. However, Schiff warns that he does not accept any responsibility for anything that happens to any individual who follows his advice; nor does he explain how to prevent the IRS from seizing property without due process of law or what can be done when such seizures occur.

Schiff maintains that the IR Code is illegal; that its administrators know this to be a fact; that the provisions therein are based on intentionally deceitful language and double-talk, in order to trick citizens into filing tax returns and paying income taxes; and that no one is legally required to do so *even under the IRS statute*, nor can anyone be legally punished for a refusal to make a return or to pay taxes. There is certainly much truth in all of this: for we have demonstrated repeatedly how the wording in the IR Code seems to require the use of the Social Security number in all financial transactions, even though the IRS knows very well that this is not so.

The IRS itself admits that all income taxation is based on voluntary self-assessment and compliance. In other words, if we do not wish to so volunteer, there can be no legal punishment for failure to do so. Actually, the income tax, to be legal, would have to be assessed and collected in the same manner as property taxes, wherein an official determines the amount due and sends the owner a bill, which can be challenged through legal channels.

Schiff holds that the use of the words "shall" or "must" in the income tax statute (or other government publications), does not mean "mandatory"; it means only "may" and constitutes a mere admonition without the force of law. For example, the Privacy Act never states that returns are *required;* therefore, we know that they are voluntary.

Schiff states that under the Amendment authorizing the income tax, no one can be required to make a self-assessment or pay any tax thereon, because it explicitly states that Congress shall have the power to *lay* and *collect* taxes, that is, the taxes must first be determined and laid by the taxing authority, which, having first computed the assessment on the basis of its own research, may then bill the taxpayer therefor, as does the county assessor on levies placed against real estate. When such a bill arrives from the IRS, the citizen would have the legal right to dispute its correctness or validity.

Filing a tax return, says Schiff, is like putting your neck into the hangman's noose; therefore, if you don't file, the IRS cannot hang you!

Irwin Schiff is now known to millions; he conducts his Untax Seminars in all parts of the country. His Freedom League, organized in 1982, is headquartered at 2140 W. Chapman, Suite 223, Orange, California, 92668. He publishes a monthly magazine, *Freedom League*, which features articles about the Federal Reserve System, the victories of tax resisters, and how to deal with government bureaucrats. The magazine gives advice on what to do if the IRS rejects the number of allowances reported on a W-4 filed with an employer, and how to achieve the exempt status from income received in the form of wages or salaries.

The magazine's staff offers a model letter to be used in writing to politicians, especially to members of Congress, and which, we believe, expresses the basic position of the Freedom League:

> I am involved in a movement to return the country to the republican form of government guaranteed us by the U.S. Constitution. I believe that 90% of the problems we are experiencing today is the direct result of the people permitting the government to subvert the Constitution. The people have stood by and watched the theft of our wealth through the creation of a fiat money system which is no longer backed by precious metals and is totally elastic to the whim of the Federal Reserve Board.
>
> Our government officials are refusing to obey the law and are running scared because the public is finally becoming educated to the fraud. I have taken a position that I will not be intimidated by the government. I am fighting for my rights and am trying to force the government into being responsive to the law.

And so, after escaping with a mere four months in detention and no fine, Schiff goes about the country as free as a bird; and, like Marvin Cooley, Charles Riely, and others who are constantly on the lecture circuit, seems to be completely untouchable. He now certainly has more income—tax free—than he had as an insurance broker in those days before he emerged as one of the country's leading spokesmen demanding restoration of constitutional government in the United States.

D. L. Kimball and the Second Declaration of American Independence

D. L. Kimball served several terms in the Iowa House of Representatives of the Iowa Legislature, as well as with the Congressional Committee of his party in Washington. In 1983, as a candidate for the Iowa senate, he proposed to introduce a memorial—similar to the ones passed in Arizona and several other states—calling for the repeal of the Federal Reserve Act.

The overall message contained in Kimball's books, *Your Choice—Freedom or Slavery*, *Freedom Is not Free*, (1983), and *The Money and the Power* (1984) is his "Second Declaration of Independence." Some of the Declaration's most significant points are the following:

"WHEN IN THE COURSE OF HUMAN EVENTS, and after over two hundred years of American Independence, and nearly two centuries of liberty under the Constitution of the United States, it becomes necessary to oppose and dissolve a trend toward tyranny and to reassert the sovereignty of the individual to which the laws of

Nature and Nature's God entitle them, a decent respect for the opinions of our fellow-citizens requires that they should publish the causes which impel them to this SECOND DECLARATION.

"Reaffirming the tenets of the Original Declaration, We assert that we continue to hold these truths to be self-evident, that all men are created equal, that they are endowed by their Creator with certain inalienable rights, that among these are Life, Liberty, and the Pursuit of Happiness, which specifically means one's wages and income and the ownership of private property. . . .

"The history of the United States for the past seventy years is a history of repeated injuries and usurpations, all having in direct object the establishment of an absolute tyranny over the people of this Republic and over the sovereign States which created the general government. . . .

". . . all three branches of the government . . . un-Constitutionally exercise the powers of the others. . . . wrongly emphasize democracy as a political form, whereas a Constitutional Republic was established by the Founding Fathers. . . . promote a kind of legalized thievery as a means to take from the wage-earner in order to redistribute wealth, but has only increased poverty among us. [Our government] has legalized a system of unfair taxation where extremely wealthy individuals pay little or no taxes. . . . It has assumed powers and prerogatives not its own and has blackmailed the States into compliance with tax money. It has pushed our people to the limits at which other nations have fallen and it has purposefully caused inflation so that they can be taxed at higher rates. . . . It has evinced an attitude that would seem to dictate the destruction of the great middle class of our nation.—It has allowed the prosecution of laws in the collection of exorbitant taxes to deny the Common Law presumption of innocence, and the denial of other rights guaranteed by the Constitution. . . . It has allowed all specie to be removed from backing our currency until it has become all but non-redeemable.—It has saddled generations yet unborn with a national debt that cannot be repaid.

"WE, THEREFORE, appealing to the Supreme Judge of the World and insisting upon our Constitutional Rights as free and Sovereign people, hereby absolve all allegiance to un-Constitutional government and insist that we are, and of right ought to be, the free people that God and the Constitution intended; that we hereby express our intent to do all possible and peaceful things to restore our Constitution and to Redeem our Republic; that WE DECLARE OUR INDEPENDENCE from all Tyranny for a Second time and in so doing we mutually pledge to each other, insofar as possible, our Lives, our Fortunes, and our Sacred Honor."

Mr. Kimball publishes an excellent magazine, *The Journal of Freedom.*

Armen Condo and Your Heritage Protection Association

In March 1975, after seventeen years experience in the vending-machine business, Armen B. Condo and some friends established Your Heritage Protection Association, which began by advising customers of their constitutional rights. The day after the first public meeting, the IRS notified the Condos that they would be audited. When the agent was confronted by eight witnesses and a tape recorder, he fled instantly. The IRS then served a summons on Condo's landlord, who, having been alerted to his constitutional rights, ordered the agent to leave the premises. Soon thereafter, the YHPA became involved in several court cases, all of which resulted in victories for the organization.

The basic purpose of the movement was to use the W-4 form to prevent any income tax deductions from employees' wages. Mr. Condo held numerous monthly or week-end seminars, and people began joining his organization by the hundreds, then by the thousands. The movement grew into a phenomenon without parallel in the United States.

It established headquarters in Huntington Beach and a bookstore and information center at 8761-9 Garden Grove Boulevard, Garden Grove, California. By July, 1979, it had 5,000 members in southern California, and even at that time it was estimated that 100,000 persons had attended classes or seminars sponsored by YHPA. In 1982, the membership exceeded 25,000.

In the monthly publication, *Your Heritage News,* and at their meetings, the leaders declared that the government has no legal function except to protect life, liberty, and property; and that the principal function of the federal government had degenerated into a vast system of bribery to induce a majority to vote for the perpetuation of this destructive despotism.

The YHPA declared that workers and wealth-producers do not owe any taxes to the government. The organization's stated objective was the restoration of a constitutional federal government, its powers strictly limited to those set forth in ART. I, Section 8, of the Constitution. It also conducted a vigorous campaign to abolish not only the federal income tax, but also the Federal Reserve System and to restore a constitutional monetary system in the United States.

On January 24, 1982, YHPA held a great conclave—called a Jamboree—in the Convention Hall Arena of Long Beach, California, with some 6,000 in attendance. On the following July 2, 3, and 4, another, smaller jamboree was held in the same place, no doubt due to the fact that in the meantime, after a five-week trial, Armen Condo had been convicted on 41 counts of tax-violation and mail-fraud, and shortly thereafter fined $92,500 and sentenced to eight years in prison. At the trial, the prosecution declared that, as a result of his activity, the government had been deprived of millions of dollars of revenue.

At the time of the July Jamboree, Condo was at liberty under appeal, but under the terms of his probation, he was (1) not allowed to associate with anyone who had been indicted or convicted for any manner of tax violation; (2) he was prohibited from encouraging others not to pay federal or state income taxes or to file W-4 forms claiming exemption from withholding; and (3) he was banned from employment by, or receipt of any compensation from, YHPA or any other entity which discourages payment of income taxes or the filing of exemption claims. Should he violate any of these restrictions, his bail would immediately be canceled.

If the government hoped to destroy the Association by silencing Armen Condo, it was quite mistaken, for, before his conviction, he had trained an extremely capable staff to take over the work. Among them are Dan Mitchum and his wife, Sandy, editor of the fine monthly, *Your Heritage News,* which features a great variety of educational material and news dealing with various aspects of the tax movement. The publication carries a calendar of seminars and events sponsored by the Association. For example, in the April 1983 issue are listed 43 meetings in California alone.

In November 1984, the IRS, with the help of local police, raided both the Association headquarters and Condo's home and carried away almost everything that could be moved. The Agency also placed a guard at headquarters and levied a fine of $1,474,000 against the Association and Condo for aiding and abetting in the preparation of "false and fraudulent" income tax returns. However, though the IRS has taken no action against those who reduced their tax obligations by filing them, I understand that, as of this writing, Armen is being held at the federal facility at Terminal Island, California, to begin serving an eight-year prison sentence.

Robert White: The Duck Book and Duck Clubs

Bob White's *Duck Book* was first issued in September 1980; and later was published monthly.

Most issues of the *Duck Book* carry the best articles from expensive newsletters, by such writers as Ben Barker, Don Bell, James Sibbet, Ron Paul, Jim Townsend, Alex Herbage, Murray Rothbard,

M. J. Beckman, Dr. George Arlen, and Colonel Archibald E. Roberts. Many of the pieces are written by Mr. White himself and some are reprinted from Liberty Lobby's *Spotlight* and other publications, such as the *National Educator* and *The Justice Times*.

Most of the issues contain investment advice and suggestions on how to insure economic survival should inflation bring on a total monetary collapse and the subsequent destruction of intangible investments. The *Duck Book* is a strong advocate of a specie currency.

A feature article by Gary North in the Spring 1981 issue compares the *Duck Book* to a hand grenade placed in the hands of American citizens. He says: "What White is doing is simple to describe, but tough to pull off. He serves as a kind of national clearing house for the true alternative press of America, the 'hard money' newsletter industry. He's getting crucially important information into the hands of literally millions of Americans—information they couldn't have assembled without help.

"Most Americans have never seen a newsletter. The newsletter industry is fast becoming the 20th century's version of the old *Committees of Correspondence*, the news network that Sam Adams created back in 1772. Those committees co-ordinated and made possible the American Revolution of 1776.

"If Bob White gets his way, the newsletter industry today will serve as the launching pad of another revolution, this time a revolution against Big Government and those who are using the system to rip off the American people.

"A new network of informed citizens is being created. You're part of it right now. Do you want to stay part of it?

"The Duck Book is only Stage One. Stage Two is the creation of a mailing list—a list that will enable you to become part of a new system of correspondence committees. Stage Three is the expansion of the Newsletter Industry. We want all people to have at least one subscription, so that this kind of information will hit every household in America on a regular basis. What you read in the *Duck Book* is only the tip of the iceberg."

Bob White's ultimate objective is to restore the constitutional principles on which our government was originally founded. He offers lifetime subscriptions (his life, not yours) for $10.00; and with a letter sent to his entire mailing list in February 1982, he included a certified copy of his income-tax return for 1981, showing that he lost $834,164 on the *Duck Book* that year.

Bob White is an integral part of the general tax-resistance movement whose purpose is restoring constitutional government. There are Duck Clubs in all parts of the country dedicated to promulgating the gospel of freedom and limited government; as of October 1981

106 cities had them. Although there are more in the West, especially in California, they are widespread throughout the South and may be found in virtually every one of the fifty states.

The Duck Clubs sponsor meetings and seminars in various parts of the country. The speakers generally are outstanding leaders in the fields of monetary and political reform. An unusually large and successful meeting was held in Costa Rica on November 5–17, 1982. The many speakers included Don Bell and then-Congressman Ron Paul of Texas. More than 800 attended, took part in workshops, studied investment techniques, and learned how to survive during an economic collapse.

Robert White no longer publishes the *Duck Book*, which has been superseded by two magazines, *The Financial Professional* and *The Financial Security Digest*.

Robert B. Clarkson: The Patriot Network

Robert B. Clarkson of Anderson, South Carolina, founded an organization in 1976 which he called The Patriot Network, whose objective was to Learn, Revive, and Preserve the Constitution. His credits include a B.A. from Clemson University, a lieutenant's commission earned during combat duty in Vietnam, and a law degree from the University of South Carolina, granted in 1971. In addition, he has served in a number of civil capacities.

The *Greenville News*, published near his home, carried an interesting article about him on November 27, 1979. When an IRS agent called to conduct an audit, he offered her an uncomfortable chair facing the bright sun, while he and a witness occupied comfortable seats. Then the Reverend Clarkson of the Church of the Holy Comforter—also the Church of Rational Morality—arose, bowed his head, and conducted an invocational service, which the IRS agent was constrained to honor by also standing with bowed head. But when Mr. Clarkson insisted on recording the proceedings, she fled in haste—which ended the conference.

For years, Mr. Clarkson supplied his clients—members of The Patriot Network—with a mass of legal or paralegal material to be used in confrontations with the IRS. Several of his documents detail techniques to be used in obtaining materials under the Freedom of Information Act. He describes methods of quashing a subpoena for bank- or other records. He has formulated a series of questions which a citizen may ask an IRS agent and which the agent is required to answer during an interview.

A model letter, intended for use by persons under investigation, includes the following:

> Recently, the IRS seized control of my bank records, including my checks and deposits. Soon, they will be contacting persons such as yourself who have had financial dealings with me. . . . I expect that you will shortly receive a . . . form letter.
>
> You have several options. . . . You can (A) cooperate totally with the tyrants; or (B) demand and receive the respect and courtesy to which you are entitled, as well as your constitutional rights.
>
> You do not have to furnish any information unless they comply with certain guidelines and statutes. Under the Privacy Act, 5 USC 552(a), federal agents must:
>
> (3) inform each individual whom it asks to supply information. . . .
>
>> (A) the authority . . . which authorizes the solicitation of the information and whether disclosure of such information is mandatory or voluntary;
>> (B) the principal purpose or purposes for which the information is intended to be used;
>> (C) the routine uses which may be made of the information; and
>> (D) the effects on him, if any, of not providing all or any part of the requested information.

Clarkson prepared an elaborate packet on how to proceed when the IRS attempts to obtain records held by third parties; if the defenses available under Section 7609(c) of the Code are fully utilized, the citizen can make it virtually impossible for the IRS to obtain any records. The packet includes a Motion to be presented in the District Court under which the citizen becomes the Intervenor. In addition, it contains a series of questions, prepared pursuant to Rule 33 of the Federal Rules of Civil Procedure, and which include the following:

> Has Intervenor been classified as a "Tax Protester"?
> Has any official definition been made of this term?
> Who has the authority to make such a classification?
> Have the tax returns of the Intervenor been accepted by the IRS?
> Describe in detail any investigation that has been made of Intervenor.
> Give names, titles, and addresses of any persons who have conducted any such investigation.
> Has the criminal division of the IRS been involved in any way?
> Has any recommendation been made to the Justice Department?
> Can any statement made by Intervenor or document presented by him be used in any criminal proceeding?
> List in detail the assets of Intervenor known to the government.
> Does the IRS expect to collect any funds from, or institute a judgement against, the Intervenor?

Another document is a demand by Intervenor that the government produce, at a given time and place, all documents in its possession pertaining to him, for his examination.

Another is a list of materials which Intervenor needs and demands in order to defend himself before the court.

Then follow detailed instructions of the steps to be taken and methods to be used in appealing any adverse decision in the United States District Court to the Circuit Court of Appeals.

Various model forms are included, such as those to be used in subpoenaing witnesses whom the Intervenor desires to examine.

If all these techniques are followed meticulously, it could be years before the IRS could see any records. Clarkson's objective was to require so much work and loss of time for IRS personnel that they will give up.

For several years, Clarkson published a periodical entitled *The Patriot Cannon, Booming for the Tax-Patriot Movement* which featured news concerning his Network. One issue was almost entirely devoted to audit procedures. When the IRS calls, tell them that all communications must be in writing; when a letter arrives setting a date for an audit, reply stating that this is inconvenient, but do not suggest an alternate time. If or when an audit occurs, the taxpayer should: deny every claim or allegation made by the agent, appeal to a higher level, and, above all, never make any admissions or affirmative statements.

The name of the game is to delay any impending audit, gain time, compel the adversary to use up his resources without obtaining any results. The taxpayer should not waste time on lengthy responses—which no one will read; he should take the Fifth as a last resort.

If the taxpayer is contacted by the IRS, via letter, for a third time, he should, before agreeing to meet, demand an exact Bill of Particulars as to what is wanted and why; still, no specific time for meeting should be offered. Throughout, however, one should be very careful never to state or write an untruth, which could result in very serious consequences.

When the information is received, further delay can be gained by using the Freedom of Information Act; the IRS should be compelled to cite its authority for every question it asks, what will be done with the information if given, and what punishment, if any, there will be for non-compliance.

All these procedures may take years; but at the end you will have a definite appointment for an audit. When this occurs, be sure to have witnesses—who need not identify themselves—and a tape-recorder in operation; if the IRS will not allow its use, demand a copy of the law or regulation that forbids it. "The tape-recorder fight alone," says Mr. Clarkson, "could easily last six months."

During the audit, never refuse to cooperate, but do ask innumerable questions; declare that you do not know or understand IRS laws or regulations, state that they are beyond your comprehension—anything to drag out the proceedings and wear out the enemy.

If you feel you have been treated unfairly when the audit is over, write your congressman and your senators, setting forth all the details of your complaint; this letter will be turned over to the IRS, which does not enjoy justifying its unethical or illegal conduct to members of Congress.

In one issue of *The Patriot Cannon* Clarkson explained why he refused to pay income taxes:

> Since I closed all of my bank accounts in November, 1977, I have been outside the jurisdiction of the IRS-Federal Reserve-Rockefeller Cabal. Our enemy has no control over us unless we voluntarily submit ourselves to his jurisdiction.
>
> Since I have removed myself from one division of the Federal Reserve, i.e., the Banks, and no longer have a privilege, i.e., a checking account, I have automatically removed myself from the other arm of the Federal Reserve, the IRS.
>
> My allegiance is to God, Family, & Country. The Washington regime is ungodly, one that no religious man could support. My tithe is to my church, to my churches' charity, not to the satanic wastrels, scoundrels, and politicians in the Babylon on the Potomac.
>
> I must be prepared to support my family, not depend on the good will of lying bureaucrats, thousands of miles away. To provide for my family's future, I need to store survival food now, survival guns, and survival currency, and not send any more hard-earned dollars to their bankrupt ponzi scheme.
>
> When I joined the Army in 1967, I took an oath to support and defend our Constitution from all enemies, both foreign and domestic. I reaffirmed that oath in August, 1969, when I accepted a commission in the U.S. Army. As yet, I have not been released from that solemn swearing.
>
> Sending Federal Reserve Notes to Washington's bloated bureaucracy is financing the destruction of our country, making more funds available to the welfare industry to increase the open-ended obligations to society's parasites.

The Patriot Cannon ceased publication in 1981, the year in which Robert Clarkson was indicted, tried, convicted and sent to prison for income tax evasion. Others can learn not only from his teachings, but from his experience.

Gordon Kahl: The Bloody Aftermath

Gordon Kahl was a North Dakota rancher who organized a Posse Comitatus group; he was one of the most colorful and extraordinary Americans of this century; and, since he was fighting a battle for what he considered freedom and a restoration of constitutional government, he deserves a place in this history.

He was no ordinary individual; he served as a gunner on a fightercraft in WW II; he stated that he shot down at least nine Japanese warplanes. For years, he worked in the Texas oil fields in the winter and returned to North Dakota in the summer; in the 1970s he became concerned that the government of this country had been subverted by international financiers, who used the Federal Reserve and the Internal Revenue System to enslave the American people; as a result, he simply refused to pay income taxes or file any returns. He was tried in 1977 in Texas for failure to file a return or pay the tax, found guilty, and sentenced to five years in prison. However, he was released in 1978, subject to five years of probation, which required periodic reports to an officer.

After his release, he reported to his probation officer for a couple of years; then, because he became convinced that this was another deprivation of constitutional rights, he simply stopped. However, not until 1981 was a warrant issued for his arrest; and it was two more years before any attempt was made to serve it or to place him under arrest.

In the meantime, he had made himself conspicuous and obnoxious to the authorities. There is solid evidence that his group, the Posse, was infiltrated by an FBI agent who fed information to the Agency.

The known facts indicate that what the government wanted was not to arrest Kahl, but to kill him or, worse, to provoke a bloody encounter in which as many as possible would be wounded or slain.

On Sunday, February 13, Kahl, his wife Joan, his son Yorie and two or three friends had attended a Posse meeting near Medina, North Dakota. Obviously he did not expect violence. Perhaps all the facts surrounding the ensuing tragedy will never be known, but certain details are incontestable:

The FBI and other law-enforcement personnel had blocked off the roads approaching the point where the shoot-out occurred. Drivers approaching the area were turned away with the warning that violence was imminent.

Several cars containing armed marshals were at the scene.

At least one ambulance was there also.

One of the marshals fired the first shot, which struck Yorie (it has been said that he had traded caps with his father and may have been mistaken for him).

Kahl fired—strictly in self-defense.

After Kahl began firing, two marshals were killed and two others wounded.

An AP news item appearing in a newspaper in Helena, Montana, declared that one of the bullets found in the body of one of the marshals had been fired by a government agent.

The next day a military force, including a tank, attacked, firebombed, and wrecked Kahl's modest home; however, he and one of his associates escaped, precipitating a nationwide search by the FBI.

Shortly after the shoot-out, Kahl wrote a letter to Jim Wickstrom, a posse comrade in Wisconsin, describing in detail how the attack upon him was perpetrated; he explained that he alone shot the government agents and exonerated his son and his friend.

It is not known how Kahl's hideout in Walnut Ridge, Arkansas, was discovered. It is probable he had been there most of the time after February 13. On Friday, June 3, heavily armed officers burst through the door of the house occupied by the refugee; before Kahl was killed and the building burned, one of the attacking assailants had been killed and another wounded.

Since autopsies performed on the sheriff and Gordon Kahl show that both were killed by shots fired from behind them, it is certain that they did not slay each other. Much of the whole tragedy remains shrouded in confusion, official cover-up, and mystery which may never be entirely unraveled.

On Wednesday, June 8, Kahl's remains were delivered to the custody of his wife in Grand Forks, North Dakota. Two days later, a Seventh-Day Adventist minister, Peter Dyke, conducted the funeral service. Hundreds of friends came to pay their respects and homage; Reverend Dyke declared, "It's so frightening. How could we ever know that a good man would get the death penalty for failure to pay an income tax?" Kahl was eulogized as a hero, a modern Paul Revere and Patrick Henry combined, while the media, there in force, looked on in amazement.

Tom Fitzpatrick of the *Arizona Republic* wrote a requiem for Gordon Kahl on June 10. Fitzpatrick had no sympathy for the principles espoused by Kahl. However, he described him as one of the kindest, most generous, and highly considerate individuals one could imagine; he wrote that Kahl was completely law-abiding in every respect except in regard to the federal income tax and related matters, that he was a devoted husband and father, and a productive worker; he had earned two Purple Hearts for service to his country; he was honest, reliable, moral beyond reproach.

The columnist notes that by the time Kahl was tried for failure to file an income tax return in 1977, he had already become too voluble—he was attracting too much attention to escape punishment: The first thing the judge declared at his trial was that he did not want to hear Kahl say anything about God or the Constitution. When the judge asked for his tax records, Kahl declared that God was keeping a perfect and complete record. Kahl was given five years in Leavenworth.

Before his death, Kahl's wife and son were tried for murder. She was acquitted—and is now penniless, as the IRS has seized her farm. Yorie was found guilty on two counts.

George Hansen: A Courageous Congressman

There are probably a number of congressmen who resent and despise the Internal Revenue Service; but their most outspoken critic, who minces no words in condemnation, George Hansen of Idaho, stands alone. I have heard him speak in public more than once; his descriptions of IRS atrocities exceeds anything I have heard from any other well-known or respected figure in American political life. He calls its agents bureaucratic brutes and the Agency itself the American Gestapo. His indictment of the Agency is found in his book, *To Harass Our People*, published in 1980, which every American, especially the middle class, should read and study.

"The people of the United States *are afraid*," writes Hansen. "They are frightened by this runaway arm of government which has powers that no business and no other government agency would dare claim or use." And he continues:

> Only IRS can attach 100 percent of a taxpayer's wage, salary, and/or property.
>
> Only IRS can invade the privacy of a citizen without court process of any kind.
>
> Only IRS can seize property without a court order.
>
> Only IRS can force a citizen to try his case in a special court governed by the IRS.
>
> Only IRS can compel production of documents, records, and other material without a court case being in existence.
>
> Only IRS can with impunity publish a citizen's debt to the IRS.
>
> Only IRS can legally without a court order subject citizens to electronic surveillance.

Only IRS can force waiver of Statute of Limitations and other citizen rights through power of arbitrary assessment.

Only IRS uses extra-legal coercion. Threats to witnesses to examine their taxes regularly produces whatever evidence the IRS dictates.

Only IRS is free to violate a written agreement with a citizen.

Only IRS uses reprisals against citizens and public officials alike.

Only IRS can take property on the basis of conjecture.

Only IRS is free to maintain lists of citizens guilty of no crime, for the purpose of harassing and monitoring them.

ONLY IRS PUBLICLY ADMITS THAT ITS PURPOSE IS TO INSTILL FEAR INTO THE CITIZENRY AS A TECHNIQUE FOR PERFORMING ITS FUNCTION.

He states that only IRS personnel are immune to law suits no matter how illegal, criminal, or outrageous their conduct against taxpayers may be.

"The IRS," he continues, "is an extraordinary example of the age-old adage that 'the end justifies the means.' The means used by the Agency is *growth*. In fact, it has a pathological fixation for growing, for consuming. The IRS reminds me of a tasteless parody of bad science fiction—a monstrous organism from another planet bent on devouring all within its path until its swelling protoplasm finally fills the entire earth."

He recounts the incredible story of an RCP (Return Compliance Project) planned for Fremont County in Idaho and approved by Howard Martin, District Director of the State, on October 16, 1975. Someone had prepared a hit list of 167 names—supposedly males between the ages of 21 and 65 who might be tax delinquents and prone to violence. Twenty-five agents, some or all of whom were to be armed, were to make a house-to-house search demanding that the residents prove that they had paid their income taxes by producing copies of their returns for the intruders to examine. These agents met and prepared for the "educational" campaign, which, however, was finally canceled.

Eventually, in spite of all IRS attempts to conceal it, Hansen obtained a copy of the "hit list," which included several women with names similar to those often given men: one was bedridden in a hospital; another was an elderly church-organist; several were young Mormons performing their two-year service in the missionary field. Some were prominent and highly respected professionals or business men who had always paid their taxes promptly. Only one had ever commited a "violent" act, which had occurred years before in a tavern.

Hansen tells the heartrending story of the destruction caused by the collapse of the newly completed Teton Dam on June 5, 1976. Floods had inundated a large area of Fremont County, causing at least $200,000,000 in damage, as well as nine deaths. As a result of Hansen's efforts, Congress appropriated the funds to compensate the victims for their losses. But then the IRS stepped in and began an almost incredible campaign of harassment. The Agency declared that the amount paid the victims above the original cost of the property (before inflation) or its depreciated basis, would be subject to capital gains taxation, unless it was replaced within two years by identical facilities. Thus, if the victim found his land useless for any purpose, he would be subject to this heavy tax; and if, for example, he could no longer raise potatoes, but shifted to wheat or some other crop, he would be required to pay this levy. Thus, after the farmers had purchased replacement machinery at higher prices or replaced their homes and barns, they would be forced to mortgage them in order to meet the demands of the tax collector. The irony is that the tragedy was due to the faulty construction of the dam, for which federal engineers alone were responsible. Actually, the farmers should have been reimbursed not only for their property, but also for their personal suffering and the deprivation of livelihood.

Perhaps the highlight of Hansen's book is his description of how the IRS almost caused his defeat for reelection in 1976. The Agency, knowing that it had no valid case against him, "leaked" information to the effect that he had been late in filing his return in 1968. If this was true, why did it take eight years to be reported? The fact was that not only did he not owe taxes for the year 1967, but he received a substantial refund because of overpayment; and he had filed his return, not in May, as the false information implied, but in February, well before the deadline.

Then followed a whispering campaign throughout his district, even more vicious than the false information which had been given to the newspapers. People began asking, "Does George Hansen pay his income taxes?" And, had it not been for some staunch and devoted friends who worked tirelessly in his behalf, he would have been defeated for reelection; as it was, he received only 51 percent of the vote.

Hansen has unearthed much about the IRS's internal operation through his investigations. He claims the Agency covertly monitors every agent and punishes those who show the slightest mercy or consideration for taxpayers. On the other hand, it rewards those who obtain the most and the quickest consent agreements, who seize property on the slightest pretext, and those who manage to drive small business men into bankruptcy. Thus, only the most cunning, merciless, and dishonest agents go to the top; in many cases, after some years of this kind of activity, they may retire with a very generous pension.

Hansen describes the fierce persecution of waitresses working hard, long hours to make a living and forced to pay taxes on tips calculated at 12.5 percent of sales, even while off duty or working as cashiers.

Our only safeguard, he declares, is an aroused public which will no longer tolerate an Agency that operates on a principle enunciated by the leftist Brookings Institution, which declared: "All income of individuals and corporations in the United States belongs to the government—whatever sums are left in private hands are a gift from the government."

George Hansen's book *How the IRS Seizes Your Dollars and How to Fight Back* (New York: Simon and Schuster, 1981) is an even harsher exposé of the IRS.

Hansen observes that: "Driving individuals and businesses into bankruptcy is not only standard procedure, it is actually organized on a competitive basis between the various IRS districts. One official IRS memorandum states, 'Certain cases must be closed in order to meet the predetermined goals and to compete with other Districts.'"

Elected officials are so terrified of the IRS that most of them dare not criticize: Those "who complain about IRS atrocities . . . will find themselves audited, investigated, and even out of a job. If no one else can bag a politician, the IRS can, whether he deserves it or not." For example, on one occasion, the entire membership of the Pennsylvania legislature was subjected to harrowing audits and investigation.

When Hansen and several other congressmen brought their findings about the IRS to the attention of the Ways and Means Committee, it, as well as the entire Congress, ignored the evidence and turned a "deaf, or, at least, a disinterested ear." They were terrified of what the IRS might do to each of them individually.

"Blackmail and extortion," adds Hansen, "are ugly words. But they are the only fair words to describe why the IRS is alone among government agencies in not being subject to scrutiny. Anyone who complains—*anyone*—is a candidate for destruction." For example, after Senator Montoya of New Mexico undertook an investigation of the IRS, he was defeated in the next election because of lies leaked to the press by the Agency.

Hansen declares that the Tax Court completely subverts law and justice; it "is a sophisticated legalistic nightmare." He warns that those who enter it, expecting to be tried by a jury, are misled; for

> [T]his never happens. [the Court] is regulated by a special branch of civil law which, contrary to all Western legal tradi-

> tion, denies the citizen, not only the right to a jury trial, but also his right to appeal to a higher court of law.
>
> Refusal to pay taxes assessed by the Tax Court is a felony. The taxpayer who has taken this course of action stands accused as a common criminal for refusal to obey the orders of the Tax Court.
>
> The IRS has done its best to take advantage of a system already heavily loaded in its favor. Tax Court judges, far from being comfortably impartial, have been, in every instance I have been able to determine, previously employed by the federal government. *Ten of the sixteen Tax Court Judges today are former employees of the Internal Revenue Service.* Four other IRS people are special hearing judges. Citizens who believe that they are assured of fair treatment in a Tax Court have been misled. . . . it is a grotesque game of making people play Russian roulette with their own rights.

Hansen concludes that:

1. IRS procedures are set up to intimidate, harass, and drive individuals and businesses into bankruptcy.
2. Promotion within the system is based upon the ruthless destruction of its victims.
3. The IRS goes to great lengths to prevent taxpayers from seeking or obtaining help outside the Agency.
4. It also goes to great lengths to hide its own abuses, especially by destroying the careers of elected officials who expose its atrocities.
5. Its procedures create a kind of cloak-and-dagger mentality among its agents.
6. It has lost all perspective as to its constitutional duty of merely collecting taxes.
7. In fact, this expanding Agency welcomes tax protesters because they create situations requiring intimidation, fear, harassment, retaliation, and punishment.

Finally, Hansen explores the illegal methods used by tax rebels—methods he does not approve of—and the steps that could lead to a restoration of justice and confidence in the federal government. Among them is a proposal that the graduated income tax, with its complicated allowances, deductions, and loopholes, be replaced by a single-rate tax, which would be assessed against all income—above a certain exemption—which was the basis of the income tax statute passed in 1894.

The IRS never rests once it targets a victim for destruction. Thus, in 1984, the Agency discovered that George Hansen had not reported certain of his wife's financial dealings. These had no relation to tax matters, but involved the unpopular House ethics rules on financial disclosure. Rep. Hansen had been assured that he need not report his wife's financial matters. However, he was tried and found guilty, by a local jury, in Washington, D.C. In spite of his troubles, he won the Republican primary in Idaho, and was defeated for Congress by a hair in the 1984 election. He is, of course, appealing his conviction.

Dr. W. Cleon Skousen and the Freemen Institute

The Freemen Institute, a 501(c)(3) organization, centered in Salt Lake City, is—except for Liberty Lobby—perhaps the most popular and successful group in America entirely dedicated to a restoration of the kind of government our Founding Fathers gave us. The Institute declares that we must jealously guard what Constitutional Freedoms are still left to us and strive diligently to regain what has been lost. Among its most revered heroes are Thomas Jefferson, James Madison, and Benjamin Franklin.

Under the leadership of Dr. W. Cleon Skousen, the Institute was founded on July 4, 1971, when it occupied two rooms adjacent to the Brigham Young University campus in Provo, Utah. At first it grew very slowly; it was not until September 28, 1976, that it moved into larger quarters in Provo. However, as its activities expanded, the organization moved to Salt Lake City, on August 21, 1979, into 6,000-square-foot headquarters.

Dr. Skousen was born in 1913, received a juris doctorate from George Washington University in the District of Columbia and was admitted to the practice of law there. He worked for the FBI from 1938 to 1952; was Chief of Police in Salt Lake City from 1952 to 1956, editorial director of the nation's leading police magazine for 17 years, and professor of law at BYU from 1956 to 1979, a position from which he retired to devote full time to the Institute.

Dr. Skousen has written more than 20 books; the most popular are a volume on Benjamin Franklin, *The Five-Thousand-Year Leap, The Naked Communist,* and *The Naked Capitalist,* a summary and critique of Quigley's *Tragedy and Hope.*

In addition to Dr. Skousen, the Board of Directors includes eleven others who have made their mark either in the professions or the world of competitive business.

In an address delivered June 18, 1982, Dr. Skousen summarized the accomplishments of the Institute:

1. It has acquired recognition in every state of the Union and even in several foreign countries.

2. It is now housed in a debt-free, modern, and well-equipped building.

3. It employs eight full-time directors in as many regions of the United States. This number is expected to rise to eighteen.

4. The history and a phrase-by-phrase commentary on the United

States Constitution has been recorded on cassette and video tapes and made available to thousands of people in a study called *The Miracle of America.*

5. More than a hundred elements which have been destroying the Constitution have been identified and documented.

6. A list of 101 constitutional questions to ask political candidates has been compiled and published.

7. Specific recommendations for the reform of the United States Congress have been compiled and published.

8. A comprehensive program for U.S. monetary reform to stabilize the economy and the American money system has been submitted to the President and Congress.

9. A comprehensive program to salvage the American Social Security system has been submitted to the President and to Congress.

10. The launching of a new series of books entitled *The American Classic Series,* has been undertaken; the first one, on Benjamin Franklin, has been published.

11. The twenty-eight ideas of the Founding Fathers, which changed the world, have been published under the title *The Five-Thousand-Year Leap.*

12. A model constitution has been prepared for Canada.

13. Freemen Institutes have been established in Canada and in South Africa; and will soon be organized in Australia, New Zealand, Mexico, and England.

14. A program of heritage tours, to the Middle East, Mexico, and elsewhere, has been undertaken.

15. An extensive study has been made of the interlocking power groups of Europe and America through interviews with about a hundred world leaders. The subjects range from the Trilateral Commission to the Foreign Policy Association and have been published in the *Freemen Digest,* a periodical published by the Institute.

16. It has conducted a number of highly successful conferences on the importance of the family.

17. It has also conducted a great number of "Constitution Rallies," addressed by speakers of national reputation.

18. Every year it presents a series of major events in various parts of the country in connection with Constitution week.

The objectives of the Freemen Institute can be summed up thus:

> Virtually every economic, political, and social problem we face in modern society can be traced to an ill-conceived departure from the sound principles taught by the American Founding Fathers. A careful study of historical developments in the light of the Founders' writings reveals that they provided workable solutions for today's problems. One of the major objectives of

the Freemen Institute is to analyze government policies and pressing current issues in terms of these sound principles, and to provide documented studies which will enable our society to return to a condition of liberty and prosperity by implementing the teachings of our Founders.

The principal activity of the Institute is to prepare, publish, and distribute material featuring the ideas and ideals of our Founding Fathers so that the present generation may obtain a sound and adequate knowledge of the constitutional principles originally established as the foundation of this nation.

The National Commodity and Barter Association

John Grandbouche, founder of the National Commodity and Barter Association, has emerged as an outstanding leader in a movement which now involves large numbers of people and literally billions of dollars and is found in every state of the Union. Its goal is to bypass all participation in the Federal Reserve monetary system and, to a considerable extent, to escape the extortion of the Internal Revenue Service. The movement has grown enormously during recent years; there are now even slick publications devoted to the cause.

The movement is based upon the well-established right to trade like for like without incurring any tax obligation when there is no gain to either party of an exchange: thus, for example, owners of two apartment projects of equal value should be able to trade the real estate without the obligation of paying taxes, whereas, if they were sold, heavy taxes might be due from both sales.

Barter has been common practice since before the founding of this nation; a farmer would bring his goods to market, where he would be given credit on its books, from which he could then draw whatever supplies he needed; at the end of the season, or the year, the books would be balanced and whatever was due from one would be paid to the other.

The present system of commodity barter is an extension and elaboration of this principle, but it goes far beyond the mere exchange of like for like, which is a basic requirement. For example, the IRS says that if a carpenter builds an additional room for a plumber, who then installs a bathroom of equal value in the home of the carpenter, both are free from income taxation; if either, however, does such work in return for legal or dental service, this is not an exchange of like for like, and both, therefore, must report the value of the work as taxable income.

The Commodity and Barter Association seeks to avoid this kind of situation by having every member deposit with the Association such assets as money, gold, silver or goods such as wheat or other merchandise. These are offered by the association to all those members who have made deposits of their own. Each depositor is given units of deposit against which he may draw whatever he may desire. Thus, the member does not trade money for clothing, or wheat for professional services, but only units for units; in other words, like for like. Receipts are never given for a specific commodity, but only units which represent its value.

The Association takes the utmost precaution to preserve the anonymity of its members. They have only numbered accounts, such as those in Swiss banks, in which all deposits and withdrawals are recorded. There is no way the IRS can discover who has these accounts, unless the individuals divulge this information themselves.

However, it was not easy to establish this privacy; after the IRS demanded the identities of depositors and the U.S. District Court upheld the Agency, the case was appealed to the Tenth Circuit Court which reversed and, in the judge's written opinion, declared that although depositors in banks, etc., have no Fifth Amendment privilege, the members of an association have the right of privacy under the First Amendment. Therefore, the identity of depositors remains immune to disclosure.

(Grandbouche was sentenced to prison, not because of any dispute over income taxes, but because he refused to turn over a client's records to the government and was therefore held in contempt.)

In his book, *A Declaration of Financial Independence*, Grandbouche explains how the Commodity Barter Association operates:

1. You enter into a common-law contract with an exchange agent, giving him the power to conduct your transactions.
2. You deposit your earnings with the agent or association.
3. You receive a warehouse receipt for whatever you deposit—money, checks, or goods.
4. The warehouse receipts are redeemable on 24-hour notice.
5. The agent at the warehouse takes care of all your pay-out expenditures or obligations.
6. Only you and the warehouse know the number of your account.
7. Your privacy is protected by the First, Fourth, and Fifth Amendments.
8. No agent engages in speculative investment. Receipts are issued only for goods or other assets actually on hand.
9. Your account authority includes your beneficiaries. Thus, there is no need for probate and you will not be obliged to pay any estate or inheritance taxes.

10. When the price of precious metals rises, the depositor receives increased value for his units. If it falls, he is guided by the price program of the association.

11. As an account holder, the depositor may be able to borrow money at low interest rates.

(It is assumed that when wages or salaries are deposited with an association, income and Social Security taxes have been deducted; and that probably these depositors make no return to the IRS, or, if they do, they will not submit to an audit.)

On April 5, 1985, armed IRS agents invaded warehouses of the National Commodity and Barter Association in seven cities. They carried away everything movable, including gold bullion, records, and all sorts of documents. Grandbouche stated that this extraordinary behavior was a reaction by the government against the burgeoning tax resistance movement; that "the IRS creates incidents to make tax protesters look like terrorists, when, in fact, the government is the terrorist."

We have no doubt that the purpose of the raid was to destroy the Association and other, similar organizations. As of this writing, the outcome of this unprecedented government action has not been determined.

4

Constitutionalist Victories in Court

The Team of Phil and Sue Long

The eight-year battle of Phil and Sue Long of Bellevue, Washington, which resulted in complete victory, is one of the most fascinating and instructive in the annals of IRS litigation. This was a civil, not a criminal procedure, and it shows what determined laymen can do.

After his father died, Bill Long, his sister and two brothers formed two corporations in 1960—Parkside and Beaconcrest—which operated 48 duplexes (96 units) until 1965–66, when they were sold to individuals for small down payments and low monthly fees. At that time, according to the IRS, the corporations became personal holding companies, required to disburse all income as dividends subject to double taxation or a penalty of 70 percent on all undistributed net income, under Sections 541–45 of the IRS Code. Total sales were about $800,000. Phil Long received a salary of $600 a month.

After auditing the two corporations for 1966, 1967, and 1968, the IRS declared that $38,144 was due, in addition to the $21,421 already paid. Since the IRS maintained that the corporations were personal holding companies and that Mr. Long's deductible compensation must be reduced, for these three years, from $20,800 to $3,600, and since the IRS assessments would be increased by interest charges and possibly by penalties for each year, it was obvious that unless the Service could be defeated, the Long assets would be confiscated by the government.

At this point the Longs decided to fight. However, they were not satisfied in simply fighting their own war; they decided to take issue with the general procedures of the IRS. They made several trips to Washington, interviewed 80 members of Congress, prepared 300 pages of briefs and memoranda, and published (at their own expense) 11 articles called "Life Under the IRS" in the Washington *Post.*

The Longs then decided to attack on another front, pursuant to the

Freedom of Information Act; they demanded that the IRS release all its manuals used to instruct agents in their dealings with taxpayers. On August 9, 1972, Judge William T. Beeks ordered the IRS to turn over to the Longs a mass of previously secret and concealed material. Ultimately, after two court hearings, the couple forced the Service to disgorge more than 40,000 pages of instructions and regulations, together with 300 manuals, a portion of which were published by the Church of Scientology as *The IRS Papers.*

Among much else, this material revealed that:

1. The IRS is extremely sensitive about its public image.
2. It attempts, as normal procedure, by bluff and deceit, to extort money not due it.
3. It does not inform taxpayers of their rights under audit procedures.
4. It will settle for little or nothing if taxpayers are prepared to go to court and have a reasonable chance of winning.
5. It is terrified of an adverse decision in a court of record, which may serve as a precedent.
6. It has a huge public relations apparatus which broadcasts victories, but carefully conceals or distorts defeats and illegal practices.
7. The more likely a taxpayer is to go to a court of record, the lower become IRS demands.
8. The IRS concentrates on small businessmen, who usually cannot afford adequate counsel and who can often be scared into paying assessments not due.
9. There is a wide disparity in settlements effected in different parts of the country.
10. In violation of Section 7214, the IRS knowingly levies heavy assessments not due, which it will settle at 10 percent or less, or drop entirely, rather than face the taxpayer in a showdown in a court of record.

Because of their battles with the IRS, the *Post* articles, their victories in court, and their testimony before congressional committees, the Longs received an enormous amount of publicity in the national media. In the meantime, they prepared an elaborate brief—praised by laymen and lawyers alike—for presentation to the Tax Court to decide whether 1) their two corporations actually were holding companies and 2) the compensation paid to their president was, in fact, too large.

The Table of Contents of the brief comprises five pages, the List of Citations includes 115 court cases, and the Brief itself covers 150 pages of fact and argument. The hearings before Judge Cynthia Hall occurred on May 24, 1973, in Washington, D.C. By this time, interest charges had increased the assessments to $41,251.72.

The Longs maintained that their corporations were not personal holding companies within the meaning of the statute, and that Mr. Long, instead of being overpaid, was grossly undercompensated for the valuable services he performed for the benefit of the corporation.

In its reply, filed July 25, 1973, the IRS contended that 1) the Petitioners were personal holding companies and 2) no more than $150 a month was due Mr. Long for services rendered.

The wheels of justice grind slowly in appeals to the Tax Court; and when this tribunal found in favor of the Commissioner (as it usually does) the Longs were faced with either confiscatory assessments or appealing to the Ninth Circuit Court in San Francisco. They decided to appeal.

The hearings before this court did not occur until nearly four years later. In a letter, dated March 28, 1977, Mr. Long wrote:

> . . . during the last seven years, we have found where the IRS is powerful and also where it is weak. We have also come to the conclusion that . . . the IRS system and the judicial system have evolved into contests much more influenced by "skills" than by "what is right". . . .
>
> On March 10, 1977, we were in the Court of Appeals . . . and we went *Pro Se*. . . . The brief and the reply brief were written by Sue and she did the 30-minute Oral Argument. . . . The questions by the judges and the review of all features make us feel that we have a good chance to win. Sue spent over half of her time for a full year on the briefs. . . . The three weeks prior to March 10, 1977, she spent about 12 hours a day reviewing for the 30-minute Oral Argument. Therefore, she was well prepared. . . .
>
> We hope to win. It will be good for all taxpayers if we win. The taxpayer who loses in court, loses not only for himself, but in the whole area of case law which will make it harder for others in the future to take their cases to court. . . . Poorly prepared cases that lose build case law that the IRS can use in the future. . . .
>
> Our efforts are mainly to get data, facts, and information on the IRS out into the open that have been kept secret. From our viewpoint, we feel that very few people really know the administrative side of the IRS and that is where the abuse of power has evolved that makes people fear and dread the IRS.

The Longs were not mistaken. On December 2, 1977, the Circuit Court ruled in their favor; they did not owe one penny of the terrible assessments which, by 1978, would probably have exceeded $60,000 which would have meant complete ruin for them.

As various news media have pointed out, the accomplishments of the Longs include the following:

1. They forced the IRS, as a result of two court confrontations, to release 40,000 pages of previously secret regulations and 300 manuals for public examination under the Freedom of Information Act.

2. Their testimony helped persuade Congress to amend the IRS Code so that the Agency can no longer issue jeopardy assessments without judicial review.

3. Their testimony also helped persuade Congress to insert a provision in the Tax Reform Act of 1976 which prevents the IRS from receiving an exemption under the Freedom of Information Act concerning its operation.

The Longs were not audited during the 1970s, and instead of paying anything of the horrendous deficiency levied against them, they received a final refund of $1,657.83 as settlement of the case.

But the Longs were not through: In 1981, they embarked on another venture—to force the IRS to surrender statistics collected under the TCMP (Taxpayer Compliance Measurement Program), which is used to analyze a great many tax returns, picked at random, to indicate which kinds and amount of valid deductions taxpayers may be expected to report. The Service contended that the release of this material would enable millions of taxpayers to cheat with impunity. The Longs maintained that these statistics are in the public domain and must be released under the Freedom of Information Act. Although the IRS admitted that the material was not exempt from disclosure, it refused to comply with the order for release issued by Judge Walter McGovern; it simply stalled, forced the Longs into more lawsuits, and appealed the case. Even when Supreme Court Justice William Rehnquist ordered the tapes released, the Agency still refused to obey. Then, in the Western District Court of Washington it won a temporary reversal.

We should note here that the Economic Recovery Tax Act of 1981 provided in Section 701(a) that Paragraph (a) of Section 6103(b) of the IR Code be amended by adding a sentence which the IRS maintained gave it the right to refuse the kind of information demanded by the Longs; however, such refusal was allowed only if the "disclosure will seriously impair assessment, collection, or enforcement under the internal revenue laws."

This did not deter the Longs from appealing the adverse opinion of Judge Voorhees to the Ninth Circuit Court, where they had been victorious in 1977. And they were again victorious; for, on December 1, 1982, the court reversed the decision and remanded the case for "the district court to weigh the relevant factors and require compliance within a reasonable time to be fixed by the court." The Circuit Court tersely rejected the IRS reliance upon the provision cited in ERTA, declaring: "There is no evidence supporting the district court's conclusion that the ERTA affected the duty of the defendants to disclose this type of document. From the record, there is no indication that the Secretary has made a determination that disclosure of this information will impair assessments."

Judge Kennedy, one of the panel of judges who heard the case in the Ninth Circuit, concurred fully with Judge Kilkenny, who wrote the opinion. He stated that in the Oral Argument, the IRS attorneys were asked whether the Agency had as yet taken an official position as to whether the provision in the ERTA applied to all IRS documents, or only to some of them; when they replied that no position had been taken on this question, the Judge concluded that its defense was haphazard and piecemeal and therefore nothing less than an imposition on the court.

Dr. Kenneth Johnson and his Questionnaire

Dr. Kenneth Johnson's victory over the IRS, with the help of attorney Merwin Grant, both of Phoenix, Arizona, was an important breakthrough for middle-class taxpayers, especially professionals.

At the time the doctor was ordered to bring in all his personal records for fiscal 1977, he had already been audited intensively for five of the preceding six years. At great cost in time and money, he had proved that no additional tax was due, except in 1971, when an inadvertently misplaced item caused a levy of $200.

At the same time, three other physicians in his office, who had filed similar returns with similar deductions, were ignored; Dr. Johnson, believing that he had been singled out for selective persecution because of certain statements he had made, decided that he had had enough.

Carl Dahlstrom, who operates the American Law Institute in Texas, has developed a technique by which to frustrate the IRS when it goes far beyond mere verification of deductions and expenditures, and seeks to examine every paper or document in any way related to a taxpayer's activity or private finances. Mr. Dahlstrom has compiled a list of questions which any government official, especially an IRS agent, is required to answer under provisions of the Privacy Act, the Freedom of Information Act, and various court decisions.

In accordance with these guidelines, then, Dr. Johnson, in reply to the vest-pocket summons from the IRS, Form 2039A, wrote to the Agency on December 4, 1978, stating that he was perfectly willing to cooperate and submit again to an intensive examination of all his papers and records, but that he intended to protect himself by insisting on his rights as enunciated in the Constitution, as well as in case and statutory law. He included a detailed list of 30 questions accompanied by the citations from case and statutory law for each question.

On May 8, 1979, and again on November 21, 1979, he sent additional letters, repeating the same questions. He never received a reply to any of this correspondence.

The following sequence of events then took place: On November 21, 1979, Dr. Johnson was served with a 2039A summons, ordering him to appear with all his books and records for 1977. When he complied, on January 3, 1980, accompanied by his attorney, he offered to submit everything to another intensive examination on condition that his questions be answered fully, explicitly, and individually. However, since he got no response, the conference was terminated.

On April 14, the doctor was served a new subpoena, ordering him to appear for an examination on May 1. It ended in the same way as the preceding one.

An affidavit was then filed in the U.S. District Court, which stated that Dr. Johnson had appeared on January 3, but had refused to comply with the terms of the summons.

On September 2, 1980, Michael D. Hawkins, U.S. Attorney for the District of Arizona, filed a Petition directing Dr. Johnson to appear with all his records. Again he did so, but still refused to give any testimony unless the IRS answered his questions.

On October 6, on behalf of Dr. Johnson, Attorney Merwin Grant filed the *Response to Petition and Order to Show Cause,* in which he reviewed the entire history of the case and refuted the allegations of the IRS. The hearing on the Show-Cause Order took place in the District Court on November 3. The transcript, which fills 56 pages, reflects the discomfort of IRS agents under examination, and blatantly showed that, for reasons best known to itself, the Service had singled out this taxpayer for constant harassment. Year after year, it had forced him to spend vast amounts of time and thousands of dollars to prove that no additional taxes were due.

(Others who find themselves in the same predicament may want to study this transcript. It is listed in the U.S. District Court as No. Civ. 80-704 PHX-WEC.)

Judge Walter E. Craig, who in the past had shown little mercy for tax protesters, was obviously impressed with the defense of Dr. Johnson. He declared: "You have a taxpayer that is very much disturbed, and I think he ought to be considered. I think somebody ought to answer his questions. Now maybe some of them can't be answered, but I think somebody ought to tell him something, give him the information.

"In addition, I think the summons is over-broad, and the motion [of the IRS to enforce audit] will be denied."

In short, the Court declared that the IRS cannot force taxpayers in situations comparable to that of Dr. Johnson to exhibit their records or to give testimony concerning their financial affairs unless the Agency agrees to answer questions mandated by the Privacy Act, the Freedom of Information law, and various court decisions.

But this was not the end of the battle. In December 1982, in another confrontation in the U.S. District Court, the judge told the disputants to work out some kind of compromise. Dr. Johnson then asked the Agency to select three areas for examination that might be suspect; when this was done, nothing wrong was found. However, a few weeks later, the IRS sent the doctor a letter detailing alleged deficiencies in other areas and demanding an immediate payment of $2,000. Through his attorney, the doctor agreed to pay this under protest; but added that he would sue for a refund in the U.S. District Court, which would then entitle him to get all his money back, at 20 percent interest plus full reimbursement for all costs of litigation, to which he was entitled under the Equal Access to Justice Act, which became effective in 1981.

At this point, the IRS threw up its hands and surrendered; it finally agreed *in writing* to accept all returns as filed, without ever collecting a penny. How much all this cost the taxpayers, we can only surmise; we do know that his victory cost Dr. Johnson untold agony, about $10,000 in legal fees, and was probably the reason he required bypass heart surgery.

The Acquittal of Norbert Stelton

The trial of Norbert Stelton, of Albany, Minnesota, for failure to file a proper 1040 occurred on April 24–27, 1978, in St. Paul. The transcript reflects intimate knowledge of the techniques used by the Agency and the methods which may be used to counteract them.

Mr. Stelton was educated at St. Cloud College and the University of Minnesota; he had been a high school teacher for twelve years, and an insurance agent and real estate broker. He was a member of the Lion's Club, the Knights of Columbus, and the American Legion, and had served two years as the mayor of Albany. He was certainly no ordinary delinquent, nor was he charged with tax evasion, for evidence was introduced indicating that he had no tax liability for the years 1973 and 1974, for which he filed Fifth-Amendment returns. He was simply charged, under Section 7203 of the Code, with failure to file a "proper" return when he admittedly had gross incomes of $18,812 and $12,200.

Mr. Stelton's original anger against the IRS was first kindled when his 1972 return—carefully prepared by a CPA—was audited, resulting in substantial deficiencies, which he was certain were incorrect and extortionary. After receiving a Ninety-Day Letter—which he ignored—he paid what he considered an unfair levy when the IRS threatened to confiscate his possessions. He noted that the computations set forth in the Letter were not binding upon the Service and that it could impose additional assessments, which he considered outrageous.

His trial revolved around the intent of the accused as contrasted with his motive, and whether he truly and sincerely believed, in good faith, that it was legal for him to file the kind of return he did.

The defense offered impeccable witnesses who testified that the integrity and honesty of the defendant were beyond reproach—to establish that if he declared his belief in the correctness of his action, willful violation could not be sustained. The prosecution attempted to turn Stelton's very honesty against him by trying to prove that none of his income derived from illegal sources and that, therefore, he could not possibly incriminate himself by revealing them; in short, that the Fifth Amendment privilege did not apply in his case. The prosecution also sought to establish that a man of his education, experience, background, and sophistication could not be ignorant of the law.

In response Stelton testified that because of his personal experiences, he had good reason to fear that no matter how honest his return or legitimate his income, the IRS could and probably would attack him unjustly by inventing some error in his return which could be used to harass, extract money not due, and even become the basis for a criminal action.

The question which the jury had to decide, therefore, hinged on Mr. Stelton's intent and state of mind: did he or did he not truly believe—as he declared under oath—that he was within his rights legally in pleading the Fifth Amendment privilege, even though none of his income derived from illegal sources? His lawyer emphasized that since his reputation for integrity was unquestioned by everyone who knew him, how could there be a reasonable doubt that he was telling the truth when he testified under oath? Over and over, the attorney hammered home this central thesis: It made no difference whether Mr. Stelton was right or wrong in his conviction—the only question at issue for the jury to consider was whether he was acting in good faith.

The jury received the case at 5:00 P.M. April 26, and returned for further deliberations at 9:00 the next morning; at 2:15, it brought in a unanimous verdict of not guilty.

Charles R. Reitz: Two Mistrials

In 1968 Charles R. Reitz of Morgan Hill, California, became deeply concerned over the question of income taxation, especially the possibility of self-incrimination under the IR Code. At his trial, in the U.S. District Court for the Northern District of California beginning August 23, 1977, and lasting seven days, the IRS had no records of any returns for 1969–72 inclusive. Reitz testified that he was uncertain whether he had filed anything during this period. However, beginning in 1973, he submitted what he called amended returns, including a mass of explanatory material, that invoked the Fifth Amendment privilege, and included discussions of the monetary issue, the loopholes and inequities in the Code, as well as other matters which the courts have ruled irrelevant.

To recap briefly: Finding that it had no returns from Reitz, the IRS sent an agent to interrogate him. He declared that he would not file because of the First, the Fourth, and the Fifth Amendments to the Constitution. In March, 1973, when interviewed by another agent, he cited court cases and read the above Amendments to the agent. On October 24, 1973, a third interview was recorded by both Reitz and the IRS agents, a significant fact, as the IRS had previously refused to allow the conferences to be recorded.

That the IRS spared no effort to convict Mr. Reitz is obvious from the time, money, and preparation which went into his trial; the transcript, not including the charge to the jury, fills 896 pages.

The defense admitted that the monetary and similar issues were invalid, but declared that in 1969, 1970, and 1971, Reitz had nothing in mind except a Fifth Amendment defense against self-incrimination. The prosecution's view was that since no returns had actually been filed before 1973, the defendant should be convicted under Section 7203 of the Code for willful failure to file. However, Reitz cited *Garner* v. *United States*, which states that the Fifth Amendment privilege may be invoked by not filing at all, and that, therefore, the fact of filing or not was irrelevant to the issue.

During the trial, it was emphasized that *intent*, a valid defense, must be clearly distinguished from *motive*, which is not. Motive has to do with an ultimate or irrelevant purpose, such as a wish to evade the income tax laws because they are harsh, oppressive, discriminatory, illegal, or unconstitutional; intent, on the other hand, deals with the state of mind that impels a person to adopt a certain position which may result in a sincere, even if illegal, action. Thus, when a citizen claims the privilege against self-incrimination, his intent is to abide by the law and to avail himself of a protection which has consistently been upheld by the Supreme Court; but if he invokes the money issue or attacks the operation of the IRS, he is *motivated* to defeat the statute, which has nothing to do with self-incrimination.

We believe that if the IRS had prosecuted Reitz only on the basis of returns that pleaded a good-faith Fifth Amendment challenge without irrelevant addenda, he would have been acquitted. As it was, the result was a mistrial in which seven members of the jury voted not guilty.

Reitz was tried a second time, in January, 1978, and again there was a mistrial.

Lynn Johnston: An Amazon in Action

Miss Lynn Johnston is a devoted and courageous Freedom Fighter who has carved for herself a permanent niche in the spreading movement to restore constitutional government in the United States. She is Director of Citizens Against Taxation, author of the CAT Amendment, Coordinator of the Michigan Tax Caucus, Regional Director of Live Free, Inc., a member of the Independent Bar Association of Michigan, a hard-money advocate, and a well-known lecturer and consultant on strategies which may be used against the IRS, and which have helped countless embattled taxpayers.

Her book *Who's Afraid of the IRS?* (available for $10 from Lynn Johnston, Drawer 2419, Ann Arbor, MI 48106), contains a wealth of material concerning the techniques useful in successfully fighting a bloated and arrogant bureaucracy.

Miss Johnston's principal objective is to help people become free and independent by ridding themselves of burdensome taxation and government interference at every level. She states that since 1975, she has paid no taxes, simply because she does not owe any; she has given herself a driver's license; she refuses to pay the telephone tax or a fine for a parking ticket; she even declares that no one should be required to obtain a license to marry—that couples should simply enter into a household contract to share their lives under a written agreement under the Common Law.

Lynn Johnston's book describes how she first became involved in the Freedom Movement, how she was victorious in a court battle, and what the enemy has done to intimidate and terrify her. Her "rebellion" began in the late 'Sixties, when she refused to pay the tax on telephone conversations, since the money "was used to fund what I viewed as an immoral, undeclared, unconstitutional war in Viet Nam."

In December 1973 she decided that she would live thereafter free of domination, subjugation, or manipulation from the IRS or anyone else; she sent up a hot air balloon that carried the sign REPEAL THE INCOME TAX.

For 1975, 1976, and 1977, she filed Fifth Amendment tax returns, accompanied by 38 pages of commentary. At her trial for nonpayment of income taxes in Grand Rapids, Michigan, she appeared *pro se*, defended herself, picked the jury, and won an amazing acquittal. Since then, she has filed nothing whatever—but at the price of being subjected to the most extreme forms of extra-legal retaliation possible.

In due course, she discovered the price of opposing and defeating the IRS: She was the victim of a hit-run "accident" in front of her house; the tires of her car were slashed twelve times, holes were punched in her car radiator and air-conditioning system, its windows broken several times, and bolts loosened on the wheels. Once, a woman backed her car into Miss Johnston's living room with devastating results. The IRS ransacked her garbage can in search of evidence, and at one time three shots from a high-powered rifle were fired at her from about a mile away. Her first-class mail was opened and much of it failed to arrive at all. She was under constant surveillance; her phone was tapped and every conversation recorded and often interrupted; she received threatening calls constantly. Undercover agents offered her large fees for telling them how to evade taxes; anyone who engaged her for a talk-in radio program or other commitment was soon audited.

This harassment went on for years. When she demanded that the IRS show her her file, under the Freedom of Information Act, the Agency disclosed only a portion, which nevertheless comprised more than 500 pages.

Charles E. (Chuck) Riely: The Golden Mean Society

On June 19–21, 1979, in the U.S. District Court for the state of Arizona, the Internal Revenue Service suffered a stunning defeat; that was when the government failed miserably in its attempt to send to prison Charles E. Riely, of Mesa, Arizona, on a charge of failing to file "proper" income tax returns for 1972, 1973, and 1974. The case went to jury on the 20th; it returned a verdict of *not guilty* on all counts the next day.

This landmark victory was won, not on a technicality, but in a direct confrontation. For 1972 and 1973 (the IRS ignored all the years following 1974) Riely filed straight Fifth Amendment returns by simply writing "Object: Self-Incrim," after each pertinent question on the tax form.

For 1974, he added 30 pages of explanatory material, almost all of which dealt directly with the danger of self-incrimination. Basically, therefore, his defense was a straight Fifth Amendment plea, available to almost all Americans.

To recapitulate: In 1971, Riely began the operation of the Tri-City Printing Company; in 1972, he established the Mesa Caucus Club, which conducted weekly meetings for two years and which developed a very successful book business. This, together with frequent seminars, took so much time that he disposed of the printing firm in 1978.

On April 30, 1975, two Special IRS agents read the Miranda Warning to Riely; the next day, his bank was served with a summons to surrender all his records; but not until August 1977 were all appeals exhausted, enabling the IRS to examine the records. However, the Agency never did obtain them, because it declined to pay the $300 the bank required for their search and reproduction.

The grand jury indicted Riely on April 14, 1979; but he was not arrested. He was told to appear for arraignment, and then was released on his own recognizance.

The government case consisted largely of Riely's conversations with IRS agents, in which he discussed the monetary system, government waste, abortions, etc. The government tried to establish that the defendant was simply hiding behind the Fifth Amendment in order to evade taxation, and that his plea was not based on a good-faith challenge. However, when the chief counsel for the IRS admitted that the returns contained none of this argument, the IRS position crumbled.

I have carefully read the transcript of the trial, which fills several hundred pages. Though Riely himself never suffered any atrocity from the IRS, he was, nevertheless, permitted to enter various exhibits that described the harassment and persecution of others. The defendant's *state of mind*—his intent—was the central issue, and the basis of which resulted from information obtained from articles, news releases, and books that described IRS operations. After the Court determined (1) that he had read these before he filed his Fifth-Amendment returns and (2) that he relied upon them, they were all admitted into evidence.

Among Riely's sources were (1) *A Citizen's Guide to Individual Rights Under the Constitution*, issued by Sam Ervin; (2) a pamphlet prepared by the Senate Judiciary entitled *Political Intelligence in the Internal Revenue Service*, an inquiry into army surveillance; (3) several articles written by John Barron and published in the *Reader's Digest* detailing atrocities perpetrated by the IRS against innocent and unoffending citizens; (4) part of the *Congressional Record* of April 2, 1967, dealing with undercover IRS operations and explaining how the careers of Senators Long and Montoya were destroyed because they criticized, and wished the investigate, the Service; (5) a letter from Sheldon Cohen, Commissioner of Internal Revenue, stating that a good-faith challenge on an income tax form is constitutional; (6) a report from *Freedom*, published by the Church of Scientology, based on an article by an ex-IRS agent, explaining how the Service is used to "get" anyone that any powerful interest in the government wishes to destroy; (7) a copy of the *IRS Special Agent's Handbook*, which explains the Fourth and Fifth Amendment rights of taxpayers; (8) excerpts from Supreme Court decisions upholding Fifth Amendment rights; (9) a story from the January 20, 1971, Mesa *Tribune* by columnist Henry J. Taylor, explaining that all information given to the IRS on income tax returns is available to 23 other government departments or agencies; and (10) a copy of the Constitution.

As this material, as well as other documents used, is in the public domain, it can be obtained and easily utilized by literally almost anyone for defense in a situation similar to that in which Riely found himself.

It is interesting that several of these items—such as a copy of the Constitution—had been strictly banned in previous trials. The judge instructed the jury that these exhibits were entered into evidence, not because they were true or false, but to enable them "to evaluate the state of mind of the defendant and his good faith [in offering a Fifth Amendment challenge to the income-tax laws]."

The crux of Riely's defense was that: (1) It is impossibe to complete a conventional 1040 without waiving one's constitutional rights; (2) since the Constitution is the Supreme Law of the Land, no government agency has the right or the power to nullify those rights; and, therefore, (3) the procedures under which the IRS operates are unconstitutional and no one can legally be required to file the kind of return the Agency demands.

In 1979, Riely and others organized The Golden Mean Society, dedicated to the objective of reestablishing constitutional government in the U.S. He also began giving seminars all over the country—sometimes with Peggy Christensen (see p. 99)—in which he explained the proposals and techniques of his organization. The Society also operates a flourishing business in the sale of books and other materials useful to citizens in their battles with the IRS.

Riely warns those taking the Fifth Amendment that it is best not to have any property which can be seized nor to leave a trail of documentable income, to have no money in any bank account, never to pay for goods or services by check or accept checks in return for services, to lease, rather than own, cars, and to convey all assets to an irrevocable trust with qualified trustees and others as beneficiaries.

Riely emphasizes that anyone under criminal investigation or prosecution should never advance other than the Fifth Amendment privilege; constitutional issues should be carried only into the Tax Court and beyond, where all procedures are civil in nature and where the IRS cannot attempt any criminal prosecution.

Riely points out that the IRS brings criminal charges against those 1) who seem to be easiest to convict, and 2) whose conviction may have the highest deterrent effect on others.

In one of his publications, he says: ". . . we very carefully distinguish the correct time in which to bring constitutional issues to court. We do not feel that it is appropriate to argue civil test-case issues in a criminal court. Therefore, the claim of constitutional right—usually based on the Fifth Amendment—is used as a buffer for the criminal court system. Once the threat of criminal court action is removed, usually after receiving the Statutory Notice of Deficiency from the Tax Court, the taxpayer can bring to light his constitutional issues."

In other words, do not argue money or any similar matters while under criminal investigation.

Over and over, Riely emphasizes the supreme importance of the jury system. When a jury acquits, that is the end of the case, for there is no appeal from such a decision. If the jury cannot agree on a verdict, the judge has no choice except to declare a mistrial; and there is no instance in which the IRS has attempted a third prosecution after two such results, or in which a person has been indicted and tried a second time after an acquittal or after serving a sentence after a conviction.

Riely offers a Tax Packet, which contains (1) the Public Servant's Questionnaire, based on the Privacy Act, and used by members of the Golden Mean Society; (2) the first page of form 1040 as filed by himself; (3) the back side of this form; and (4) the voluminous tax return appendix, including letters and affidavits, which accompanies the 1040 form.

He carefully avoids any mention of such subjects as the Federal Reserve System, government waste, abortion, etc.; any argument dealing with such matters would destroy the return as a good-faith Fifth Amendment challenge. Instead, he focuses exclusively on the danger, likelihood, or possibility of self-incrimination, and sets forth the citizen's rights to protect himself under existing and statutory law.

Peggy Christensen: Paralegal Supreme

In 1969, Peggy Christensen and her husband decided to dedicate themselves to the Freedom Movement after they had observed that church organizations and most trusts afforded citizens little protection when the government decided to seize their property. Therefore, they got rid of their possessions, especially their real estate, so that if the government should move against them, there would be little or nothing to take.

Mrs. Christensen began to study the Constitution, and in due course, she teamed up with Charles Riely and became an integral part of the Golden Mean Society as a paralegal, with an office in Missoula, Montana. Her job is to aid those patriots who refuse to file income tax returns or submit to IRS demands. That her work has been remarkably successful is demonstrated by the record, which consists of thousands of pages of court transcripts of trials in which she has participated as a paralegal and in which the IRS has been defeated. To date, she has over 65 victories to her credit, in trials in which the accused have obtained jury acquittals.

Mrs. Christensen explains how to make the best use of the Fifth Amendment right. After the IRS sends three form letters to people from whom no returns are on file, "an agent will pick about one out of ten letters to investigate." If the Agent receives a reply by mail or telephone or finds a person at home when he calls, he will exert pressure to obtain a return. This, says Peggy, is a good time to file a 1040 return claiming your First, Fourth, Fifth, and Ninth Amendment rights of the Constitution. The point of all this is that when a taxpayer signs his 1040 under penalties of perjury, he does so voluntarily and waives all constitutional rights. But if the government forces him to submit a return on pain of punishment, this is compelled testimony which can never be used to convict in a criminal prosecution; citizens should therefore seek official demands that returns be made under pain of definite punishment; if these are filed, it should be under protest.

Peggy describes a technique by which the charge of wilfullness can be negated: e.g., the revocation of a constitutional return which has already been filed. When this is done, the government has no basis for a charge of *wilful intent.*

As previously noted, Peggy has assisted in 65 cases that resulted in jury acquittals. She has available, at $25.00 each, the transcripts of 15 such victories.

In almost every case, there was some exculpatory element, the result of which the IRS could be portrayed in a bad or questionable light. In one case, for example, a man could not understand why he could not file exempt on his W-4 form, since he had been overwithheld the previous year, had not received a refund for this overwithholding, and believed that this would cover all possible tax liability for the current year. In another, a more or less unlettered orator, who had persuaded the accused not to file a return, was permitted to address the jury for an hour with the result that an acquittal followed.

In all the trials, the defense forced the government to recognize the supremacy of the Constitution; and, although not required to do so, the defendant took the stand and told his story, which thus became evidence instead of argument; this was so persuasive that the jury simply could not conclude that he was guilty of specific intent to wilfully violate any constitutional law.

What we find in all these cases is that defendants have now become far more sophisticated than they were even ten years ago; it is now possible to routinely force the courts to permit testimony and procedures that were simply banned on pain of contempt of court in the early 'Seventies.

5

Willis E. Stone and the Liberty Amendment

The material in this chapter—slightly revised—was supplied by Willis E. Stone, the founder of the movement to repeal the Sixteenth Amendment. He relates the origin, development, and growing support for this vast undertaking. Armen Moths, whose career we describe elsewhere, has become the principal collaborator in this endeavor, especially in the petition drive for signatures in support of Yes on 23 Proposal.

There is nothing new about tax rebellions. They have been going on throughout human history. Tyrants have been overthrown only to have new ones replace them with other usurpations and consequent oppression.

Only once, in all history, was this crucial problem met and solved—by the establishment of the U.S. Constitution. Thomas Jefferson declared that its purpose was to bind down those in government "from mischief by the chains of the Constitution." This document performed that miracle.

In a single century under our Constitution more progress was made than during 6,000 years of previous history. After little more than 100 years of true constitutional government, however, we began to desert the concepts of "government by law" and to renew the power struggles by personalities, partisanship, and policies of the ancient tyrannies of government by force.

Several violations of our Constitution at the start of the 20th century have survived and become the basis of a pattern. Various federal bureaucracies, greedy for power, initiated a constant flow of new intrusions upon our lives and energies, as the memory of freedom and self-reliance began to fade.

The violations of our Constitution continue. The total expenditures of our government from the time it was organized until 1913—when the Sixteenth Amendment was imposed upon us—amounted to just over $25 billion. During this period we advanced from national obscurity to become the richest and most powerful nation on earth. Consider this: The federal deficit in 1982 amounted to nearly five times as much as the total cost of our federal government during our first 125 years! Another yardstick: Spending in 1982 under what was called a "tight budget" was 30 times as much as it cost to run the government during its first 125 years!

The following statistics show how inflation, deficits, and taxes have gone hand in hand in order to reduce a sovereign people into a state of servitude.

Election Year of	Consumer Index	Buying Power of 1940 Dollar	Individual Income Taxes	Gross Federal Debt
1940	40.5	100 Percent	$ 1.110 billion	$ 50.7 billion
1944	53.6	76 "	20.179 "	204.1 "
1948	82.8	49 "	19.310 "	252.0 "
1952	88.6	46 "	27.310 "	259.1 "
1956	90.7	45 "	32.188 "	272.8 "
1960	94.9	43 "	40.741 "	290.9 "
1964	94.7	43 "	48.697 "	316.8 "
1968	102.5	40 "	68.720 "	369.8 "
1972	119.1	34 "	94.700 "	437.3 "
1976	183.0	22 "	131.600 "	631.9 "
1980	258.6	16 "	238.700 "	892.8 "

Since 1980, the deficits and total debt have increased even more. However, the madness can be stopped—with the passage of the Liberty Amendment, now pending in Congress as H. J. Res. 23.

One morning in Van Nuys, California, a group met to discuss the increasing threats to our constitutional government from within. All agreed that the Constitution should be restored and the federal government's activities limited to those mandated therein. But, *how?* And *with what means?*

An industrial consultant who wrote a column for the weekly Sherman-Oaks *Citizen Tribune* felt that because federal bureaucracies believe that they are empowered to do anything not specifically prohibited to them by the Constitution, a specific provision would have to be added thereto to prevent all their illegal activity. The words of such a provision would need to be so clear and precise that even a federal bureaucrat could not fail to understand them.

To accomplish this objective, it was mandatory to amend the Constitution. As a beginning to this end, the Sherman-Oaks paper carried an article on June 2, 1944, in which the following was printed: "THE GOVERNMENT OF THE UNITED STATES OF AMERICA SHALL NOT ENGAGE IN ANY BUSINESS, COMMERCIAL, OR INDUSTRIAL ENTERPRISE IN COMPETITION WITH ITS CITIZENS."

It was a beginning, but no more.

In order for this concept to accomplish its grand design the knowledge and expertise of some 130 top constitutional authorities across the country were recruited to prepare the precise language that would withstand any attack.

It took nine years to complete the first three sections of the present Liberty Amendment, which was submitted to, and approved by, the Illinois legislature in 1953. Section One, similar to the wording printed in the Sherman Oaks paper, reads:

"THE GOVERNMENT OF THE UNITED STATES SHALL NOT ENGAGE IN ANY BUSINESS, PROFESSIONAL, COMMERCIAL, FINANCIAL, OR INDUSTRIAL ENTERPRISE EXCEPT AS SPECIFIED IN THE CONSTITUTION."

These twenty-four words do not change the Constitution; instead, they restate the laws already there, which limit the power of those in government so they cannot invade, take over, or encroach upon the properties, enterprise, or lives of the people, except as the Constitution itself clearly permits or provides.

While these words restore the economic rights and powers of the people, they also establish the specific obligations of government to exercise only those limited powers enumerated in the Constitution and enforced by the Ninth and Tenth Amendments. However, since this provision would need protection from the avarice of both foreign and domestic cabals, a second section was added, which provided that:

"THE CONSTITUTION OR LAWS OF ANY STATE, OR THE LAWS OF THE UNITED STATES, SHALL NOT BE SUBJECT TO THE TERMS OF ANY FOREIGN OR DOMESTIC AGREEMENT WHICH WOULD ABROGATE THIS AMENDMENT."

All those preparing the amendment believed that its first two sections were quite capable of restoring to the people all the rights, powers, lands, properties, etc., which had been usurped, and would provide the means of preserving that state of liberty with full human rights to life, liberty, and property from the avarice of domestic and foreign contrivances.

The potential blessings for the American people through the restoration of their Constitution are of amazing dimensions. How much, for example, would the sale of unconstitutionally held lands produce? Estimates of the value of this land (as of 1980) run from a trillion to a trillion and a half dollars. If more than three quarters of it was returned to state jurisdiction and private enterprise, and, therefore, sold, even at half of present appraisals and under unfavorable conditions, it could bring close to half a trillion, cutting the federal debt by that amount, which would reduce the interest charge by at least $50 billion a year. It would also place about 30 percent more land in private enterprise and on the tax rolls to support local, county, and state governments, increasing productivity and general well-being.

And if half of the federal debt could be thus expunged, nearly all the remainder could be erased by the simple expedient of repossessing without payment all securities now held by entities that never paid for them in the first place—including the Federal Reserve System, its member banks, and a variety of federal trust funds.

These amazing data demonstrate that, using the simplest equation of all, a dollar cut from federal spending means a dollar reduction in federal taxes. By restoring the Constitution to its full force and effect, government would have to relinquish those powers, properties, and other perquisites it had taken without authority and return them to state jurisdiction.

At last, thirteen years after the research began, what is known as the Liberty Amendment proposal was completed. It concludes with the following provision:

"THREE YEARS AFTER THE RATIFICATION OF THIS AMENDMENT, THE SIXTEENTH ARTICLE OF AMENDMENTS TO THE CONSTITUTION OF THE UNITED STATES SHALL STAND REPEALED AND THEREAFTER CONGRESS SHALL NOT LEVY TAXES ON PERSONAL INCOMES, ESTATES, OR GIFTS."

Public support, necessary for ratification, increases steadily. As of late 1982, the Amendment was pending in Congress as House Joint Resolution 23, co-sponsored by former Representative Ron Paul (R-Texas) and the late Larry McDonald (D-Ga.). A resolution memorializing Congress to submit this to the people for approval or rejection has been formally approved in the legislatures of Wyoming, Texas, Nevada, Louisiana, Georgia, South Carolina, Mississippi, Arizona, and Indiana. It is pending in several others. When 34 states have approved such a resolution, Congress must submit it for ratification to the states.

The proposal has been presented for discussion before many organizations, large and small, across the country; more than 8,000 of them have endorsed resolutions in support of it.

A petition—the Yes on 23—sponsored principally by Armen Moths and his United Taxpayers' Union has already gathered several million signatures.

The concept of liberty is as strong as it was 200 years ago, as evidenced by the extent of the tax rebellion. Grass roots opposition to the federal takeover of land, enterprise, roads, water, crops and countless other things that belong to the people proves that the passion for freedom is alive and well in America.

The source of all these problems is the same: the violation of our

Constitution. And all can be resolved by the same means—the restoration of the Constitution to full force and effect as operative law.

These may seem like abstractions, but how real and personal they become when they affect us individually. Just imagine! No more tax form 1040. Instead, a full day's pay for a full day's work. And plenty of employment. Legislation has never produced a single job; only producers and customers can do that.

6

The Social Security Swindle

Had the bureaucrats who devised the Social Security System announced their ultimate objective at the beginning it is very doubtful that it would have been enacted or that it could have survived a Supreme Court challenge. Social Security was sold as an insurance program, never as a major support in old age: It was meant only as a small supplemental income to that from other forms of savings. It was foisted upon the American people in 1935—in the midst of the Great Depression—when tens of millions were unemployed and when the purchasing power of the dollar was at its peak. It was touted as an aid for the poor and deprived; it was believed that it would be a true form of insurance, in which funds would be vested and funded and from which beneficiaries could receive death benefits comparable to those paid by private insurance companies in return for equitable investments.

But such was not the intent of those who engineered the legislation; their objective was to use Social Security to build an empire of unimaginable dimensions. They knew—as we know now—that every dollar sent to, and expended by, the federal bureaucracy gives it more power, more intrusive capacity, more control over the lives and destinies of the people.

The SS number, which was never meant to be used for identification, has now, as the TIN (Taxpayer's Identification Number), become a principal means by which American citizens are regimented. SS numbers are needed for every kind of transaction and in most situations. Even infants must have their numbers. The IRS demands that we disclose our numbers even where no law requires it.

How did this system, which began so modestly, burgeon to such dimensions? Eventually, various categories of additional people were brought into the system, such as the self-employed, the disabled, wives of retirees, widows and widowers, alien parents, ministers, and even felons serving long-term prison sentences. And in legislation enacted in 1983, all new federal employees will be enrolled; no longer will the employees of other governmental units or of charities be permitted to leave the system. In fact, in due course, very nearly the entire workforce, public, private, charitable—even the lay employees of churches—will be forced into the system. The pretext for such a devastating law is that additional "contributions" obtained in this way will keep the program—now foundering in bankruptcy—solvent for the foreseeable future. Actually, of course, it will make its funding even more oppressive when the new enrollees are ready to retire.

The bureaucrats have been equally diligent in providing benefits of some kind for more and more people; thus, they bring more and more individuals into their orbits of taxation. Consider the following:

THE GROWTH OF THE SOCIAL SECURITY PROGRAM[1]
(Numbers in Thousands)

Year	1941	1950	1960	1970	1975	1979–81
Workers Covered with Taxable Contributions	35,393	48,283	73,000	93,000	100,000	111,000
Beneficiaries under OASDI	17	651	10,310	16,870	21,831	22,421
Total Beneficiaries	113	3,012	14,299	26,229	32,086	36,006
Trust Fund Balance (millions)	$2,398	$12,893	$21,663	$18,235	$48,200	$20,500
Average Payment to Retirees	$22.60	$41.40	$74.00	$118.00	$206.00	$386.00

[1] These statistics from *SA* 1956 p. 260; *ib.* 1963, p. 286; *ib.* 1966 p. 293; *ib.* 1982–83, p. 253, 325, 326.

In 1983, 122,200,000 workers contributed to SS; the average monthly benefit was $419 (*ib.* 1984 *SA* pp. 376, 379).

In 1941, there were only 17,000 beneficiaries for 35,393,000 contributors; in 1950, the ratio was 1 to 16; in 1960, it was 1 to 7; in 1970, it fell to 1 to 3½; and in 1979–81 to about 1 to 3. Furthermore, since the population as a whole is aging and people are living longer, it is likely that within two or three decades there will be only two contributors for each recipient; and, with inflation, the burden on the producers will become intolerable. Note also that while the trust funds increased from $2,398 million in 1941 to $48,200 million in 1975, they decreased sharply to $20.5 billion in 1981, much of which came from the General Funds of the nation. In addition, payments to retired workers (there are several other categories of recipients) increased from $22.60 in 1941 to $386.00 in 1981.

In 1982, the total trust funds in Social Security were exhausted for

SOCIAL SECURITY INCOME AND EXPENDITURES[1]
REVENUES (in millions)

	1965	1970	1975	1981
OASDI				
Contributions	$16,017	$20,256	$58,816	$122,627
General Fund		449	425	674
DISABILITY				
Contributions	$1,188	$4,481	$7,444	$16,738
General Fund			90	168
MEDICAL				
Contributions	$3,152	$4,881	$11,509	$32,959
General Fund	312	874	689	900
SUPPLEMENTARY MEDICAL-CARE				
Contributions	$640	$1,096	$1,918	$3,722
General Fund	923	1,093	2,648	11,291
TOTALS	$22,242	$43,130	$83,539	$189,079
	1,245	2,416	3,852	13,033
BENEFITS DISBURSED				
OASDI	$16,737	$28,796	$58,509	$122,796
DISABILITY	$1,573	$3,067	$6,414	$17,200
HOSPITAL	$3,353	$5,124	$11,318	$30,342
SUPP. MED. CARE	$1,197	$1,975	$4,273	$13,113
TOTALS	$22,860	$38,962	$80,514	$183,451

[1]Statistics from 1982–83 *SA* p. 325.
In 1983, OASDI collected $172.2 billion and disbursed $170.5 billion; $59.5 billion was collected for health insurance and $57.3 disbursed (1984 *SA* p. 317).

the first time; even in 1981, with $13,033,000,000 from the General Funds, the system had barely enough income to meet its self-imposed obligations. In spite of collections for health care totaling $36,681 million, it required an added infusion of $12,191 million from the taxpayers to meet expenditures of $48,872 million.

I have been predicting for years that sooner or later the Social Security System would reach the crisis of 1982–83. I have advocated that the government, instead of trying to place the Social Security noose around the necks of more people, should do everything in its power to reduce or terminate its involvement therein, which it should never have undertaken in the first place. When it began, the maximum payment from an employee—matched by the employer—

was $30 a year, at a rate of 2 percent on $1,500 of income. However, under the rates enacted in 1977, the maximum combined tax rose to $2,885.40 in 1979 at the rate of 12.25 percent on $22,900; this rose to $4,562,60 in 1983; and is scheduled to become $6,709.50 in 1987,when the levy will be 15.75 percent on $42,600. The rate of the self-employment tax, which was 9.35 percent in 1982, equaled the combined rate on employees and employers in 1984. However, there is a credit of 2.9 percent of such income from 1984 to 1988, after which there is to be an appropriation from the General Funds to help pay the cost.

More than 25 percent of all people who begin paying into SS at the age of 22 do not live to receive one penny in return for their payments, which otherwise invested might have created multi-million dollar estates. Could there be a greater inequity or injustice? SS should be a form of retirement insurance: instead, it is a discriminatory tax used to establish and finance a form of the Welfare State. I knew a woman who invested $6 and drew $10,000; but I have known others who, after contributing many thousands over a long period of time, received nothing—nor did any of their heirs—because they died as they were approaching retirement.

SS is not insurance; it is neither funded nor vested; it impinges with terrible impact upon young families attempting to establish themselves; personal payments into the system are not even deductible from taxable income.

Should inflation begin to rise rapidly again—which will be inevitable unless the federal government starts to exercise a high degree of fiscal responsibility—an income of $42,600 will be barely sufficient to maintain a decent living standard for a family of four in 1987. After this family and its employer contribute more than $6,800 in SS taxes, in addition to an equal amount paid by the family alone in state and federal income taxes, there will scarcely be enough depreciated Federal Reserve units of exchange remaining to pay for the bare necessities of life.

Congress must realize that deficit spending must cease and debt obligations drastically reduced. It has been estimated that the real national debt, including SS obligations, was more than $5 trillion in 1975 and $9 trillion in 1982; in addition, the private debt, for mortgages and goods purchased on time, now exceeds $3 trillion. This fiscal insanity can only lead to chaos and destruction.

ARTICLE I, Section 8 of our Constitution lists the only functions, activities, and powers which may be exercised by the federal government. No authority to establish or operate a welfare state or an annuity system, or anything resembling Social Security is conferred.

In recent years, there has been a vast proliferation of private profit-sharing and other pension plans. In 1980, 43,877,000 workers were enrolled in both private pension and group health insurance plans; another 4,126,000 were in pension plans alone. Funds invested by private, insured systems totaled $188 billion; another $293.2 billion was invested by uninsured plans. State and local government employees had plans with funds totaling $221.3 billion. (*SA* 1982–83 p. 230–31.)

All this constitutes a development in the right direction.

Even more important are individual annuity plans, now sanctioned by law. In 1964, Section 404(e) was incorporated into the Internal Revenue Code, which allowed self-employed people to deduct up to $2,500 of otherwise taxable income as a contribution to a personal (Keogh) trust fund. Effective January 1, 1974, this was expanded by permitting 15 percent deductions, not to exceed $7,500. In 1975, Section 219 was added to the Code, permitting wage earners to deduct 15 percent of income up to $1,500 for an Individual Retirement Account (IRA), provided no other form of annuity was in place. Section 221 now provides that spouses may establish joint IRA with exempt contributions up to $2,250. The Tax Equity and Fiscal Responsibility Act of 1982 provides that the Keogh Accounts may now deduct up to $15,000 a year from taxable income. Anyone receiving wages or a salary may now invest $2,000 in an IRA, even if that is the entire income. Couples with separate incomes may each establish their own IRAs with deductions of $2,000 a year.

Almost any bank, trust company, or savings and loan association can administer such funds, which are guaranteed up to $100,000. The annuitant can begin drawing benefits at age 59½, or wait until reaching the age of 70½.

These retirement provisions are steps in the right direction and could help to pave the way for the eventual termination of the federal SS System.

To force the producing generations to support those who have retired is an outrageous imposition. The present system places an intolerable burden upon the young; yet, the amounts received by the old is only a pittance; still the burden becomes greater and greater as the retirees increase in number and longevity while the number of contributors is reduced because of the falling birth rate. The system creates enmity between the young, who must pay, and the old, who receive an inadequate disbursement.

If this nation is to remain happy, prosperous, and on a solid social and economic footing, we must replace the present Social Security System with one providing much greater benefits at much less cost with no burden whatever upon the producing generations.

There is a simple way to accomplish these objectives: it is a proposal I call the Universal Trust Plan (UTP). Under this, every individual receiving an income would establish his own irrevocable trust account in a qualifying financial institution, very much like the present IRA or Keogh account plans. These trusts could be of any size; but would require that a minimum of five percent—to be deducted from taxable income—be placed in such trusts every year until retirement. Human nature being what it is, this deduction would have to be mandatory; otherwise too many people would set aside nothing for their own old age. A person earning $25,000 a year would deposit a minimum of $1,250, or about $104.00 a month; or could elect to set aside any larger amount, up to 15 per cent—as under present IRA or Keogh rules. In short, the UTP would simply be an extension of a system already in operation.

The extraordinary benefits of UTP are almost incomprehensible; instead of the current expensive and inequitable welfare system, which leaves millions of annuitants at a near-starvation level, it would repay everyone on the basis of his contributions and create for him or her an irrevocable estate. Each UTP account would increase phenomenally year after year as compound interest is added to the deposited principal; this increment would in due course create tens of millions of estates and a society consisting of comfortable—even affluent citizens.

Each individual would contribute only to his own trust; the support of the old would not fall upon the younger generations.

One of the great blessings of the UTP is that it could and *would* eliminate the need for fractional reserve banking, that gargantuan swindle by which bankers annually collect about $300 billion of interest on credit loans created, on their books, out of thin air. Thomas Jefferson once wrote that no one should be permitted to lend money except those who have money to lend; but the Federal Reserve Act makes it possible for financiers to collect these enormous profits without lending any actual money or value in return for mortgages by which they almost literally own all the property in the United States. The amount borrowed for the financing of homes, apartments, shopping centers, etc., would remain the same or be increased; but instead of the $300 billion going to the financiers, this would accrue to retirement trusts and estates owned by virtually the entire American population.

These statistics illustrate the fantastic power of compound interest. The UTP would, in effect, transform virtually the entire population into money-lenders and estate-builders, thus reducing banks and trust companies into what they should be: fiscal managers, who would perform this service for a reasonable fee.

In 1981, the federal government paid benefits—in addition to

BUILDING AN ESTATE WITH $125 PER MONTH

Years of Contributions	Total Investment	At Five Percent	At Ten Percent	At Twelve Percent
5	$ 7,500	$ 8,531	$ 10,003	$ 10,965
10	15,000	19,720	27,082	31,101
15	22,500	33,492	54,873	68,217
20	30,000	51,470	100,789	136,137
25	37,500	63,267	176,222	261,106
30	45,000	104,691	294,511	497,107
35	52,500	141,948	492,186	912,600
40	60,000	190,515	828,126	1,687,763

medical care—totalling $140,905,000,000 to 36,000,000 recipients under the SS System (an average of $386 per month to retired workers and less to other beneficiaries, except the disabled who averaged $413 and who totaled 2,777,000); there were 20,196,000 retired workers; there were 3,549,000 couples; 4,430,000 children; 548,000 widowed mothers; 4,508,000 widows or widowers; and 91,000 classified as parents or persons receiving social payments. (1982–83 *SA* p. 326.) Compare these benefits with what would be available under the UTP at a small fraction of the present cost of SS.

If the retiree dies before exhausting the corpus of his trust, the remainder will accrue to his heirs or devisees.

What are some of the other advantages of the UTP?

1. The SS bureaucracy, which now employs about 60,000 people, costing taxpayers about $2 billion a year, would be abolished; all its activities would be handled without cost to beneficiaries by private financial institutions.

2. The UTP would remove the federal bureaucracy from an area of activity in which it should never have been engaged.

3. The UTP provides a permanent source of capital for sound investments of all kinds at reasonable cost.

Obviously, during the transition from the SS System to the UTP the federal government must keep faith with the millions who are now on SS and other millions now approaching retirement. At the same time, the government should be seeking and implementing every logical method by which to reduce the number of potential annuitants in order to accomplish more easily the ultimate phaseout of the program.

We suggest that the following steps be taken:

1. Every self-employed person who so desires should be refunded whatever sum he has already contributed to the system when he leaves it (as is done with federal employees upon termination). How-

ever, such a refund should be made on condition that it be deposited in a Koegh-type account and that the recipient continue to contribute at least five percent of his adjusted gross income to it thereafter until retirement.

2. Every wage-worker or salaried individual who so desires should be refunded his actual cash investment in the system on condition that he/she deposit such refund in an IRA-type account and that continuous deposits equal to at least five percent of AGI be made into it until retirement.

3. As soon as feasible—say, in ten or fifteen years—the entire present SS System should be terminated.

This phaseout should begin as soon as possible; the longer it is delayed, the more expensive and difficult it will be.

Under any method of transfer, retirees now on SS must continue to receive their benefits, though other sources of funds must be found to finance such payments. Of the 21 million current retirees, about 1.5 million will die every year. Within fifteen years few will remain provided no new beneficiaries are added. Thus, the annual cost should drop from the present $140 billion to about $35 billion in 1998; and eventually become negligible.

In order to finance the transfer—especially the refunds to millions who will terminate—the federal government would need considerable money during a fifteen-year period. We suggest the following as the means of solving the problem:

1. The Department of Health and Human Services' current budget of $285 billion, scheduled to increase to $435 billion in 1988 (including the Social Security payments) can include the cost of financing the transfer. By simply eliminating waste and fraud, it could save at least $10 billion a year.

2. Until the majority of SS retirees die, a portion of the interest paid on UTP accounts could be used to meet federal commitments to those already in retirement. In ten years, the trusts would total at

MONTHLY BENEFITS UNDER THE UTP

Trust Fund	At Eight Percent: Interest Only	At Eight Percent: Exhaust Fund in 20 Years	Approximate 40 Year Investment	At Twelve Percent: Int. Only	At Twelve Percent: Exhaust Fund in 20 Years	Total Potential Disbursements
$50,000	$334	$417	$3,000	$500	$550	$132,120
100,000	667	836	4,000	1,000	1,101	264,240
200,000	1,335	1,673	7,000	2,000	2,202	528,480
300,000	2,002	2,509	11,500	3,000	3,303	792,720
400,000	2,668	3,340	15,000	4,000	4,404	1,056,960
500,000	3,337	4,182	19,000	5,000	5,505	1,321,200

least $1 trillion and in twenty years about $3 trillion. If the revenues from these trusts were taxed at 25 percent, they would provide from $15 to $45 billion a year, which alone would be sufficient to meet most of the obligations to existing retirees after eight or ten years.

3. The trusts could pay an estate tax of 25 percent during the transfer period. Since heirs would not have contributed anything to the funds, there would be no injustice in taking a portion of them to finance the transfer to the UTP.

4. The elimination of one million federal bureaucrats would reduce the federal budget by enough to pay for most of the suggested transfer.

5. By leasing or selling oil shale deposits and encouraging production therefrom, the government could obtain enough money to finance the transfer for several years.

6. By eliminating the unnecessary paperwork the federal government foists on American business, the cost of government could be reduced by $50 billion.

7. By selling a portion of its 760,532,000 acres—which comprises 33 percent of the entire U.S. land area and includes some of our most valuable mineral and forest reserves—the federal government could realize enough to finance the entire transfer from the present SS System to the UTP.

8. As a last resort, the federal government could issue bonds to finance a portion of the transfer cost; the interest on these and their amortization could be financed by taxes levied on the income accruing from the trust accounts.

7

The Battle for Constitutional Money

The Background

Our Founding Fathers were determined that (1) the federal government have exclusive power to issue our currency, and (2) that it should consist of, or be redeemable in, specie. Therefore, they provided that Congress alone shall have power to coin (issue) money and regulate the value thereof; and that no state shall make anything except gold and silver coin a tender in the payment of debt. This means, of course, that the currency must be issued by the Treasury; and that fiat money or bills of credit shall be banned forever—for how can the value of irredeemable currency be regulated? Since these provisions are still in the Constitution, those who support and defend the present Federal Reserve System are deceivers and betrayers.

Thomas Jefferson fought a bitter battle over this crucial issue with Alexander Hamilton, who succeeded in establishing a banking system basically similar to that which now exists; it was approved by congressional action and was given the power to issue currency, to expand or contract credit, and thus to create inflation or deflation at will. This was what the financiers of that day—like those of the present—desired; by it, they made fabulous fortunes; and, as Jefferson declared, were able to form an aristocracy based on moneyed interests.

Jefferson had a simple and practical solution for the monetary problem, which, had it been adopted, would have made the United States the most secure, peaceful, and prosperous nation ever known, and any emergency—even the expense of a great war—could have been met without borrowing money or imposing additional taxes. Jefferson proposed that the Treasury issue all currency to consist of, and be redeemable in, specie; during a war or other emergency, the Congress would issue interest-bearing notes in small denominations, which would be universally acceptable, either for savings or exchange, and which would be redeemed in specie and destroyed when the emergency was over.

Hamilton's First United States Bank was established in 1791, with a 20-year franchise; however, in 1811, Madison vetoed the attempt to renew its charter, and there was no national bank until 1816, when the Second United States Bank, also with a 20-year franchise, was established because of the debts created by the Second War with England. The attempt to renew its charter was vetoed by Andrew Jackson in 1832. The national debt was liquidated in 1835.

Because the people were so suspicious of any central banking authority, no such institution existed from 1836 to 1863: state-chartered banks issued their own currency. There were some 12,000 different currencies in circulation during this period, many of them fraudulent or actually counterfeit. The vision, power, and statesmanship necessary to establish a monetary system on Jeffersonian principles evidently did not exist. However, the cost of the Civil War—when Lincoln issued $450,000,000 in fiat Greenbacks, which could not be used to pay import or export duties or the interest on the national debt—brought on a new crisis, which allowed the financiers to force through Congress the National Banking Act of 1863, giving them much of the power they craved. Under this Act, the banks could buy government bonds with Greenbacks—purchased at thirty cents on the dollar—at face value; they then collected seven percent interest in gold; and were permitted to use the bonds for the issuance of their own currency up to 90 percent of the face value of the bonds.

When Lincoln tried to borrow money, the financiers demanded 28 percent interest and, so, in spite of the tax- and interest-free Greenbacks, they obtained at least that rate of return on most of what had become the $2.7 billion national debt at the close of the Civil War.

The Financiers Establish a Central Bank

The period 1865–1910 was generally one of prosperity and expansion, interrupted only by severe panics in 1873, 1893, and 1907. However, as the Civil War debt gradually declined after 1866, the reserves on which to create currency were reduced in equal ratio, to about $1 billion shortly after 1900. There was, therefore, an insufficient reserve on which to create credit money for loans; and, in due course, the bankers made elaborate plans to establish a monetary system similar to those operating in England and other European countries. Most of these were under the control of the Rothschilds, the Warburgs, and other great private banking interests.

To accomplish this in the United States was not easy; but it was eventually done through a series of deceitful maneuvers almost without parallel in political history.

In November 1910, a group of bankers, politicians, and collaborators journeyed in great secrecy to Jekyll Island, off the coast of Georgia, for the purpose of hammering out proposed legislation which would create in the United States the kind of monetary system the conspirators desired. It would be a private corporation, but established by congressional statute. Among those who met there were Nelson Aldrich, a New York Senator-banker and the maternal grandfather of the Rockefellers; the German emigre, Paul Moritz Warburg, representing the Rothschild interests of Europe; representatives from Kuhn, Loeb, and Company, and other financiers representing the great banking interests of the Eastern Seaboard, and closely allied with their European counterparts.

Paul M. Warburg was the genius who, more than anyone else, created the Federal Reserve. With $500,000 of Rothschild money, he had purchased a partnership in Kuhn, Loeb, & Co.; he was given a then tax-free annual salary of the same amount and an indefinite leave of absence, which he utilized by traveling the country promoting the monetary system he envisioned. He realized that the desired institution could be established—in the face of the existing opposition—only if the members of Congress could be deceived into believing that it was actually a governmental institution. He wanted to call it the Federal Reserve System, in order to disguise its real nature. In addition, a variety of features were to be incorporated so that the public could be made to accept it as a true federal agency, although, of course, it was to be nothing of the kind. And this objective was achieved.

The promoters assured Congress and the public that under the proposed legislation there would never again be any inflation or deflation, panics or depressions, or any shortage of money for necessary business purposes. And there would forever be a stable and dependable currency.

However, the incumbent president, William Howard Taft, had, by endorsing the proposed Nelson Aldrich Bill—which made no attempt to conceal its purely private nature—committed political suicide; had he been re-elected in 1912, the Federal Reserve Act could not have been passed. It was therefore necessary to find a more suitable person for the presidency: The man chosen was Woodrow Wilson, then Governor of New Jersey, who, financed by the very interests he denounced throughout his campaign, went up and down the country condemning the Wall Street bankers and all they stood for. Since the Democrats were then a minority party, Wilson could not have been elected were it not for Teddy Roosevelt and his Bull Moose Party, which was financed by the bankers whom he also assailed. With the Republican vote thus split, Wilson was elected by a plurality of 42 percent. Taft came in a poor third after Roosevelt.

W. J. Bryan, who had run for the presidency three times and who had always been an outspoken critic of the financiers, was named Secretary of State by Wilson in order to hold the Party together.

Henry Parker Willis, a professor from the University of Chicago was drafted by Carter Glass, Chairman of the House Banking and Currency Committee, to prepare the text of the proposed legislation. He drew up one draft after another; after the third version was completed it was submitted to Bryan, who demanded four conditions which he declared were absolutely necessary to obtain his approval:

1. that the Federal Reserve notes look as if they were issued by the Treasury;
2. that these notes be declared obligations of the federal government;
3. that the members of the Board of Governors be appointed by the President with the advice and consent of the Senate; and
4. that government control of federal funds be assured.

When Glass told Wilson privately that the proposed Fed was not a public institution, the President observed that the people, the Populists, could have the Shadow so long as the financiers retained the Reality. President Wilson signed the bill a few hours after its passage on December 23, 1913. Warburg had previously written to Carter Glass that the law was what he had hoped for and that, in due course, any desired changes would be implemented by an obedient Congress.

Of all those involved in the passage of this Act, only Warburg, Wilson, Aldrich, Glass, and a few others really knew what a monster they were creating. Professor Willis published a huge volume in 1923 in which he praised it; Senator Robert Owen wrote another in 1921 lauding it. Willis turned against it in 1927 and Owen in 1935. Bryan was not disillusioned until much later. Warburg published a two-volume work about it in which, with apparent great satisfaction, he explained in detail just how the whole thing was accomplished.

Only one man—as far as is known—at the time fully understood the Act's potential dangers and did his utmost to defeat it. Charles Augustus Lindbergh, Sr., Congressman from Minnesota, wrote three books analyzing and condemning it, declaring that the Act would lay the foundation on which panics and depressions could be created scientifically in the future by the financiers. He lost his seat in Congress and died soon thereafter.

The History and the Structure of the Fed

The first great accomplishment of the Fed—in collaboration with the newly established Internal Revenue Service—was to finance the first World War, which increased the national debt from $1 billion to $26 billion, and which made profits of at least $25 billion for the financiers.

The Fed's second great accomplishment was the fierce depression of 1920–21, in which millions were thrown out of work and hundreds of thousands of farmers lost their property.

The third was the stock market speculation of 1928–29, in which those on the inside made fortunes, but millions of others lost everything.

The fourth was the Great Depression of 1929–40, in which the Middle Class was almost extirpated; money virtually disappeared from the American scene and nearly all city property went through foreclosures.

Franklin D. Roosevelt was elected to the presidency in 1932 on a very conservative platform, which he totally ignored by establishing policies the exact opposite of those he had advocated in public. His first act in office was to close all the banks; next he gave the gold in the Treasury to the Federal Reserve System; then he made it a crime for Americans to retain their own gold coins. He increased the price of gold from $20.67 to $35 an ounce, but gave Americans only $20 Federal Reserve notes for their $20 gold pieces. He said he would reduce federal costs by 25 percent and then increased them by 3,000 percent. He said he hated war, but he conspired by every conceivable means to drag the nation into global conflict.

Under FDR's leadership, the Federal Reserve Act was amended in various ways, all of which strengthened the power of the financiers. The Secretary of the Treasury was replaced by a private banker appointed as Chairman of the Board of Governors, thus severing the last link between the government and the System. The Open Market Committee was established, operating out of the New York Branch, which gives the Fed almost total control over the economy. It has the power to buy unlimited amounts of federal securities and to pay for them either with newly-ordered Federal Reserve notes or by writing checks against the U.S. Treasury. In 1982, it held a portfolio of such securities totaling more than $139 billion, which was the principal portion of its book assets, which exceeded $190 billion. Under this computation, its gold reserve is valued at only $42.23 an ounce; but at the current price of gold, the assets of the Fed now exceed $300 billion.

When the price of gold was set at $35 an ounce in 1934, the Depression was at its worst, and gold could be produced for $12 or less. Therefore, gold began flowing into the United States, increasing the Fed's hoard from about $3 to more than $25 billion by 1942; at that time every Federal Reserve note in existence could have been redeemed five times over in gold. The Fed purchased most of its gold from foreign financiers, who made an estimated profit of at least $15 billion. Then, about 1954, when the cost of producing gold began to exceed the statutory price, the Fed began selling it back to the foreign investors. It continued to do so until 1972, when bullion exceeded $125 an ounce. However, the gold bars were not shipped abroad, but simply transferred from Fort Knox to the vaults of the New York branch of the Fed, where, earmarked to foreign ownership, some 18,000 tons are stored at taxpayer expense for the benefit of the actual owners. Under Sections 892 and 895 of the Internal Revenue Code, there will be neither taxation nor disclosure when the foreign owners sell this vast treasure at a possible profit of several hundred billion dollars.

The Federal Reserve System consists of 12 branch or regional banks, each of which is governed by nine directors. These are divided into three classes: Three directors are elected directly by the member banks; three by the stockholders in their locality; and three are appointed by the Board of Governors. With two-thirds of the directors elected by the private banks, obviously those appointed by the Board are mere supernumeraries.

Section 5 of the Federal Reserve Act provides that member banks must subscribe 3 percent of their capital and surplus in payment of stock.

Section 7 provides that a tax-free dividend of 6 percent be paid annually on such stock.

Section 10 provides that the seven members of the Board of Governors be appointed by the President with the advice and consent of the Senate, to staggered 14-year terms.

Section 12 creates the Federal Advisory Council, consisting of representatives from each of the regional banks.

Section 13 provides that every member bank "may discount notes, drafts, and bills of exchange arising out of actual commercial transactions" or "based on the importation or exportation of goods. . . ." It also precludes the use of bank credit for speculation (a provision violated especially in 1928–29, when the banks extended credit of billions for the purchase of stock on margin).

Section 14 provides that the Open Market Committee may buy and sell government securities in the open market.

Section 15 provides that government funds may be deposited in Federal Reserve Banks, which should act as fiscal agent for the government.

Section 16 provides that Federal Reserve notes shall be issued at the discretion of the Board of Governors for the purpose of making advances to the Federal Reserve banks, said notes to be obligations of the United States and be receivable for all taxes, customs, and public dues.

This section also provides that every member bank may obtain from the regional reserve bank such quantities of Federal Reserve notes as it may need by using discounted commercial paper or government securities as collateral. It also provides that each of the regional banks shall have the power to obtain such notes for the cost of production from the Bureau of Printing and Engraving.

Section 19 provides that the Fed shall have the power to establish the reserve requirements for the creation of credit in what is known as fractional reserve banking; such reserve requirements may vary anywhere from 10 to 26.

We find, therefore, (1) that the System is immune to income taxation; (2) that all stock is owned by the private, commercial banks, which are members of the System; (3) that it obtains Federal Reserve notes for the cost of production, and charges even this to taxpayers; (4) that it determines the reserve requirements of member banks; (5) that two-thirds of the directors of the regional banks are elected by the member banks or their stockholders; (6) that the Fed controls prices of government securities through the Open Market Committee and thus is able, in effect, to set interest rates and determine the value of the currency.

We find also that it creates or contributes to inflation by printing currency to buy government securities; that it is now and always has been immune to any meaningful audit; that it operates completely independent from government control; that member banks obtain government securities for nothing, then collect interest on them, and use them for the creation of credit on their books by fractional reserve banking; that the Fed is a public institution only in the sense that it was created by congressional statute and may be abolished by an act of Congress, as provided in Section 30 of the Act; and that, as a result, it is far more responsive to the interests and demands of the financial community than it is to the authority of Congress or to the needs and welfare of the American people.

Some apologists for the Fed make a great deal of the fact that it is required to make annual reports to the Congress and that some of its operations are subject to scrutiny. However, the GAO (Government Accounting Office) may not delve into or investigate any matter dealing with monetary policy, discount window operations, securities credit, Open Market operations, and various other areas which are the very crux of the System.

It is ironic that, while the federal government has embarked upon hundreds of programs specifically outlawed by the Constitution, it has turned over to a private corporation one of its most important duties and mandates: the issuance of money and its regulation—that is, the determination of its intrinsic value. Congress has no more authority to transfer its monetary authority to a consortium of financiers than it would have to give it the power to lay and collect taxes or to declare and wage war.

If there is any lingering doubt that the Fed is a private corporation, consider these facts: (1) Its personnel do not work for the government, have no tenure, and never enjoy any General Service rating, as do all federal employees; (2) its employees do not participate in the retirement system in which all federal employees are enrolled; (3) the Fed pays postage on all the mail it sends; and (4) it pays local real estate taxes on all its properties. Under these conditions, how is it possible to regard the Fed as a governmental institution?

The Purpose and Power of the Fed

The Fed itself was not established and is not operated as a profit-making entity; from a total income of $16,517,385,129 in 1982, it paid the Treasury slightly over $15.2 billion from revenues obtained mostly from federal securities. Its purpose is to make it possible for its member banks to amass profits and wealth. Each of the 12 branch banks can order Federal Reserve notes from the Bureau of Printing and Engraving, in any desired quantity, for the actual cost of production. Member banks can also obtain government bonds without actual cost, on which they collect interest which is *not* returned to the Treasury. In 1981, the member banks held federal securities with a face value of $116 billion, which could be used as the basis for the creation of credit-money by the technique of fractional reserve banking; such credit-, debt-, or check-book money is then used to obtain mortgages on real estate and other assets representing solid collateral. This can be done without actually lending any real money at all.

The Fed enables its member banks to obtain vast assets by creating loans in this way. The Board of Governors determines the ratio of reserves necessary for doing so. Thus, when easy money or inflation is desired, it reduces the ratio to ten, which means that credit equal to ten times the cash assets or the value of the bonds may be created. When the Fed wants a depression, it may increase the reserve requirement to any desired level, which means that credit will be drastically curtailed, loans will be called, and bankruptcies will be frequent occurrences.

The Fed could at any time order enough Federal Reserve notes printed to liquidate the national debt; but we can be sure that will never happen, for it desires *more,* not less, debt on which to collect interest.

The Fed can also set the interest rate at any level it wishes; it could reduce it to 2 or increase it to 40 percent. Its power is without limit or control, except as it may fear an outraged electorate, which might force some drastic congressional action to monitor it.

Let us see how a bank creates a mortgage lien on a house: A man who owns a building lot and has $20,000 needs an additional $75,000 to build a house. If the banker finds the collateral sufficient, he may credit the man's checking account with $80,000—minus several points for expenses—against which checks can be written to pay for construction. When the house is completed, it will have a thirty-year lien at 12 or 15 per cent. After working thirty years to liquidate the debt, the owner will have paid perhaps $300,000 for something that did not cost the banker a dime in the first place. This is the magic of fractional reserve banking.

We may estimate that the bankers in the U.S. currently have a collective annual income of possibly $300 billion—on which they pay only a minimum of income taxes. The Chase Manhattan Bank of New York has not paid any such levies for years; David Rockefeller, once Chairman of its Board, told the House Ways and Means Committee in 1969 that *he* did not owe any income taxes either.

There have been sporadic attempts in Congress to do something about the Fed. In the early 1940s Jerry Voorhis introduced a bill to abolish it. Congressman Wright Patman, chairman of the House Banking and Currency Committee, criticized the Fed severely, and called for a complete audit. The most outspoken enemy of the Fed, Louis T. McFadden, another chairman of Banking and Currency, lost this position in 1931, was defeated for re-election in 1934, and died in 1936, under questionable circumstances. None of this opposition had any effect on controlling the power of the Fed.

The Growing Opposition to the Fed

When I wrote *The Federal Reserve and Our Manipulated Dollar* in 1974, there had as yet been very little public interest in, or understanding of, the Federal Reserve System. Only occasionally had anyone challenged its validity. At first gradually, then in greater numbers, however, one articulate voice after another was raised in opposition to it; today, there is a powerful grass-roots movement with one insistent slogan: Repeal the Federal Reserve Act and establish a constitutional monetary system.

Of great significance is the increasing opposition to the Fed emerging from state legislatures. Four states have already passed resolutions calling for the repeal of the Federal Reserve Act and similar actions are pending in at least twenty others.

The following is the first Resolution of its kind in the United States:

THE MEMORIAL RESOLUTION OF THE ARIZONA STATE LEGISLATURE DEMANDING THE REPEAL OF THE FEDERAL RESERVE ACT

To the President and the Congress of the United States of America:

Your Memorialist respectfully represents:

Whereas, Article I, section 8, Constitution of the United States, provides that only the Congress of the United States shall have the power "to borrow Money on the credit of the United States;" and

Whereas, Article I, section 8, Constitution of the United States, directs that only the Congress of the United States is permitted "to coin money and regulate the value thereof" . . . and

Whereas, the Federal Reserve Act of 1913 transferred the power to borrow money on the credit of the United States to a consortium of private bankers in violation of the prohibitions of Article I, section 8, Constitution of the United States; and

Whereas, the Congress of the United States is without authority to delegate any powers which it has received under the Constitution of the United States established by the people of the United States; and

Whereas, Article I, section 1, Constitution of the United States, provides that "All legislative powers herein granted shall be vested in a Congress of the United States, which shall consist of a Senate and House of Representatives;" and

Whereas, the Federal Reserve Act of 1913 was imposed on the people of the State of Arizona in violation of the provisions of Article I, section 1, Constitution of the United States; and

Whereas, the Federal Reserve Banking System has threatened the integrity of our government through arbitrary and capricious control and management of the nation's money supply; and

Whereas, the United States is facing, in the current decade, an economic debacle of massive proportions due in large measure to a continued erosion of the national currency and the resultant high interest rates caused by the policies of the Federal Reserve Board; and

Wherefore, your Memorialist, the House of Representatives of the State of Arizona, the Senate concurring, prays:

1. That the Congress of the United States immediately enact such legislation as is necessary to repeal the Federal Reserve Act.

2. That the Secretary of the State of Arizona transmit copies of this Memorial to the President of the United States Senate, the Speaker of the House of Representatives of the United States, and to each Member of the Arizona Congressional delegation.

(Approved in the Second Regular Session of the thirty-fifth Legislature, 1982.)

A grand jury in Salt Lake City, Utah, returned a criminal indictment against the Fed in March and June 1982, in a document comprising about 3,000 words. The following excerpts are indicative of its general thrust and content.

"The Grand Jury finds that:

"The power to print paper money or to issue bills of credit was never given to the federal government and it is contrary to both the letter and the spirit of the Constitution for it to do so.

"While the power 'to coin money and regulate the value thereof, and of foreign coin' were both delegated to the Congress, the power to print money was never given. A proposal was made to the constitutional convention to give Congress this power and it was defeated by a vote of nine states to two. . . . But the wording of the Constitution itself denies such power to Congress. It provides that 'No state shall make Anything but gold and silver Coin a Tender in the payment of debt.' This being so, when the Federal government issues irredeemable paper as a tender in payment of debt, it compels them to violate this prohibition. Inasmuch as the laws dealing with lawful money are still intact (gold and silver coin), the federal reserve system, in ignoring these laws, is also violating these statutes. . . .

"An irredeemable currency is directly contrary to the spirit of the Constitution which was designed to protect contract rights. There is a specific provision contained in the Constitution which says: 'No state shall . . . pass any law impairing the obligations of contracts.' The same law shall apply to the federal government. By printing worthless currency and compelling state courts to use it as a legal tender in payment of debts, it forces them to disobey the Constitution. Recognizing the danger of allowing state governments to pass laws destroying contract rights and also desiring that states should act honorably, this prohibition was adopted. Morally and legally, it is equally applicable to the federal." (The point of this is that as fiat currency declines in value, debts can be repaid in declining values, and therefore the obligations of contracts are impaired.)

This indictment was dismissed on July 9, 1982, by the United States District Court Judge.

Senator Jack Metcalf and the Washington Legislature

One of the principal leaders in the movement to abolish the Fed and restore a constitutional monetary system is Senator Jack Metcalf of Washington. Under his leadership, its legislature passed SCR 127 in 1982 calling for a Supreme Court challenge of Congress's delegating to a private corporation the power to create money and regulate its value.

This was the first such legislation enacted. And, although the State Attorney General refused to bring suit, Senator Metcalf is optimistic that when other states take similar action, the Supreme Court will be forced to hear and adjudicate, once and for all, this vital issue, and declare whether or not the Federal Reserve Act is constitutional. The Senator also arranged congressional hearings on the question, in which various members of Congress participated and at which a number of leading economists testified.

Senator Metcalf wrote: "In 1980, Congress passed what I believe history will record as the most dangerous piece of legislation in its entire history. It was the Monetary Control Act of 1980. . . . This Act allows the Fed to 'monetize' (bail out) the debt of foreign nations! The taxpayers of the United States are now being saddled with the debts of the whole world! Between April 21, 1981, and August, 1982 this provision was used 65 times, allowing the Fed to monetize $3.3 billions of foreign debts."

But this, of course, was only the tip of the iceberg. In June 1983, the Senate passed a bill to give the IMF another $8.4 billion for the same purpose. There is no doubt that the megabanks intend to compel the American taxpayers to repay them for at least $175 billion of bad loans which they have made to foreign countries, including communist ones.

The Fed is Worried

Because of rising opposition and criticism, Fed bureaucrats are deeply concerned; they issue extensive reports attempting to establish the belief that the entity is constitutional and that it is a true government agency. Once, after I had given a talk, reported in the local newspaper, the Director of Public Relations of the Federal Reserve Bank in San Francisco wrote a long letter to the editor, which he hoped would be printed, attempting to refute my statements.

Donald J. Winn, Assistant to the Board of Governors, in a letter written at the request of a certain congressman to one of his constituents, stated that, since the Fed is supervised by a Board of Governors appointed by the President, with the advice and consent of the Senate, and since its currency is an obligation of the government, it is, in fact, a corporate instrument of the United States, established for a public purpose. These were just the provisions William Jennings Bryan insisted be included in the Act before he would endorse it.

Winn goes on to say that since the stock owned by the member banks (5,465 in 1983) cannot be transferred or hypothecated, it does not confer control or constitute private ownership. He mentions that the 6 percent interest rate paid on the stock is less than the current rate. However, he neglects to point out that it is tax exempt and that the same rate prevailed when the government borrowed money at 2½ percent.

He emphasizes that the Fed is not operated for profit, as if this were proof of public ownership or control; he makes much of the fact that in 1982 it returned to the Treasury about 90 percent of the $15 billion it received in interest on government securities. But he does not explain how the Fed, without investing any funds of its own, came to possess about $140 billion of government securities, or that it pays its operational expenses largely out of this income.

He states that "although the Board is an independent agency, Congress does have ultimate authority" over the System. "The Board is required to make an annual report to Congress." So, by the way, is every private corporation in the United States—except churches and a few "charities"—to the Internal Revenue Service.

Perhaps the crux of Winn's argument is his statement that the Congress has "exclusive power to coin money and regulate the value thereof"—a function that has been "broadly construed by the Supreme Court to authorize the regulation of every phase of the subject of currency. . . . Congress used this constitutional power when it passed the Federal Reserve Act in 1913 and specifically authorized the Reserve Banks to issue currency."

All this is a subtle twist of logic: We are told that, since Congress has the exclusive power to coin money and regulate the value thereof, it has also the authority to delegate this power to anyone it wishes! Thus, by the same reasoning, it could farm out the business of collecting taxes and pay the collectors a fifty percent commission for doing so!

Winn cites *Juilliard* vs. *Greenmann* as his principal authority. However, when this decision was handed down in 1884, it stated specifically that only the federal government, since it had sovereign power, may authorize only the Treasury to issue notes of legal tender. And, at that time, such notes were redeemable in specie.

Even so, the eminent historian, George Bancroft, wrote a pamphlet entitled *A Plea for the Constitution*, published in 1886, condemning the Opinion and predicting that it would some day be used to justify a monetary system which would be a total perversion of the Constitution. He called the words of the decision "the language of revolution"; and declared that the Court was not interpreting the Constitution, but legislating powers which are specifically forbidden in that document.

Winn cites other court decisions written in extension and elaboration of *Juilliard* which, he says, make it clear "that Congress is empowered under the Constitution to authorize the Federal Reserve System to issue currency in the form of Federal Reserve notes and that these Federal Reserve notes are lawfully issued."

Perhaps Winn's most glaring deceit is his attempt to sidestep the implications of the Ninth Circuit Court decision in *Lewis* vs. *United States*, entered on April 19, 1982, in which a man who had been injured by an automobile owned and operated by the Federal Reserve Bank of San Francisco sued for damages in a federal court. The court declared that since the Federal Reserve System and its twelve branch banks are private corporations, the Federal government could not be held responsible.

The language is explicit. "Federal Reserve banks are not federal instrumentalities for purposes of a Federal Tort Claim Act, but are independent, privately owned and locally controlled corporations in light of the fact that direct supervision and control of each bank is exercised by a board of directors; federal reserve banks, though heavily regulated, are locally controlled by the member banks; banks are listed neither as 'wholly owned' government corporations, nor as 'mixed ownership' corporations; federal reserve banks receive no appropriated funds from Congress and the banks are empowered to sue and be sued in their own names."

The Opinion continues: "The liability of the United States for the negligence of a Federal Reserve Bank employee depends, therefore, on whether the Bank is a federal agency. . . ." It is true that the Federal Reserve Banks perform certain functions which are, or should be, governmental in their nature; however, "[T]he fact that the Federal Reserve Board regulates the Reserve Bank does not make them federal agencies. . . ."

Thus, the Federal Reserve is neither a wholly-owned government operation, nor one of "mixed ownership" and operation, nor does it qualify as a federal agency. Therefore, the Fed is a federal agency only in the sense that it was created by congressional statute.

Archibald E. Roberts and the Committee to Restore the Constitution

Among those now engaged in the struggle to reinstate the Constitution, surely Colonel Archibald E. Roberts of Fort Collins, Colorado, stands in the forefront. He has focussed his criticism on the Federal Reserve System and its illegal operation. He has appeared before various state legislatures, urging them to pass Memorials demanding that Congress repeal the Federal Reserve Act and establish a constitutional monetary system.

He has organized chapters of his Committee to Restore the Constitution throughout the country, assembling a prestigious group of officers and council members, including ex-congressman John Rarick as chairman, publisher Don Bell, Curtis B. Dall of Liberty Lobby, author Howard Kerschner, Dr. Revilo P. Oliver, and many other individuals with national reputations.

On March 7, 1983, Colonel Roberts appeared before the Idaho State Legislature in support of a proposal that it adopt a Memorial similar to those passed in Arizona and Alabama. He stated in part:

> Article I, Section 8 of the Constitution directs that the Congress is authorized to borrow money on the credit of the United States, and to coin money and regulate the value thereof. Federal agents are prohibited from modifying the Constitution or transferring these vast powers to a private banking cartel. There is no authority in the Constitution permitting such usurpation of power. . . . The Federal Reserve is not a government agency. It is a private banking cartel. This is the crux of the issue. . . .
>
> It is obvious that when the power to control money is transferred from the people to a private banking monopoly, as is now proven to be the case in America, the sovereignty of the people is surrendered also. Control of wealth confers upon those who control the final decisions in the domestic and international affairs of the nation. When an invisible government of monetary power usurps the coin of the realm, the people are disfranchised and real political authority is transferred into the hands of a financial aristocracy. I believe that an invisible government of monetary power will continue to control the American destiny and the lives of the people until informed citizens dismantle the Federal Reserve System. . . .
>
> The Monetary Control Act of 1980. . . . brings all U.S. depository institutions under the authority of the Federal Reserve Sys-

> tem. . . . It also expands the definition of collateral for Federal Reserve credit and Federal Reserve notes in circulation. This means that any asset the Fed may purchase on the open market can be used as an asset against such borrowing. The cartel thus has a lien against all property in the United States, because all of the banking and lending institutions under the Federal Reserve today use their collateral as authority to create money out of thin air. This, then, is the means by which the internationalists have placed their control over all real estate in the United States, and, of course, all individuals who own private property of any kind.
>
> For example, the Feds can now purchase such collateral as FHA and VA-backed mortgages or corporate debt obligations. . . . the Fed can bail out the Chase Manhattan Bank . . . or any other bank with the acceptance of federally backed mortgages from such banks . . . placing the burden of repayment for these bad loans upon the backs of the American people. . . .
>
> Under the provisions of the Monetary Control Act, the foreign debts granted by our various banks are all based upon the ability of the American taxpayers to pay. All of these debts, under this alleged authority, are subject to monetization. . . . the taxpayers become subject to paying, not only the interest on these horrendous debts, but also the principal. The International Monetary Fund is exercising that alleged authority to place the burden of repayment, not on the resources of the host country . . . but on the backs of the American taxpayers.

Colonel Roberts emphasizes that because the states, under the Constitution, are superior to the creature they have created—i.e., the Federal government—it is their constitutional responsibility, and that of their elected officials, to enforce the articles of the Constitution. And one of the first things to be done is for the state legislatures to demand the repeal of the Federal Reserve Act.

Tupper Saussy and *The Main Street Journal*

In 1981, Frederick Tupper Saussy established the magazine, *The Main Street Journal*. Though Saussy works closely with Irwin Schiff, Charles Riely, and others in the tax resistance movement, his journal concerns itself with the violation of only one part of the Constitution: namely, ARTICLE I, Section 10, with which our entire financial and monetary superstructure is inextricably involved. If it is obeyed, no State can make any payment except in specie, nor require anyone to make payment in any other medium. And, because there cannot be two kinds of legal currency circulating in the nation—one on the federal and another on the State level—, it is obvious that any money that does not consist of, or is not redeemable in, specie is patently unconstitutional.

Based on this focal point, Saussy has built an important movement, which now involves thousands of highly vocal and determined individuals in all parts of the country. Among their heroes are Roger Sherman, who is credited with leading the movement for a specie currency preceding the ratification of the Constitution; and the great historian, George Bancroft, whose *Plea for the Constitution*, published in 1886, following the Supreme Court decision in *Juilliard* vs. *Greenmann*, demonstrated the terrible effects which would ensue from this decision. Bancroft established beyond doubt that the Founding Fathers were determined that fiat, paper currency should never be permitted.

Saussy is the organizer of the Roger Sherman Society, dedicated to the restoration of constitutional money.

In July 1984, Tupper Saussy was charged with failing to file proper income tax returns and with not paying taxes for the years 1977–79. At a bizarre hearing held in Nashville, Tennessee, on February 24, 1985, he denied the jurisdiction of the court and was sentenced to 90 days for contempt; he was then whisked off to a federal penitentiary in Atlanta. His trial is set for May 7, in a place hundreds of miles from his home, where, probably, few friends will be present to support or encourage him.

The publishers of *The Main Street Journal* are well aware that victory can come in only one way—not from the politicians, the media, the churches, the colleges and universities, any other of the well-fed segments of society, all of which are pampered by the monetary subverters. The solution must come from the concerted action of the people, themselves, who live on "Main Street" throughout the country. When enough of them rebel, and refuse to knuckle under to the enemies of the Constitution, this holy instrument will be restored in its pristine purity.

A Farmer Exposes the Fed

In 1983, Edward Kennedy published a book called *The Fed and the Farmer*. Born in 1894, the author was raised in an Iowa farm family. In due course, he became a leading protagonist for agricultural rights, and in the progress of this struggle, discovered the role of the Federal Reserve and its allies in pauperizing the independent farmers, and in trying to eliminate them entirely from the American scene.

Kennedy's first encounter with corruption occurred when he was

25, when he found that a certain contractor was paid for the construction of at least 110 bridges which were never built. Mr. Kennedy led a movement that exposed this crook, forcing him to pay back the county for the money he had received, and which led to his eventual ruin and bankruptcy.

His first encounter with the Fed came during the devastating Agricultural Depression of 1920–21. In 1918–19, the Fed had encouraged farmers to borrow funds to improve their farms, construct buildings, and buy new machinery, etc.; then, suddenly, around mid-1920, it called in their loans, raised interest rates, and foreclosed several hundred thousand farmholds. Kennedy helped the farmers, the local bankers, and the town merchants to survive, while throughout the state at least one-third of them were going bankrupt, as loans were called, credit curtailed, and farm prices declined by more than 50 percent.

Kennedy's book also describes in detail how the Fed "ballooned the stock market with easy credit" before 1929 by permitting its members to advance billions in loans to purchase stocks on margin. "Then, one Monday in late 1929, it pulled the rug from under the market—and from under all those who had borrowed money to buy stocks on margin. All this set the stage for the continuation of the Great Depression through the Thirties to Pearl Harbor," he writes. "The Fed continued the restriction of money and credit to prolong the depression for nearly 13 years, until we entered World War II." It worked in tandem with the Board of Trade and the U.S. Department of Agriculture to keep the depression going and bankrupt the farmers. For one thing, it reduced the money supply by $6.5 billion and refused to place any more in circulation until the advent of WW II, when it opened its pursestrings without limit to finance the destruction.

One of Kennedy's principal themes is the operation of the commodities, or futures, market by the Chicago Board of Trade, which deals in agricultural commodities in somewhat the same way the New York Stock Exchange handles corporation securities. Speculators purchase futures of 5,000 bushels of grain, 40,000 pounds of beef, or 30,000 of pork; they never own an ounce of these, but buy and sell the rights to purchase in order to make a quick profit. In any one year, the total grain transactions can total ten or more times the domestic production. In 1970, for example, wheat production totaled 1,357,538,000 bushels, but 19,010,125,000 bushels were exchanged in the futures market. The Board of Trade operates in tandem with the Fed and other federal agencies to control and depress farm prices. The principal speculators cause the market to rise or fall by giving out selective information. By various techniques, the Board of Trade can make sure that the farmers will never receive enough to cover their actual cost of production.

The federal government forces all farmers to restrict various kinds of production by enforcing quotas, paying subsidies, and penalizing those who do not qualify. The ostensible reason for these policies is to eliminate supposedly huge surplusses, which cause depressed prices. Kennedy, however, demonstrates that domestic production never equalled consumption—the "surplus" was the result of imports used to depress the domestic market and drive the American farmers into bankruptcy. Such practices have been federal policy since Roosevelt became president in 1933.

Kennedy led the movement that resulted in a national moratorium on farm mortgage foreclosures in the 'Thirties, which, he said, while alleviating the crisis, did not solve the problem. A greater victory resulted from a battle he led in 1941 when the Federal government imposed a penalty tax of 49 cents on every bushel of wheat and 36 cents on every bushel of corn produced, *even for its own use*, by those farmers who did not qualify for subsidies by meeting quotas. He helped organize a revolt so powerful that Congress was forced to repeal this outrageous and unconstitutional levy.

Since 1944, says Kennedy, the Fed has "gone in for the kill. It has manipulated interest rates as its principal instrument of destabilization. During these 35 [sic] years, the Fed has increased the prime rate ten times totaling 38 percent. It has decreased the prime rate nine times, totaling 22 percent. By the end of 1980, the net increase was 17 percent. . . .

"For thirty-five years there has been no period of income stability. . . . Business could not plan for any long term to increase its facilities and production to employ the new crop of workers which come on each year."

The farmers especially have suffered from being forced to borrow and pay excessive interest. In 1953, their mortgage debt totaled $7,240,937,000; by 1980, this had risen to $63,303,316,000. Added to other indebtedness, the total skyrocketed to $194.5 billion—a burden simply impossible to bear or liquidate.

To obtain a copy of Edward Kennedy's book, write to him at P.O. Box 164, Pismo Beach, Calif. 93449.

Richard Solyom and the Sound Dollar Committee

More than a hundred years ago, the grandfather of Richard Solyom of Fort Lee, New Jersey, purchased some land in Rockville, in Montgomery County, Maryland, which was bequeathed to a number of heirs. The Maryland Park Commission, which had previously bought five acres of this land, wanted an additional 1,253 square feet, claiming its right to it under its power of eminent domain. Solyom demanded payment in specie for his one-ninth interest; but at a hearing before the Commission, his request was denied by Judge Fairbanks of the Sixth Circuit Court who ruled that Article I, Section 10, of the Constitution does not require states to pay eminent domain claims in gold or silver coin. The Judge also held that state courts have no jurisdiction in such matters, since the power to declare what shall constitute lawful money is vested solely in the Congress of the United States.

Solyom then demanded a jury trial, which occurred on November 30 and December 1, 1981; however, the judge ruled that the jury could not hear any testimony dealing with the monetary issue. It was determined that $1,462 would constitute fair compensation, which Solyom refused to accept unless payment was in gold or silver coin, as set forth in the Constitution.

On February 26, 1982, the Park Commission filed a motion asking the Court's permission to pay the $1,462 into the Registry of the Court, and, in return, acquire title to the disputed land; on March 12, Solyom filed a motion in opposition, unless payment were made in specie. On March 23, the judge issued an order granting the request of the Commission, which then took title on April 1, 1982, pending appeal.

On June 8, Solyom filed a 174-page brief in the Court of Special Appeals in Annapolis; when the Commission responded with new arguments, he filed a reply on June 26. On August 10, then-Congressman Ron Paul and Senator Jesse Helms filed an amicus curiae brief prepared by Henry Mark Holzer, Professor of Constitutional Law at the Brooklyn Law School. This Appeal was heard by a three-judge panel on October 31, which rendered its Opinion on December 8, 1982, denying Solyom's Motion and upholding the action of the Commission. The panel declared that it has long since been established, "in this country, that the federal government did have power to emit paper money. . . . In the last of the legal tender cases, *Juilliard* vs. *Greenmann*, 110 U.S. 421 (1884), the Court stated that Congress, under its power to borrow money on the credit of the United States and to issue circulating notes for the money borrowed, was authorized to establish a uniform national currency, either in coin or in paper, and to make that currency, dollar for dollar, legal tender for the payment of all debts, public and private." The Court then cited 31 USCA #463 (1933) to the effect that all debts could be paid in any coin or currency which at the time of payment is legal tender for public and private debts. In 294 U.S. 240 (1935) the Supreme Court abrogated the "gold clause" in all pre-existing obligations and declared that these could be met with the current legal tender currency.

On March 24, 1983, the Court of Appeals in Maryland—the highest tribunal in the State—reaffirmed, without comment, the decision of the three-judge panel. It simply ignored the issue entirely.

Again, *Juilliard* vs. *Greenmann* did not permit the issuance of fiat currency, even by the Treasury, much less by a private corporation like the Federal Reserve; nor did either of the other references cited do so, for at that time all Federal Reserve notes were redeemable in specie. Thus, the citations offered are irrelevant, and do not support the Opinion of the Maryland courts.

In the course of Solyom's battle, Dr. Edwin Vieira, Jr., became his principal collaborator and theoretician. After years of research, Dr. Vieira completed an excellent and powerful 45-page manuscript entitled *The Monetary Powers and Disabilities of the United States Constitution*, which was distributed to members of Congress and others. (This has now been expanded into a large book published by Devin-Adair.)

Dr. Vieira declares the Federal Reserve System is a "domestic corporate-state banking monopoly [which has been given] unlimited, uncontrollable license . . . to generate Federal Reserve notes . . . as legal tender tokens irredeemable in silver or gold coin. . . . The United States government has the highest legal obligation and authority to disestablish the Federal Reserve System . . . as soon as possible, even if [this should] greatly exacerbate the international crisis."

It may be said that the "crimes" Congress has committed in the field of monetary degeneration are: (1) the demonitization of gold and silver coin, (2) the creation of the Fed, with power to emit fiat currency in unlimited quantities, (3) the extension of a legal tender character to this currency, and (4) the effective repudiation of these notes by refusing to redeem them in specie.

Ron Paul: Leading Critic of the Fed

Ron Paul, former congressman from Texas, is one of the nation's leading critics of the Federal Reserve. Among his statements the following appeared in *The National Educator* of April 1983:

> As a member of the House Banking Committee, I have long believed that our present economic difficulties are caused principally by our centralized banking system headed by the Federal Reserve, and by the use of irredeemable paper money.
>
> Article I, Section 8 of the Constitution grants Congress the exclusive power of coining money, not printing it. But seventy

years ago, in 1913, Congress enacted the Federal Reserve Act establishing our present banking system. At the time, we were still on a gold standard, and the harmful effects of the Federal Reserve System were meliorated by the continued use of gold and silver as coins and as backing for paper currency. Still, the Federal Reserve has succeeded in causing the worst depressions, inflations, recessions, unemployment, and interest rates in our history.

The conflicting elements in our monetary system in 1913—central banking and the gold standard—could not coexist, and the gold standard had been totally eliminated while the Federal Reserve grew in power. In 1933–34, President Roosevelt confiscated privately-owned gold, devalued the dollar by over 40 percent, and ended domestic redeemability of paper currency. In 1944, an international monetary system was established at Bretton Woods which further attenuated the role of gold in international transactions. In the late 1960's, the use of silver in coinage was ended, and silver certificates were replaced by irredeemable Federal Reserve notes. In 1971, President Nixon severed the last link between our paper currency and gold by ending international redeemability of paper for gold. Since 1971, we have endured the highest interest rates, business failure rates, and inflation rates in our entire history. Now, double-digit inflation and interest rates have caused double-digit unemployment rates.

I am convinced that there is no permanent solution to our severe economic problems that does not involve thorough monetary reform. This is why I have introduced four major pieces of legislation. The first bill H.R. 875 would repeal the Federal Reserve Act of 1913, thus ending our 70-year experiment with paper money, an experiment that has obviously failed. To achieve that end, I have also introduced a bill requiring, for the first time in history, a complete audit of the Federal Reserve, H.R. 877. I believe that a thorough audit and investigation of the Federal Reserve would reveal enough damning information about the Fed that virtually all members of Congress would support its abolition.

Third, I have introduced the Monetary Freedom Act, to end our paper money system and to restore gold and monetary freedom. The first step toward such a restoration of honest money is the re-introduction of genuine American gold coins, which would be accomplished by my American Eagle Gold Coin Act, H.R. 878.

The Monetary Control Act of 1980 gave Federal Reserve banks the power to monetize foreign debt; that is, they can buy the worthless bonds issued by defaulting nations and use them as collateral to print more Federal Reserve notes—a highly inflationary process. It is estimated that these debts now total more than $850 billion, owed by Third World and communist nations. "The fact," says Ron Paul, "that the debt structure is so large and the banks holding the debts are so influential, causes me to predict that our government will do a lot more inflating to 'bail out' the private holders of foreign debt through this mechanism. . . . The banks will get their payments, the socialist dictators will get our dollars, and the American middle class will get the bill. . . ."

Paul, an ardent advocate of a specie currency, has published a 36-page pamphlet, *Ten Myths about Paper Money*, in which he sets forth his ideals with great lucidity:

Myth #1: *Paper Money is Wealth.* Paper money is *not* wealth, which must come from production; there is no other way to create it. Capital also comes from production and consists of what can be saved from the excess of production over consumption. Paper-money advocates claim that economic growth results from the emission of paper money; but when such money is created out of thin air, the harmful result is that the formation of capital through savings is discouraged or eliminated.

Myth #2: *"Easy" Money Causes Low Interest Rates.* This misconception is the result of the belief that interest rates can be controlled by the government. For instance, if a usury rate is set at a point which is below the market, no money will be available; this will always happen. The market, not the government, determines interest rates.

Myth #3: *Paper Money is Elastic.* The fact is that *the paper money bubble expands until it bursts.*

Myth #4: *Paper Money Gets Its Value from the Economy.* The only reason money has value is because people place value on the things they use as money. They will accept it in exchange for goods and services because they know that someone else will also accept it. But money became acceptable in the first place only because it was a commodity with intrinsic value, not merely a medium of exchange. Government cannot make money out of nothing. It can fool many people for a while, but not everyone forever; sooner or later people will discover what real money is.

Myth #5: *Legal Tender Laws Instill Trust in Paper Money.* Legal tender laws are intended to make it illegal for real money to compete with the government money monopoly. A monetary system such as our present one is doomed to failure, for people cannot prosper under a false concept of money. The opponents of gold consider redemption in specie old-fashioned. Replacing real money with a politician's promise destroys the very essence of money.

Myth #6: *The Low Cost of Printing Paper Money is an Economic*

Advantage. Because gold must be mined—obtained by effort—it has value of universal desirability. Printing money costs little, but the result is a cheap kind of money, which can be reduced to nothing at all.

Myth #7: *Paper Money Can Pay for the "Good" Things Government Does*. Government can never turn stones into bread or create good things for people to consume. The cruel hoax that it *can* do "good" things for people must be destroyed; government can, however, take from taxpayers to give to others. Paper money can only destroy; gold, on the other hand, preserves wealth and encourages savings and capital accumulation.

Myth #8: *Paper Money Eliminates the Business Cycle*. Instead of paper money acting to smooth out business cycles, it makes them worse. The fact is, paper currency has caused more inflationary booms and deflationary depressions than anything else in our history.

Myth #9: *A Managed Paper Money Gives Stable Prices*. The fact is, fiat currency has created the most unstable price system ever known. Because of it, there are wild swings in interest rates, which cause the economy untold ills. Property and medical costs have soared into the stratosphere. These distortions are inevitable under a paper-money system. Although the explicit aim of the Keynesians was to achieve stable price levels, the exact opposite has happened.

Myth #10: *Politicians Can Be Trusted with a Printing Press*. The fact is that no one—especially politicians—can be trusted with the power to create paper money for history shows that this power has *always* been abused. Sometimes it is used for personal gain, at other times to serve special interests for political reasons, to promote wars or to establish the welfare state. Ron Paul states:

> The Administration is mistaken if it believes that nation's $3 trillion economy can be successfully managed by Mr. Voelker or any other man or any body of men. Since Voelker took office in August 1979, we have had the highest interest rates, unemployment rates, and bankruptcy rates in 40 years. The Federal Reserve System is a disastrous way to run a supposedly free-enterprise system.
>
> In little over a decade, from 1971 to 1982, the Fed . . . caused three recessions . . . by manipulating the nation's money supply.
>
> The Federal Reserve, the nation's central bank, was created by the Congress in 1913 for the purpose of smoothing out or eliminating the booms and busts of the business cycle. In its 70 years, the Fed has induced the deepest depression in American history and many less severe recessions.

> Central banking is a throwback to central economic planning, and central economic planning has failed wherever it has been tried. It is time to end the over-70-year experiment and allow money decisions to be made in the marketplace, not in Washington, D.C.

In 1984, Paul left his seat in the U.S. House of Representatives to run for the Senate. Unfortunately, he was defeated by the money powers. However, he has established his own organization, which publishes a great deal of material explaining his position. The hope is that he will run for office again in 1986—and be elected.

A Practical Proposal

Constitutionalists are in general agreement on three points: (1) The Federal Reserve Act should be repealed; (2) the Treasury should issue the national currency; and (3) the stability of this should be insured. (On other questions, such as whether a return to specie is necessary or desirable, there are sometimes differences of opinion.) Merely repealing the Act would not be sufficient. It must be replaced by a statute setting forth in detail what the new monetary policies will be; that defines the relationship to be established between the Treasury and the private banks, how the new system will operate, and what kind of currency will be issued.

Congress should enact legislation to 1) repeal the Federal Reserve Act of 1913, and 2) replace the Fed with a publicly owned facility to operate as an integral part of the Treasury under the supervision of a board of trustees or directors, appointed by the President with the advice and consent of the Senate, for terms of a given length, and a majority of whom would be drawn from, and represent, other than financial interests.

A new act should, in addition, contain the following provisions:

1. Repossession of the entire Federal Reserve System by reimbursing—with Federal Reserve notes—the present member banks dollar for dollar for their investment in stock.
2. Turning over to the Treasury all the assets of the System, including real estate, Federal Reserve notes, governmental securities, the gold stock, and miscellaneous properties.
3. Repossession without compensation of all securities held by the member banks of the Fed and obtained by them without actual cost.
4. Replacement of such securities with government certificates of deposit on which interest would be paid at current rates.

5. Replacement within a certain period—perhaps one or two years—of all outstanding Federal Reserve notes with government issue.

6. The establishment of such reserve requirements for private banks as are necessary before fractional reserve banking can be abolished entirely, which should be replaced as soon as practical by actual savings collateral—possible a few years after the establishment of a Universal Trust Plan.

7. The establishment of rules and regulations for auditing and governing private banks and other financial institutions to guarantee their solvency and proper operation.

8. Requiring the federal government to balance the budget.

9. Requiring the federal government to place its trust funds in private, interest-bearing accounts.

10. The gradual reduction of the national debt through the redemption of federal securities.

11. Maintaining present insurance corporations to insure the safety of all deposits in private financial institutions.

12. Limiting the function of the Treasury primarily to the issuance of currency and supervision of private financial institutions.

13. A return to a specie standard within a given period, and regulation of the value of the dollar by defining its gold content.

8

The Internal Revenue Service and the Churches

The Harassment of the "Non-Traditionals"

When few except "traditional" churches existed, the IRS bent over backwards to confer upon them all possible advantages—many of which would seem to be unconstitutional: for does not the First Amendment declare that Congress shall make no law respecting an establishment of religion? Many provisions of the IR Code enable religious organizations and personnel to accumulate wealth otherwise beyond their reach. We can scarcely expect a minister who receives a salary of perhaps $40,000, largely exempt from income taxation and immune to Social Security contributions, to object to a system so beneficial to him—especially when doing so would cause the loss of such advantages. Nor can we reasonably expect an organization with a multi-million-dollar income deriving from commercial investments which are immune both to taxation and disclosure to find any fault with this situation.

The IRS is well aware of the sensitivity involved in administering laws which impinge upon the taxation of churches. Undoubtedly, this is why the word "substantial" is used in Section 501(c)(3) of the IR Code which describes the amount of effort a church or other exempt organization may devote to a prohibited activity without endangering its preferential status. Since this area is ambiguous, the IRS is able to assume broad discretionary powers, which may result in a highly discriminatory diversity. For example, the Service would not dare apply the same criteria to a powerful denomination that it might to a small or independent church which dares to question IRS activities.

There is little doubt that if the IRS were to enforce the same rules against wealthy and well-established "traditional" churches that it applies to the so-called "illegitimates," many of the former would lose their exemptions. For example, one church was charged with a violation because it accumulated a building fund. One minister wrote that after his church had organized its own school in order to escape forced busing of children to distant places, the Agency audited the returns of every member and disallowed all contributions to the general fund on the ground that some of the money might have been used to support segregated education.

There is, no doubt, a valid question as to whether some of the so-called mail order churches and ministers really qualify as religious organizations and personnel or were created simply to evade taxation. It is therefore not surprising that the IRS has been actively harassing them.

However, during recent years, the Service has been equally intent on destroying well-established, independent churches which evince any sign of dissent against the principles espoused by the federal bureaucracy. It focuses especially on churches that have established schools which, in the opinion of the IRS, were created to avoid racial integration. Thus, religious officials and congregations which have as much right to tax immunities as Baptists, Presbyterians, Episcopalians, Mormons, Christian Scientists, and Roman Catholics, have been subjected to harrowing ordeals. In perpetrating such action, the IRS engages in an activity totally unrelated to the collection of taxes, but whose purpose is only to achieve a social or political objective.

In some cases, the IRS has demanded that a particular church bring in for examination all its books and records, including a list of all members, in spite of the fact that such examination is forbidden in Section 7605(c) of the Code *even if the church is in violation of some law or is engaged in an unrelated business activity which could result in a tax liability*.

One questionnaire, sent to a church in Georgia, demanded replies to 31 specific questions, including the following:

Have you ever filed an application for recognition of exemption with the Internal Revenue Service? (This requirement is specifically waived under Section 508[c] of the Statute.)

Have you submitted a conformed copy of your creating instruments and by-laws? (Such submission need be made only to state authorities, and not necesssarily even to them).

Does your organization file annual information returns (Form 990T)? (These are never required from churches.)

Does your organization have a recognized creed and form of worship? Explain in detail. (This should not concern the IRS or any government agency—many well-established churches have no particular creed; and some do not even have a statement of faith or belief.)

State how many members your church has. Has anyone been rejected for membership, and, if so, on what grounds? (The IRS is here probably trying to find out whether the church has a color-line; but it has no authority to demand such information.)

Provide a complete history of your church from the date of its founding. (This is outside IRS authority.)

Provide a complete list of officers and directors, including a resumé of backgrounds. (This is totally inappropriate.)

State in detail whether you pay compensation or make any other payment to or for individuals who perform services for your organization. (No church is required to make such disclosure.)

Identify contributors who have given $500 or more during your most recent accounting year. (The IRS has no authority to demand such information.)

Submit a complete schedule of receipts and expenditures. (This is precisely the kind of information that Section 7605[c] forbids the IRS from attempting to obtain.)

Ironically, the IRS letter concludes by stating: "Submission of this information . . . does not constitute an examination of your books and records."

The IRS wrote a long letter to a church in Oklahoma demanding detailed information concerning its creed, beliefs, precepts, discipline, organizational structure, number of members, their voting rights, method of selection, etc.; it also demanded copies of service bulletins, newsletters, a description of bookkeeping procedures, general ledgers, cash receipt journal and bank statements, together with a listing of assets and liabilities; also a roster of the ten largest contributors and their relationship to the founders, elders, and ministers of the church.

Such questions, which covered several pages, constituted demands for information that not even a private corporation for profit could be forced to divulge.

This is the method used in respect to perhaps hundreds of independent churches; the IRS proceeds under the alleged authority of Section 7605(c) of the Code—added in 1969—which was inserted precisely for the purpose of preventing the IRS from interfering with, or making any inquiries into, any religious activity, even if this could involve it in a tax liability because of Unrelated Business Income. This Section states:

> No examination of the books of account of a church or association of churches shall be made to determine whether such organization may be engaged in the carrying on of an unrelated trade or business or may be otherwise engaged in activities which may be subject to tax under part III of subchapter F of chapter 1 of this title (sec. 511 and following, relating to taxation

> of business income of exempt organizations) unless the Secretary or his delegate (such officer being no lower than a principal internal revenue officer for an internal revenue region) believes that such organization may be so engaged and so notifies the organization in advance of the examination. No examination of the religious activities of such an organization shall be made except to the extent necessary to determine whether such an organization is a church or a convention or association of churches, and no examination of the books of account of such an organization shall be made other than to the extent necessary to determine the amount of tax imposed by this title.

This explicitly states that no records or books of account of a church may be examined even if it is engaged in an activity which involves tax liability; in any case, no one below the status of Regional Commissioner (there are ten such officials) may note such activity; and if any inquiry is to be made, notice must be given in advance and nothing may be examined except what may have direct bearing on such liability.

However, the IRS has seized upon the words "except to determine whether such organization is a church" to justify demands and intrusions which it could not even make in the affairs of a private corporation for profit or of any individual. The law states specifically that the IRS may make no inquiry except to determine the extent, if any, in which the church is engaged in an unrelated business activity. Questionnaires, such as those described, to established churches are, therefore, in violation of the IRS's own law.

When facing this situation, I suggest that churches invoke a provision in the Privacy Act of 1974 which provides that when the IRS demands information from *anyone*, it must, upon request, state its authority for seeking it, explain the purpose of the interrogation, state what will be done with the information if it is given, and declare what will happen if it is refused. The church should also ask whether such questionnaires are being sent to all churches, and, if not, why it has been singled out.

In addition, under the Freedom of Information Act, harassed churches have another powerful weapon of defense. Since the IRS states, when serving these questionnaires upon churches, that it is merely trying to determine whether they qualify as religious organization, the Agency *must have an official definition of what constitutes a church*. Upon receiving a questionnaire, therefore, the church should at once demand that the IRS supply a specific and detailed definition of a church. Even if the IRS could do this, which is unlikely, it would have to supply legal authority, which could be challenged and refuted.

Then, if the IRS refuses to reply or gives an irrelevant answer, the church would be fully justified in refusing to comply with IRS demands. In the event that the Agency rescinds its certificate of exemption, previously issued, the church should file suit against the Agency for taking actions outside the periphery of its authority. Other harassed churches should be ready to contribute to the cost of the litigation, as they would all profit by victory.

Social Security and Other Church Exemptions

All members of recognized religious (apostolic) orders who have taken a vow of poverty are immune to SS taxation (Section 501[d]). However, they may enrol by election (*Regulation No. 4*, Subpart K, 404.1015[a]).

Furthermore, ministers, priests, Christian Science practitioners, and members of religious orders who have not taken the vow of poverty, automatically come under the SS program as self-employed individuals unless they file Form 4361 during the first two-year period in which they receive income for services in such capacity. If they waive SS benefits, the action is irrevocable. However, if an individual had filed a waiver of exemption previous to 1967, he/she may not leave the program. Since all such personnel are treated as self-employed, they are required to file their own returns and contribute to SS (Section 1402[e]). However, all such people are entitled to a very important Housing Allowance (Section 107), which involves a substantial reduction in taxable income.

What of the lay employees of churches, such as stenographers, bookkeepers, choir members, janitors, etc.?

A law passed in 1983 provides that all church lay employees, as well as employees of all other private "charities," must be enrolled in Social Security. Because this forces churches to pay taxes, there is widespread resistance to this provision, which may eventually end in outright revolt by many churches.

The question is often raised that, since Section 508(c) of the IR Code states that "churches, their integrated auxiliaries, and conventions or associations of churches" are not required to file for exemption, why would any do so? The only answer I can offer is that by so doing the organization will be listed in the *Cumulative Index of 170 Organizations* so that contributors may be certain that their gifts will be tax deductible. However, by making such disclosure to the IRS, the organization may invite examination and harassment.

Is or is not a school operated as an activity of the church an integrated auxiliary thereof? It obviously is; and, therefore, should enjoy the same mandated exemption from filing accorded to churches and associations or conventions of churches.

The 1979 *Publication 557* states specifically that religious schools enjoy the same immunity as churches; however, *Publication 1023*, on the same subject, omits any direct reference to schools, *per se*. Furthermore, since we have been unable recently to obtain copies of *Publication 557*, we wonder whether the IRS has been planning on withdrawing its automatic exemption from some church schools. If so, it would be in line with IRS accusations of racism and its attempts to declare that church schools organized since 1960 are in the same category as corporations-for-profit and therefore subject to audit and intensive investigation.

The Church of Scientology

Many churches have incurred the enmity of the government, but none more than the Church of Scientology. There is no question that it qualifies as a religious organization legally, just as do thousands of others on whom the Agency confers its blessings. The crime Scientology has committed is not to be found in its doctrines, discipline, or operation, but in the fact that it has dared to challenge and expose some of the activities of the federal colossus. What the government has done to this group is such as one might expect under an authoritarian regime using extreme police measures to crush and destroy dissent. The manner in which the IRS and other government agencies, including the FDA and the FBI, have violated constitutional protections in their vendetta against the Scientologists is enough to make an American wonder whether we are not engulfed in a totalitarian society.

One of the "crimes" committed by the Church of Scientology was the publication, in 1972, of secret material, called *The IRS Papers*, which the Agency had been forced to disgorge under court proceedings brought by Phil and Sue Long of Bellevue, Washington. But the conflict between the Church and the federal government had begun long before 1972.

The harassment suffered by the Church, and recorded in the book *The American Inquisition*, has continued almost without interruption since 1950. Government agents have infiltrated and spied upon the organization, made secret tapes of discussions at meetings, monitored and opened its mail, and raided its offices in one city after another.

On January 4, 1963, the Church headquarters in Washington, D.C., was invaded and looted by a small army of United States marshals and deputized agents who roamed through the structure, entered bedrooms where couples were in bed, and, escorted by motorcycle policemen, carried away documents and other personal property which filled two large vans.

Because of this raid, the Church sued the government for a return of its property in litigation that dragged on for more than ten years; finally, in October 1973, after the United States Circuit Court of Appeals had declared the original raid unlawful, several tons of property were returned, including 5,000 bound volumes, 20,000 pamphlets, and 65 E-meters. However, the Church was compelled to pay the cost of storage for the illegally seized property, not all of which was returned or accounted for.

In July 1977, by actual count, 134 government agents burst into three of the buildings occupied by the Church in Los Angeles and in Washington State. The pretext was that the Church had infiltrated government agencies in an attempt to discover and copy documents pertaining to the Church. The irony is that under the Freedom of Information Act, the government is under mandate to release all such materials to affected parties upon request.

During the raids goons used axes and sledge hammers to batter down doors while officials of the Church stood by, offering to open the doors for the invaders. Property worth many thousands of dollars was destroyed and tons of literary material was carted away.

James J. Kilpatrick pointed out in a syndicated column of August 14, 1977, that a federal judge had declared the July raids illegal and ordered the restoration of the seized property; but Jackson observed that the harassment suffered by the Church had been terribly expensive. As in other situations, even if the IRS cannot prevail in court against its victims, it hopes to bankrupt them and ruin their reputations so that public sympathy will be lost and the financial support from the public drastically reduced.

Among its various publications, the Church of Scientology offers an excellent pamphlet dealing with the Freedom of Information Act and how to use it. It also issues a periodical called *Freedom*, with a circulation of several hundred thousand, which exposes the FDA, the medical profession, the abuses committed by the IRS, and other federal agencies. It also quotes statements of ex-agents explaining why they can no longer tolerate the mendacious existence required by the Agency. No wonder the Church of Scientology is a thorn in the flesh of the federal Establishment; no wonder the goverment has spent millions to destroy it.

However, in spite of everything done or attempted by the federal government against this organization, it has continued to grow in size and influence; it has thousands of devoted members who declare that they have profited by its teachings and ministrations; it has one very large headquarters on Berendo Street in Los Angeles and another in Florida. The fact is, the Church is more prosperous and flourishing than ever.

Kirby Hensley and the Universal Life Church

One of the most colorful figures to emerge on the American scene in recent years is Kirby Hensley, who organized his Universal Life Church in 1959 and incorporated it in 1962, with headquarters in Modesto, California. Although he can neither read nor write, and even though he was once a hobo, he had, I understand, twice made and lost a million dollars before he became deeply involved in religion. He does not accept the creeds or tenets of any of the traditional churches; he has prepared his own abbreviated version of the Bible—both Testaments. Within the book, Hensley's "Testament of Today" discusses such subjects as The Mystery of God, What Is Man?, What Is Truth?, The Second Coming of Jesus, The Second Coming of Christ, The Church and State, The Resurrection, and The Coming Kingdom of Man. His religion is one in which personal happiness, health, and success in the here and now become the prime objectives.

On one occasion, I had a long conversation with him at the home of a mutual friend, where he conferred upon me the Honorary Doctorate of Divinity. When I asked him to what article of faith those ordained by him were asked to subscribe, he declared that his basic religious tenet was "To Do That Which Is Right." You can be a Roman Catholic, a Methodist, a Lutheran, a rationalist, an atheist, or whatever in the ULC, since the only dogma is that everyone observe the highest ethical standards. Hensley defines God as a Universal Presence which constitutes all existence—a belief similar to that found throughout the New Thought Movement.

His main purpose was to establish constitutional principles as they relate to church and state. He was opposed to the privileges and immunities conferred upon the mainstream denominations by a multiplicity of tax and other laws which actually constitute an establishment of religion, in violation of the First Amendment.

What, then, was his real objective? He declared that he would be perfectly willing to have his churches pay taxes, provided all others were to do the same. But so long as all they enjoy special benefits, he insisted that new and non-traditional churches be given the same advantages.

After 1962, the success of Hensley's operation was phenomenal. By 1978, the staff included 28 people; more than six million had been ordained and some 35,000 churches had been chartered, an activity that generated a multi-million-dollar income.

At a convention of the Southern Baptist Churches, I once heard its president say that the proliferation of non-traditional and illegitimate churches must be stopped, or *all* churches would be in danger of losing their privileges. It was not surprising, therefore, that, in the early 1970s, the IRS attacked Hensley's church with vigor. The Agency declared that the operation did not qualify as a church or for the immunities so generously conferred on other religious denominations; and it forced the ULC to pay an income tax of $10,370.20 for the fiscal year ending April 30, 1969. While the IRS admitted that the Church could qualify as a religious entity, it based its action on two contentions: (1) that the granting of charters and the issuance of honorary doctor of divinity titles constituted substantial activities which do not further any religious purpose; and (2) that the issuance of such degrees is either illegal or in violation of public policy and the California Education Code.

Attorney Peter Stromer represented the Plaintiff in its suit to recover the tax paid. The case came to trial on September 17, 1973. The Court found that granting charters and ordaining ministers was normal procedure among churches, that this activity was not substantially without religious purpose, and that the granting of honorary divinity titles did not violate the Education Code.

On March 4, 1974, the Court ordered all monies levied upon the Church returned with interest. The IRS had no stomach for an appeal.

Although its incorporation as a non-profit corporation was approved by the state of California in 1962, it was not until April 13, 1976, that the ULC received its official Letter of Exemption from the IRS.

As the Church continued to expand, thousands of local "churches" and perhaps hundreds of thousands of ordained ministers were filing for exemptions which impinged upon both property and income taxation. Hensley and his Church were no longer a joke; instead, by 1980, they had become a very serious problem for the IRS and for local tax assessors all over the country. In Hardenburgh, New York, more than 200 residents—sick of the great number of local tax exempts—declared their homes to be sanctuaries and filed for immunity to taxation. It was said that by doing so a man with $20,000 income would so arrange his affairs that he would pay little or no income tax.

The ULC now has at least two or three hundred congregations which could certainly qualify as tax-exempt entities.

The Church states its Belief as follows: "The Universal Life Church has no traditional doctrine. We, as an organization, only believe that which is right. Each individual has the privilege and responsibility to determine what is right for him—as long as it does not impinge on the rights of others. We do not stand between you and your good. We are active advocates of the First Amendment to the United States Constitution."

In 1980 the IRS attacked Hensley's central organization, determined, by one means or another, to have it declared illegitimate and therefore not qualified for religion-related benefits. However, this was not so easily accomplished: The ULC held an Official Letter of Exemption, no allegation could be made that it had engaged in any unrelated business, and there was no evidence that its operation in 1981 differed in any way from what it was in 1975–76. It would seem that in order to sustain its action, the IRS would have to show that the Church had in some way violated the basis on which its original exemption was granted.

The IRS sent 22 questions to the Church on June 30, 1980, which, the Agency stated, were in accord with Section 301.7605-1(c) of the Procedure and Administrative Regulations. Some of the questions were simply frivolous; others asked for information already in the IRS's possession. Other questions would have been intolerable under even a communist regime.

1. Does the organization issue church charters or ministerial certificates? If so, furnish all information surrounding these transactions (e.g., include a current list of members to whom charters have been granted, copies of agreements between issuer and recipient, specific criteria used in determining recipients, consideration received for the charters or certificates, copies of advertisements or other literature related to these areas, copies of charters and or certificates, etc.).
2. Give a narrative description of the activities presently carried on by the organization, and those that are planned for the future. This narrative should specifically identify the services performed or to be performed by the organization.
3. In what state or states has the organization been incorporated?
4. In what year was the organization incorporated?
5. Furnish a conformed copy of the organization's Certificate of Incorporation, as well as a copy of its by-laws or other, similar code of rules regulations. In addition, please furnish any amendments to the Articles since incorporation.
6. Is the organization associated with any profit/non-profit or-

ganization(s)? Give the name(s) and address(es) of such organizations.

7. What specific method of record-keeping does the organization employ? (I.e., checkbook only, cash receipts and cash disbursements, etc.)
8. Is the organization associated with any church or religious order? Give the name(s) and address(es) of such organizations.
9. Where does the organization maintain its checking accounts?
10. Where does the organization maintain its saving accounts?
11. Where are the books of account and other records of the organization physically located?
12. What requirements must an individual meet in order to qualify for membership in the organization?
13. How many members does the organization currently have?
14. Does the organization pay any compensation to any individuals? If so, please discuss, indicating the person or persons compensated, amounts paid, and the services for which such compensation is paid.
15. Does the organization make grants or loans? Please list the recipients of these grants or loans along with the amount.
16. Does the organization furnish property for the use of any individual? If so, please discuss in detail.
17. Does the organization own, control (directly or indirectly) or operate any other entity (i.e., business, church, etc.)? If so, please discuss in detail.
18. What is the structure of these businesses? (I.e., corporation, partnership, association, etc.)
19. Describe in detail all properties owned by the organization, indicating how such properties are used.
    a. State if income is generated from any property.
    b. State if any such properties are used by anyone other than the Church.
20. Has the organization sold any property? List the properties sold since 1976, date of sale, purchaser, and selling price.
21. Do any individuals receive a parsonage allowance from the organization? If so, please discuss in detail.
22. Please submit budgets for the organization, including schedules of receipts and expenditures and assets and liabilities for the current and following fiscal years (1978 and 1979).

The IRS demanded a full reply in 15 days; had it been given, there is no doubt that another and then another questionnaire would have been sent, each more elaborate than the one before.

Instead of complying, the Church, through its attorney, Peter

Stromer, filed a class action suit asking for declaratory and injunctive relief. The suit stated that the number of member churches exceeded 50,000 and that there were more than ten million ordained ministers. The suit charged also that the ULC had been singled out for harassment and persecution because it was "non-traditional and because it conferred mail-order charters and ordinations," which had been declared legal by the courts. It charged further that the IRS had engaged in a conspiracy to deprive the ULC and its members of their constitutional rights and that, in so doing, violated the laws under which it operates. By singling out mail-order or non-traditional churches for prosecution, the IRS was denying them equal protection under the laws; and its action constituted an impermissible establishment of religion in violation of the First Amendment. The request to answer the 22 questions did not even come from the Regional Commissioner, as required by the IR Code, but from a mere District Director. The IRS failed to recognize that all member churches were parts of the One Church and therefore entitled to the same exemptions and immunities conferred upon the parent organization by the Letter of Exemption issued in 1976.

The Brief closed with demands that the Court:

1. Make a declarative judgment that the action of the IRS violated the First Amendment rights of the Plaintiff.

2. Issue preliminary and permanent injunctions enjoining the IRS from engaging in the activities complained of in the suit, which are beyond its statutory authority.

3. Issue a mandamus ordering the IRS to make corrective statements wherever it had released false and erroneous information concerning the Plaintiff.

4. Declare that a judgment of $10,000,000 be assessed as compensatory damages to the Plaintiff.

5. Allow, also, reasonable costs and attorney's fees to Plaintiff.

6. Give such other relief as may be just and proper.

On March 16, 1981, the government filed a 28-page document in support of its Motion to Dismiss the suit for lack of jurisdiction. On December 14, 1981, a Magistrate in the District Court recommended that the government's Motion be granted for a number of reasons, among which the most important was that since this was a tax matter and since the United States enjoys Sovereign Immunity, it could not be subject to a suit of this kind. Stromer then filed a brief which held that such immunity did not apply in the instant litigation, because no tax matter was at issue, but, instead, activity by the IRS which was unconstitutional and beyond its statutory authority. On February 18, 1982, he filed a Supplemental Memorandum.

On June 16, 1982, Judge Edward Dean Price of the U.S. District

Court signed an order requiring the ULC to turn over all its records, including a complete list of members, to the IRS by July 7. Instead, the ULC filed a motion asking for a stay, pending appeal. The Court granted the Motion, but only on condition that the records, which filled 35 large cabinets, be surrendered *under seal*, pending final outcome of the Appeal. The Church did not turn them over, but filed a Motion to Appeal.

Following a hearing on November 8, 1982, the Court, completely ignoring the arguments advanced in several briefs, held the Church in contempt. It ordered the Church to pay a fine of $100 a day until it purged itself of the charge. The Church was forced to permit an examination of its records. IRS agents thereupon invaded the Church headquarters in Modesto and spent several months there in a diligent search for incriminating evidence.

In a personal interview, Hensley declared that no membership lists had been, or ever would be, surrendered; and that, as far as he could learn, the agents were principally interested in finding some proof that Hensley himself had converted Church funds to his own personal use. In this, he stated, they had been, and would be, completely frustrated.

The battle between the IRS and the ULC continues; as of this date, the outcome is uncertain.

William Conklin and the Church of World Peace

The Church of World Peace, headquartered in Denver, was established by William Conklin in November 1977. He was raised a Methodist; for a time he traveled in Mexico and Alaska as a pioneer in the Bahai faith; in due course, he rejected all existing religious creeds, and decided to found his own church. Convinced that true religion cannot exist among the conventional denominations because all disagree in their dogmas, he established a church dedicated to religious freedom and world peace. Although it has close ties with the Universal Life Church, it is a separate and independent entity with its own Letters of Exemption—from the IRS (August 11, 1978), the State of Colorado (August 27, 1978), the City-County government of Denver (October 24, 1978).

The Church and its ministers are legally empowered to perform marriage ceremonies; it also issues certificates for gay and lesbian marriages (which are valid only for the persons involved). The Church has a Model Ordination Ceremony; a Model of Marriage Vows; a Model outlining the duties of a pastor or missionary; an Exorcism of Guilt; a Sacrament of Enjoyment; a Sacrament of Divorce—a consolation for those who are undergoing the trauma of this experience; and the Holy Sacrament of Extreme Unction, to be performed at the bedside of a dying friend.

In view of the nature and operation of The Church of World Peace and the personal convictions of its founders, it was to be expected that the IRS would begin its classic form of harassment, first by demanding that long lists of interrogatories be answered. This harassment continued for years, finally culminating in a suit in the U.S. District Court on November 10, 1981, in which the judge dismissed the suit on the grounds that the government cannot be sued for injunctive relief in a case dealing with taxation. The circumstances were detailed in an article by Patricia Cummings, entitled "IRS Church Audit Draws Federal Court Ire," appearing in the March/April 1984 issue of *Colorado Liberty*.

> In August of 1983 a Federal Court censured the IRS for its underhanded attempts to coerce the Church of World Peace (a Denver-based group) to provide information the IRS already had in its files.
>
> The story reads like a plot for a novel: A small, non-mainstream church pitted against the giant Internal Revenue Service. The tiny congregation applies for tax-exempt status just like the big religious groups. A raft of forms are filled out diligently by the minister and returned to the Service. These initial forms seem to be the ones every minister or priest would receive to be completed and filed in some IRS computer. The questions are financial: source of expected funds, salaries of employees, disbursements of various kinds.
>
> The church is even granted nonprofit status when it incorporates in the State of Colorado. But apparently the name of the church, or its nonaffiliation with anything tagged Catholic, Baptist, Mormon, or other majority religion, attracts the attention of the moles at IRS. With a name like Church of World Peace, it must be a subversive organization, right? Maybe Communist, maybe even worse, a tax-evasion set up!
>
> So several pages of questions arrive for the busy minister to answer. Are these financial questions? No, most of them are requests for descriptions of the belief systems and ceremonial practices of the new Church. Now aren't you comforted to hear that the IRS is protecting us all from fake religions? Do you wonder what they can do with the information requested?
>
> The minister, Rev. Will Conklin, answers these searching theological questions exhaustively. His effort is an obvious good-faith (no pun intended) effort to satisfy the rampant curiosity at the IRS about his religious beliefs. The three financial questions (out of 16) are also answered thoroughly.
>
> Is the IRS satisfied that this is indeed a religion, a tax-exempt organization? One has the feeling that if Rev. Conklin had called

his group "St. Mark's Methodist Church of World Peace," he would have been tax-exempt after the first set of forms. But another letter (from a different IRS officer) arrives, with more questions to be answered: Do you provide counseling? Who will write your religious texts? Describe in detail the specific activities that will develop universal love and religious acceptance. Who ordained Rev. Will Conklin?

However, arrogant though the questions are, Rev. Conklin answers them. He does, however, note in his answer whenever the question is of a theological nature, rather than financial, and wryly congratulates the IRS officer on his "quest for religious knowledge." All the questions are again answered thoroughly.

Back comes another request for information from Michael Gompertz of the IRS. This time, he begins with financial questions, several of which were asked in previous letters, but he quickly returned to his probing of the Church's belief system: Who leads prayer and meditation meetings? Describe some of your ceremonies. What is the meaning of the phrase "Eternal Essence" and what is its significance in your teachings? How many homosexual weddings have you performed?

More ominous is the closing paragraph of this letter, appearing here for the first time: failure to provide requested information in a timely manner will be considered as a failure to take all reasonable steps to secure the ruling (tax exemption) requested by you.

Rev. Conklin replies again, thoroughly answering all questions, although he now includes in his letter a request for justification from the IRS for asking religious questions. Nevertheless, every question is answered, even those he has been asked before. He even includes a "suggested" wedding ceremony in description of one of the ceremonies.

Finally, on August 11, 1978, tax-exempt status is granted to the Church of World Peace. A year later, the Church's name mysteriously vanishes from the role of tax-exempt organizations, but this is due to an "administrative error" and apologies are tendered, as well as reassurances that the Church is still tax-exempt.

But one month after this reassuring note from the IRS, another letter arrives, with 23 questions to be answered "within 15 days." Many of the questions have been asked and answered by poor Rev. Conklin, some more than once. Again, the nasty terminal paragraph informs Rev. Conklin that his tax-exempt status may be in jeopardy unless he responds in a "timely manner." The deadline of 15 days is in the first page, this vague "timely manner" on page 4. The letter is signed by Richard Anderson of the IRS.

For the first time, the response from the Church of World Peace is short, brusque. Rev. Conklin requests the IRS to get the answers he has already written from their files, instead of pestering him to re-write them. Still, the new questions are answered exhaustively, in the requisite "timely manner"; and with a bit of good humor Rev. Conklin bestows Sainthood (a ceremony of the Church) on Anderson for his unending quest for the truth.

Now Richard Anderson disappears, and a "follow-up letter" arrives from a different IRS agent, Roy Henley, asking for "clarification" of several points. Rev. Conklin's response is decidedly testy. He asks what use the IRS plans to make of the information they request, and states in his letter that he believes their object is to "harass deeply religious people who have a commitment to their church." He points out that the IRS also has an obligation to abide by their own regulations.

This seems to be what the IRS was waiting for, and warning against in that grim terminal paragraph. An audit of the Church's books is announced in a letter which concludes again in the "timely manner" threat, this time spelled out more thoroughly: If you do not provide the information, we will . . . deny your exemption from Federal income tax.

The Church responded by filing an action in the courts, seeking a declaratory judgement that the Service and its agents were acting beyond their authority, and were not entitled to examine the books, plus a request for an injunction to prevent the IRS from continuing the "harassing" requests for information. This action has to date gone all the way through the Tenth Circuit Court of Appeals. In August of 1983, the Tenth Court found for the IRS, but with such stringent language that the decision constitutes a slap on the hand for the Service.

The Court "strongly disapproves of the attempt by the Service to coerce compliance" by the threat in the terminal paragraph of the last letters from the IRS to the Church, and pointed out that the threat was an empty one; the *IRS must go through the Courts to enforce a summons for information.* The court reviews the summons to prevent abuse (such as *harassment or pressure on a taxpayer by requiring him to furnish information already in the Service's possession*).

Finally, the Court pointed out that although the Service did not have the power to issue the injunction requested, but must decide the exemption on the basis of what information it already had—a decision which could then be appealed by the Church with *no prejudice to its rights resulting from its good faith failure to turn over the requested information.*

And there it stands. The Church of World Peace is still, at last report, a tax-exempt organization. The IRS got one in the eye from a Federal judge for its unscrupulous tactics. And I do not doubt that many more letters have gone out of IRS offices since August with that threatening final paragraph attached.

When this was written the Church of World Peace had more than 150 congregations with at least 2,000 members, in addition to a peripheral audience of several thousand. However, I learned from Will Conklin that because of the constant harassment and the heavy expenses incurred, he had become discouraged. I have heard little from him lately; his future and that of his church are uncertain at this time.

9

The Growth and Revolt of the Middle Class

Definition and Characteristics

The term Middle Class usually means that large segment of the population—a clear majority—who earns their own living, is self-dependent, supports themselves and their families, pays various taxes, and thus constitutes the basis for social and political stability. However, in a more specific and restricted sense—which we are chiefly concerned with—the Middle Class refers to those economic independents who:

1. invest both their labor and capital in the economic activity from which they derive their livelihood;
2. are never employees and most of whom have no employees;
3. keep their own books and records, make their own reports, and offer their services or goods to the general public in competition with others; and
4. usually ask nothing from the government except protection against violence and other forms of crime. Consequently, they resent interference from government in their daily lives, especially in their businesses, and voluntarily accept only reasonable taxation.

Since the incomes of these independent proprietors cannot be determined accurately by the IRS, the Agency hates and is suspicious of them, and seeks by all possible means to harass, impoverish, or destroy them.

Our Founding Fathers were able to create a truly republican government and give us our Constitution and Bill of Rights because the majority of the population were members of an economic class—such as farmers and independent tradesmen—who earned their living by operating their own freeholds.

The preservation of a republican, constitutional government in the United States mandates that the economic base of the Middle Class be protected and its interests reflected in every legislative act passed by the Congress. More than any other segment of our population, Middle Class independents believe in the Constitution, for it reflects their needs and interests. Therefore, the battle these people are now waging against federal taxation is a struggle to restore the Constitution in the form left us by our Founding Fathers.

Every authoritarian government hates and fears the Middle Class because its members cannot be controlled or regimented, and based on the economic decisions they must make in order to prosper, even to survive, they are generally independent politically. Therefore, in the United States, the labor bosses, the federal bureaucrats, the central government, the financiers, and various other forces have always done their utmost to oppress, bankrupt, and destroy the Middle Class. In 1920–21 the Fed created the Great Agricultural Depression in which hundreds of thousands of farmers lost their freeholds. The same entity caused the 1926–29 expansion of the stock market and the subsequent depression of 1930–40 in which the urban middle class was virtually eradicated.

During this dreadful decade, when money almost vanished from the American scene and when nearly everyone—except the great corporations—went bankrupt, the Middle Class was driven to the lowest position it had ever known. Nearly all city properties were lost through foreclosure; the only reason the same fate did not befall the farmers was that they, armed with shotguns and rifles, prevented it by threatening a violent revolution.

In 1942, the Office of Price Administration (OPA) was established to prevent small landlords from sharing in a prosperity which made the financiers and their allies fabulously wealthy. The purpose of the OPA was not, as stated, to keep rents down for the benefit of tenants; the real objective was to eliminate the small landlords. The program was so successful that something like six or seven million of them lost their investments entirely.

Today, the same federal government uses inflation to destroy the value of Middle-Class savings and thus reduce these citizens, during retirement, to virtual wards of the state.

Middle-Class Expansion

The efforts of their enemies notwithstanding, the Middle Class is an increasingly powerful segment of society. The following statistics are significant.

Though the number of sole proprietors increased from 5,689,000 in 1945 to 12,330,000 in 1979 and their reported receipts from $79 to $487.7 billion, net incomes were only $13 and $61 billion, an average of $2,110 in 1945 and $4,947 in 1979. Since these amounts are ridiculously low, we know—as does the IRS—that drastic underreporting is almost universal among the millions of sole proprietors.

While proprietary retail establishments increased from 1,554,000

SOLE PROPRIETORSHIPS IN THE UNITED STATES[A]

	1945	1965	1979
Number	5,689,000	9,978,000	12,330,000
Receipts	$79,000,000,000	$199,325,000,000	$487,700,000,000
Net	13,069,000,000	27,000,000,000	61,000,000,000
Average	12,970	21,911	39,550
Av. Net	2,110	3,084	4,947
Business under $50,000			10,134,000
Retail Establishments	1,414,546[B]	1,554,000	1,986,000
Receipts		77,850,000,000	146,000,000,000
Net	5,019,000,000	7,300,000,000	
Average		50,090	73,510
Av. Net		3,230	3,676
Service Establishments	559,559[C]	2,208,000	3,654,000
Receipts	8,578,162,000	29,789,000,000	83,320,000,000
Average	15,330	14,390	22,800
Net		11,008,120,000	25,500,000,000
Av. Net		5,000	6,962

[A]Data for 1945 from 1963 SA p. 489; for 1965 from *ib.* 1968, p. 473; for 1979 from *ib.* pp. 528–29.
[B]This is for 1950 and taken from *ib.* p. 210.
[C]This total is for 1948 and taken from *ib.* p. 270.
In 1980, there were 12,702,000 sole proprietorships and 1,350,000 small partnerships with respective gross incomes of $505.9 and $286 billion (1984 *SA*, p. 532).

in 1965 to 1,986,000 in 1979, and the average receipts from $50,000 to $73,510, the net reported average incomes were only $3,230 and $3,670. Service proprietorships increased from 559,559 in 1945 to 3,654,000 in 1979 and their gross receipts from $8,578,162,000 to $83,320,000,000—an extraordinary proliferation, which included establishments of almost infinite variety from barber and beauty shops to entrepreneurs offering income tax services and many other kinds of help.

In spite of efforts to repress the growth of the Middle Class, it has increased at a ratio far greater than the general population; and its gross income has expanded even more phenomenally. In addition to 12,330,000 proprietors (in 1979) there are millions of others who belong in the Middle Class: for example, in 1980–81, 3,528,000 full- and 2,822,000 part-owners of 2,434,000 farms; about 6,000,000 landlords; more than 600,000 physicians and dentists; 581,000 lawyers; about 3,000,000 brokers, agents, and commission salesmen; plus several hundred thousand others in a variety of professions.

There are, therefore, about 30 million economic units who are not subject to Social Security or income tax withholding on their incomes.

The available evidence indicates that, in 1984, the income of proprietors alone was probably more than $600 billion; added to the revenues of everyone else who belongs to the Middle Class it would certainly be well in excess of $1 trillion. The tax on 40 percent of this amount would probably range somewhere between $150 and $200 billion. But much of this income is unreported, and, therefore, untaxed.

The Rationale of Middle-Class Growth

What is the force that has powered this extraordinary development?

For example, how can any independent businessman—say, a paint and wallpaper dealer—not only survive, but prosper, in the face of competition from the large, chain department stores? He can, because the employees of the latter have little or no personal interest in the business; too often they are clock watchers, concerned primarily with getting their paychecks. The horrendous overhead, taxes, and other costs of running these giant stores are unavoidable. The independent is willing to work 60 or 70 hours a week as the price of success, he believes that hard work, close attention to business, and the best possible prices and service for customers will lead to independence—even to affluence.

Take, for example, a typesetter who operates a one-man office, or perhaps, one with the single addition of a partner. Ordinarily, he has plenty of work to keep him busy; but accepts additional jobs on a contract basis, does the work after hours or on weekends, and completes the work for less than half of what it would cost in a union shop in New York or Washington. Even so, he may earn more per hour than the union employee takes home because he has no additonal overhead, nothing is snipped from his pay, and he has every incentive to produce at a maximum rate and at minimum cost.

This is the real story of millions of Middle Class proprietors and entrepreneurs. They succeed because they offer better service and lower prices than the large corporation with its unionized labor force. Above all, they are interested in serving their customers, for they know that satisfied clients mean more business and more net income.

The fact is and will be forever that no incentive to work and produce can ever equal that in which the laborer has an overwhelming interest in his project *because he personally receives the profit from his endeavors.* Millions perform their work on this basis; even if they pay all taxes required by the government, they can still undersell their competitors. However, a great number of such workers operate as part of the subterranean economy, with the result that they can reduce prices still further and, at the same time, retain more of their earnings.

The Middle Class continues to grow because millions of Americans are willing to pay whatever price is necessary to achieve economic independence. No wonder, then, that the corporations cannot compete with them. And no wonder that the bureaucrats, the labor bosses, and the financiers fear and hate them, for they constitute the bedrock of our republican government and the great hope for a peaceful revolution that will restore constitutional government in the United States.

Techniques of Middle-Class Resistance

The IRS knows that millions of proprietors have for years been underreporting their net incomes. So long as books are kept in good condition and bank deposits are in agreement with reported gross income, the IRS is virtually helpless to do anything about this kind of fraud. For example, if a merchant with a real income of $100,000 reports only $85,000, the latter sum is what he deposits in his bank accounts; however, this 15 percent reduction in gross income may mean a reduction of 40 percent in his net, or taxable, income. In this manner, millions of entrepreneurs are retaining large amounts of money which would otherwise be taken for taxes.

The Chicago *Sun Times* published a series of articles on this phenomenon, concluding that "a substantial portion of our supposedly respectable fellow-citizens are nothing better than common thieves. . . ." The biggest ripoff is "the common small business practice of understating receipts by a standard percentage on the books for tax purposes."

One bar owner boasted: "I've got a bookkeeper who knows the score. I'm making $1,400 a week and reporting $400. That means $4,000 to $5,000 a month tax free. Listen, when I started this business, I was broke. Now I've got half a million. I make 30 to 40 grand a year. If you looked at my tax returns, you'd think I was on food stamps."

The normal procedure is to keep two sets of books—one showing only 60 percent of gross income. Accounting firms that specialize in this field sometimes re-create the phony accounts from correct ones supplied by the businessman. When one tavern keeper consulted ten tax accountants, all but two recommended fraud by skimming off the top, keeping two sets of books, and thus underreporting the net-taxable income anywhere from 20 to 70 percent.

The IRS tax code is filled with traps and snares for the purpose of destroying independent proprietors. Since these businesspersons do not have the time to study tax and case law, and since reliable counsel is often unattainable or too expensive for them, thousands have fallen victim to IRS bluff, dishonesty, and misinterpretation of the law.

But now the Middle Class has developed various techniques of defense, such as learning how to use the loopholes in the Code—as the rich have always done—in order to build modest estates, sufficient to insure a comfortable retirement at a not-too-advanced age. They profit from the ownership and operation of commercial, depreciable property; they invest in gilt-edge, tax-exempt securities; they buy gold and other precious metals: In short, they are making sure that most of their personal income—sometimes all of it—will remain tax exempt.

Members of the Middle Class are persuaded that the government is wasteful and extravagant to an extent that beggars description; thus, they no longer feel any moral obligation to support it. They have, therefore, developed various sophisticated techniques by which to frustrate the tax collector.

The Underground and Subterranean Economy. These are economic activities performed by one person for another which are not subject to income tax withholding and are not reported to the IRS. One man paints a house for another; or an employee of a plumbing firm moonlights in the evening, on weekends, and holidays.

Barter and Exchange. This activity is legally tax exempt if there is an actual exchange of like work for like work. However, when, for example, a carpenter builds a room onto a lawyer's or dentist's house and receives legal service or dental work in return, the IRS declares that this is not an exchange of like for like and is, therefore, taxable to both parties. However, if no report of the work is made by either party, the Agency may never be able to discover the transaction. What the IRS considers illegal tax-free barter runs into tens of billions of dollars.

Income from Illegitimate Sources. Several Supreme Court decisions (as *Marchetti*, *Grosso*, and *Garner*) have declared that a person who derives income from illegal sources may utilize his Fifth Amendment privilege by making no disclosure of such income. Thus it was that 15,000 prostitutes in Detroit who earned an average of $30,000 in 1980 were not required to file any tax returns. They declared that if the IRS wanted to collect from *them*, it would have to do its own research, prepare the tax returns, and attempt to collect!

Imagine if the IRS had to do that in respect to all the honest taxpayers with legitimate incomes.

Underreporting by the Self-Employed. This practice, previously touched upon, is perhaps the cause of the greatest loss of monies sustained by the Treasury. Millions of proprietors and service establishments are underreporting their incomes by substantial ratios. And there is little the IRS can do about it: There are simply too many delinquents. It is impossible for the IRS to prove unreported income in most instances; and even if it could, it would rarely be able to collect much of the tax due.

In this and in other ways the Middle Class is winning its war with the IRS.

The Government Finally Takes Notice

In 1979 the IRS issued an extensive *Manual Supplement* that described eleven techniques commonly used by tax resisters to evade income taxation. These included (1) constitutional objections to payment, (2) the fair-market value of current "dollars" in comparison with specie, (3) the gold/silver money argument, (4) submitting blank or Fifth Amendment forms; (5) non-payment based on various types of protest, (6) reduction of payment based on illegal government operations, (7) mail-order ministries, (8) protest letters and cards, (9) family estate trusts, (10) excessive allowances, and (11) amended or 843 returns demanding refunds. However, the manual did not even mention the three most important forms of protests: (1) not filing any returns at all, (2) underreporting, especially by the self-employed, and (3) the underground or subterranean economy.

After trying for years to ignore these facts, the IRS finally testified to them in detail in hearings held on September 5 and 6, 1979, by the House Committee on Government Operations. According to the Commissioner of Internal Revenue:

> Non-filers are difficult and expensive to deal with. . . . unreported income from self-employment is a problem area. . . . Self-employed non-compliers are difficult to identify and costly to audit. . . . The self-employment "gap" ranges from $33 to $100 billion. . . . Non-compliance by independent contractors is widespread. At least 47 percent of such workers reported none of their compensation for income tax purposes. Social Security tax compliance is even worse. About 62 percent paid none of the Social Security taxes due. . . . Over one-third of the workers with adjusted gross incomes between $15,000 and $20,000 failed to

report any of their compensation for income tax purposes and over fifty percent failed to pay the Social Security tax. . . .

During the hearings the Associate Director of the General Accounting Office, stated that it is impossible to determine the extent of lost revenue, because the income of non-filers is not even considered in estimating of Treasury losses. The IRS has been unsuccessful in determining where fraud exists or what its extent may be. Most "underreporters are not pursued and some are not even identified. . . . [the] IRS does not know how many underreporters or how much unreported income" there may be.

It was further determined that the Service cannot possibly handle this staggering job. Since it does not know the extent of the rebellion and does not have the manpower to identify and pursue more than a small fraction of known tax cheaters, millions of people can avoid paying untold billions of taxes. As of 1979, there were at least five million non-filers, out of which fewer than 600,000 were investigated; by 1980, there was a backlog of at least 700,000 incomplete investigations. Even when the IRS identifies evaders and assesses deficiencies against them, it is unable to collect much of the money due.

Other authorities believe the actual losses of government revenue through tax evasion to be even greater than what has been documented.

Professor Peter M. Gutman, for example, of the College of the City University of New York, stated in an article in *Business World*, March 13, 1978, that the underground economy alone, at that time, was at least $195 billion, including losses from underreporting, barter and exchange, and other forms of tax evasion. Various other sources placed the losses at even greater totals, in one case $521 billion of unreported income.

In an April 1, 1979, article in the Philadelphia *Daily News* it was reported that barter and exchange—some legally exempt but much of it taxable according to IRS regulations—totaled not less than $15 billion.

A report in the October 22, 1979, *U.S. News & World Report* estimated that the underground economy alone involved between 15 and 20 million individuals who failed to report incomes totaling more than $500 billion. The author of the article declared that approximately 4.5 million people derived their entire incomes from such activity, while the remainder were "moonlighting" and "forgot" to report their income therefrom. For example, a young, New York actress worked as a bartender for $30–$35 a week, helped out in her father's jewelry store, and performed occasionally at a cabaret in a Greenwich Village night spot—and made no reports or paid taxes on any of this income.

Techniques of evasion are legion: A great many people take in boarders or rent rooms or apartments; one woman made a career of weekly garage sales; another earned $200 a week making children's clothes; farmers operated roadside vegetable and fruit stands; a musician earned $8,000 a year giving guitar lessons; an employee of a large garage had his own shop behind his house where he did car repairs for his friends at very reasonable prices; thousands, perhaps millions, sell various kinds of merchandise door-to-door; taxi drivers keep reported income below taxation levels, or report nothing at all; a self-employed illustrator reported no income from work done at home; many people even collected unemployment benefits while earning all kinds of unreported income; some people with low or no income collect on bets, made by others, at race-tracks.

The methods of Middle-Class tax evasion are obviously without number and limited only by the ingenuity of the perpetrators.

10

How to Protect Yourself Against the IRS

Nothing is more likely to trigger an audit than what the IRS considers excessive deductions; therefore, when large deductions are reported, the taxpayer should be prepared to verify them fully—should the necessity arise—with invoices and canceled checks.

There is little likelihood that returns will be selected for audit unless the deductions substantially exceed the norm. The 1984 edition of the *Master Tax Guide,* published by the Commerce Clearing House, which works in close collaboration with the IRS, contains the chart below.

Though most percentages remain fairly constant over the years, the average dollar amounts increase with rises in inflation. Thus, the totals were much larger in 1981 than in 1974 or 1977. Interestingly enough, the ratio increased in the lowest bracket from 35 to about

AVERAGE ITEMIZED DEDUCTIONS FOR 1981
(1984 Master Tax Guide, #1070)

Adjusted Gross Income Ranges	Medical	Taxes	Contributions	Interest
$4,000– $6,000	$1,894	$ 852	$502	$2,420
6,000– 8,000	2,066	928	650	2,244
8,000– 10,000	1,494	969	623	2,306
10,000– 12,000	1,413	1,056	678	2,523
12,000– 14,000	1,314	1,176	696	2,397
14,000– 16,000	1,163	1,284	646	2,626
16,000– 18,000	995	1,329	667	2,720
18,000– 20,000	887	1,488	651	2,654
20,000– 25,000	756	1,718	670	2,887
25,000– 30,000	672	1,983	697	3,122
30,000– 40,000	605	2,496	834	3,483
40,000– 50,000	553	3,211	1,079	4,282
50,000– 75,000	676	4,400	1,567	5,586
75,000–100,000	859	6,637	2,512	8,312
100,000 or more	1,387	14,166	9,522	16,414

113 percent—which meant that in many instances the deductions would wipe out the tax liability. However, the ratios remained very nearly identical in the brackets above $16,000.

To repeat: Unless there is some other reason for conducting an audit, the IRS will probably not disturb any taxpayer unless he exceeds substantially the ratios indicated in the above table.

The "Cooperative" Audit

Every taxpayer should know that if he refuses to verify the deductions on his return, the IRS may recompute the tax as if there were none at all, levy a deficiency assessment, and seize property unless the dispute is contested through the administrative channels of the Service.

Therefore, let us outline the preliminary steps one should take in anticipation of an audit. If he receives a call proposing an audit, the taxpayer should tell the agent that the proposed conference must occur at a time and place convenient for him, such as his home or office. He should also state that no arrangement will be made except in writing.

Sometimes agents declare that audits must take place at IRS headquarters. However, this rule can be enforced only when a district court so orders.

If the taxpayer discovers, after a suggested appointment has been made by the agent in writing, that the time is inconvenient, he can write by certified mail, return receipt requested, asking that a different time, mutually acceptable, be arranged. Such delays may occur two or three times.

Agents sometimes appear unannounced at homes or offices. If such an intrusion occurs, the taxpayer should declare politely but firmly that no conference can take place except by previous arrangement.

It should be understood here that we are dealing with the taxpayer who wishes to avoid any serious trouble with the IRS, who is sure he can verify all deductions, who has been careful to keep all invoices, receipts, and canceled checks, and who has studied the IRS Code sufficiently to feel certain of his position.

John B. Dougherty, who left the Service after fifteen years to become a tax preparer, offers some practical advice for taxpayers, and which, he says, would eliminate 95 percent of IRS abuses.

1. Never accept any verbal assurances, agreements, or statements of fact or opinion from IRS personnel—force them to commit everything to writing.

2. Never allow an IRS agent to copy or remove any paper, record, or personal document of any kind from your premises.

In addition, no taxpayer should ever permit the IRS to conduct a "fishing expedition"; nor should he permit access to his bank records or other records held by third parties such as bookkeepers, lawyers, or accountants. In refusing, he is fully protected by Section 7609, which was added to the Code in the Tax Reform Act of 1976.

In his preliminary correspondence with the IRS, the taxpayer, while agreeing to cooperate in every legal demand, should insist firmly—pursuant to the provisions in the Privacy Act of 1974—that he receive in writing a precise list of what information is desired, why it is wanted, and the specific authority on which the demand is based. He should also study carefully *Publication 556*. At his conference with the IRS, therefore, he will have the necessary data—but no more—on hand.

In 1976, Congress passed a law providing that, if an audit does not increase tax liability, and, if the Service re-examines the same taxpayer in either of the next two years, with, again, no resulting increase, the IRS must reimburse the taxpayer for the entire cost of these transactions. The Tax-Equity and Fiscal Responsibility Act of 1982 went even further; it provides that, whenever the taxpayer spends money during an audit to prove that there is no additional tax liability, the Agency can be forced to reimburse him for the expense.

Publication 556 states: "You may represent yourself at your appeals conference, or you may be represented by an attorney, a certified public accountant, or an individual enrolled to practice before the Internal Revenue Service." The taxpayer should be aware, though, that any person who represents him must be given power-of-attorney, which means that the representative could make a deal with the IRS, thus betraying his client.

IRS agents sometimes maintain that no one except such persons as those mentioned above can be present during an audit or examination; this can only be a bluff, however, as it happens to be untrue. *Publication 556* explicitly states: "You may bring witness to support your position," which means that, not only may friends be present, they may also speak in your defense. And they need not even identify themselves.

Therefore, when the agent arrives to conduct the examination, you will have with you a lawyer, an accountant, or a tax-preparer, depending on your wishes and whether any of them are involved in your tax situation. However, if you have prepared your own return, we suggest that you have two or three friends present who will not only act as witnesses, but who will also corroborate your position. If the agent objects to their presence, read his own law to him.

Generally, IRS agents are extraordinarily wary when taxpayers use tape recorders during an examination. Because they fear making misstatements, contradicting themselves, or failing to properly answer pertinent questions, it is extremely important to them not to be recorded. An unrecorded statement can always be denied. Therefore, the taxpayer should have two recorders on hand during an audit, including one for the use of the agent, who may declare that his *Manual* forbids the use of recorders except in cases of criminal investigation; that they can be permitted only by special authority. However, it is now officially established, by various court decisions and the IRS itself, that no taxpayer can be denied the right to record as long as the IRS agent is permitted to do the same.

The taxpayer should not volunteer any information about his own taxes or financial situation; he should present only what is essential to verify deductions or expenditures claimed on his 1040. If an agent requests any information beyond this, the taxpayer should cite the Privacy Act, and ask the Agent to cite his authority. For example, if an Agent should ask what allowances you give your children, what your spouse spends for clothes or cosmetics, whether you own any tax-exempt securities, or how much you spend for vacations, you should state that such information is outside the scope of the examination. *Never accept anything an IRS agent tells you at face value: Force him to reveal explicit authority therefor.*

Should the IRS make disallowances or "adjustments" that result in increased tax liability, but seem in any way questionable, prepare to pursue your defense through a conference at the district level, then in the Appellate Division, and, if necessary, in the Tax Court. The Service wants to obtain the greatest possible amount of money with the smallest possible expenditure of time and effort. It should be your objective to force it to work overtime for every dollar it may extract from you.

Remember, as tax returns become more complicated and confusing, audits require more time, and the IRS does not have the manpower to handle as many of these or in as great detail as it would like. In 1979, it audited 2.11 percent of all individual returns; in 1980, 2.02 per cent; and in 1982, only 1.55 per cent. If you do not itemize—i.e., if you use only the zero deduction—your chances of being audited are much reduced, unless, perhaps, you have a business that claims a large operating loss.

The Contested Audit

Let us now consider the taxpayer who has made a proper return and paid all taxes due, but who, nevertheless, has decided that, IRS request notwithstanding, he will not submit to a "routine" audit.

Upon notification that his return is to be examined, the taxpayer should follow the procedure outlined above, in regard to written communications and to a conference to be arranged at a time and place convenient for him. He should also take immediate steps to protect documents which could have a bearing on his tax liability by not leaving them in the custody of any third party—such as a bookkeeper or a CPA.

One of the favorite ploys of the IRS is to serve its Form 2039A, or "vest-pocket," summons, upon record holders, demanding that documents pertaining to a particular taxpayer be surrendered, including papers belonging to people with whom he has had any financial dealings. Bankers have often acceded to this IRS demand because of possible retaliation, without even notifying the individual involved that they have been ordered to produce for examination every conceivable kind of record or memoranda pertaining to the taxpayer.

In the past, bank depositors tried to protect themselves by citing *Reisman* vs. *Caplin* and other court decisions. Now, however, they can cite Section 7609 of the IR Code, part of the Tax Reform Act of 1976, which provides protection for all records held by third parties. If the IRS issues a summons to any third-party record holder, notice of such summons must be sent to the taxpayer within three days and at least 20 days before the contemplated examination is to take place; and this notification must be accompanied by full instructions as to how compliance may be delayed or prevented. The summons, must, furthermore, identify the taxpayer and include specific information enabling the record holder to locate the desired material easily. The IRS must also pay any expense involved.

The taxpayer need only send a letter by certified mail, return receipt requested, to the record holder and to the IRS stating that the examination is not to be permitted without the consent of the writer. If the IRS then appeals to a U.S. District Court for a show-cause order, the taxpayer has the right to intervene before any determination may be made; and also to appeal an adverse decision to the United States Circuit Court of Appeals. In the meantime, the IRS cannot enforce any assessment or initiate any action.

If, at any time, the IRS turns over its investigation of a taxpayer to its Intelligence Division, it becomes a criminal procedure, and the IRS is required to read the Miranda Warning to the taxpayer, who will, from that point on, refuse to answer any questions. If, on the other hand, the case goes into the Tax Court, it becomes a civil procedure, and no criminal action can be taken.

A pamphlet entitled *How to Protect Yourself from the Internal Revenue Service*, published under the alias of A. Patrick Henry, outlines the rights of the taxpayer and advises him how to conduct himself during a first meeting with an auditing agent. The author declares that his approach has been carefully researched in the law, court cases, and the Constitution and is guaranteed to accomplish the desired results. The law, he declares, makes adequate provision for the protection of the taxpayer under the Constitution, and he should retain the perjury line in the 1040 for his own protection.

At the time appointed for the revenue agent to visit you, be certain that you have at least three witnesses present; also a tape recorder with the microphone in such a position that it will pick up all the voices of those present.

If the agent objects to the presence of witnesses, he should be told that even according to IRS publications it is the taxpayer's *right* to have them, and that there is no law, rule, or regulation against the use of a tape recorder; that several District Court judges have sanctioned its use; that it is going to remain; that the conversation will be recorded; and that otherwise there will be no conference.

Also, according to A. Patrick Henry:

> There is no provision in the Code making it mandatory for you to prove the figures on your income tax return.
>
> The Internal Revenue Code provides that the IRS has the right to examine your records. This must be done, however, only with your permission or by court order.
>
> If your return is incorrect, you can invoke the Fifth Amendment to the Constitution and you cannot be compelled to furnish any evidence or give any testimony that may tend to incriminate you—even *with* a court order.
>
> The courts have stated time and time again that although the Congress does have the power to tax, this power is limited by the provisions of the Constitution; therefore, the enforcement of any of these provisions is limited by the protective elements of the Constitution.

As noted, IRS agents are very much against the use of tape-recorders. Nevertheless, contesting taxpayers should insist on their use. If an agent refuses to proceed with the examination unless the tape recorder is removed, the taxpayer is within his rights in declaring that no audit may go on without it, as long as the agent has one at his disposal.

To repeat: A taxpayer should never volunteer information, but state only what is essential concerning his financial condition. He should also obtain the agent's name and service number to make certain of his identity; if the agent leaves any documents, he should be required to write his name on them. If the agent states that the taxpayer has violated any IRS law or regulation, he should be required to produce and leave with the taxpayer a copy of such law or regulation. This is the taxpayer's absolute right under the Privacy Act.

During any conference that occurs in a home or office, the taxpayer should observe the agent closely to discover any unauthorized procedure. If it seems that illegal assessments are being proposed, or if, after an audit, the IRS continues to harass the taxpayer, he should prepare a statement carefully describing his experience, which he may want to sent to his U.S. senators, his congressman, and to the chairman of the Senate Appropriations and Finance Committee. The IRS finds it highly embarrassing to explain to a member of Congress why a constituent is being hounded. If the taxpayer has a good case, it might even be expedient for him to air his complaint in the newspapers. The IRS fears nothing more than adverse publicity.

Summary

Although we by no means imply that a taxpayer can rid himself of the IRS by using any of the above methods, there are instances where it has happened. At the very least, the Agency will have failed in its attempt to obtain a quick assessment; it will realize that it is going to take time and effort to collect any money from such an individual.

However, if the IRS is persuaded that a substantial sum—at least $500–$600—can be obtained, it will probably pursue the taxpayer by all means provided in its cumbersome statute. However, if the Agency thinks it will fail, it may forget the whole thing, and the citizen will have removed the IRS millstone from his neck forever.

It is obvious that, after making "routine" audits, the IRS not only violates the Constitution, but also such Supreme Court decisions as *Boyd*, every day. It finally admits that private personal papers may not be obtained under criminal sanctions; but if these documents are not forthcoming, the Service simply disallows valid deductions and proceeds to assess a deficiency, without evidence, that additional tax is due. Actually, what it does is far worse than what is strictly forbidden in *Boyd*. Returns are filed under penalties of perjury: The taxpayer, who, under duress because of possible fraud, has already laid himself open to heavy fines and imprisonment, must permit the IRS to examine his records—in violation of the Fourth Amendment—in order to prove his innocence, or his property will be confiscated without due process of law—in violation of the Fifth. If the audit reveals fraud, the taxpayer's own testimony, or lack of it, is used to prosecute and convict him, also in violation of the Fifth. Since property seizure without due process constitutes a criminal act, the IRS violates *Boyd* as well as the Fourth and Fifth Amendments every time it disallows a deduction simply because a taxpayer declines to verify it in order to prove his innocence.

It is a very serious mistake for a besieged taxpayer to pay a few hundred dollars when a questionable assessment is made because it is easier or cheaper than resisting; for by such submission, the taxpayer may become an annual target for extortion.

The procedures suggested herein are effective and available to all taxpayers; yet we must warn that their use may not only frustrate the IRS, but also produce reprisals. However, the taxpayer who follows our suggestions is completely within his legal rights; and it has been demonstrated countless times that those who cannot be bluffed or intimidated fare much better than do those who knuckle under without resistance or objection.

By refusing to permit agents to examine his records during a first conference, the taxpayer is only wagering his own time against that of an agent; and even if the IRS continues to pursue the taxpayer, he still has at his command all the rights and privileges under administrative law that he had in the first place. In short, he has nothing to lose but some of his time; he has a world to gain.

He can carry his case to a conference at the district level, the Appellate Division, to the Tax Court, and even to the Circuit Court of Appeals. There are those who have done so successfully without the aid of a lawyer.

(Procedures to be followed during such appeals are explained fully in my manual, *How to Defend Yourself Against the IRS*, available from Liberty Lobby.)

Using the Fifth Amendment

Among the various methods to combat the IRS, use of the Fifth Amendment on the tax return is a favorite with a growing number of people; the citizen simply gives his name and SS number on the 1040, writes *Object: 5th Amend* on every pertinent line, and signs the document. Such returns give the IRS a huge headache; and, since it cannot know whether the individuals involved are really entitled to make such a report (as are all people whose income derives from illegal sources), it cannot make a *prima facie* determination.

Thus, no criminal sanctions can be enforced simply for taking the Fifth and declining to show records. However, if the IRS can document unreported income of a taxable nature, it can bring charges under Section 7203 for failing to file a proper return; it can also bring civil proceedings for the collection of taxes. Finally, it can seize property if the levies are not paid and if appeals are not made through administrative channels.

There is no doubt that a Fifth Amendment plea can be a very powerful and effective weapon; but anyone considering using it should be aware of the possible consequences. The IRS may declare such returns to be the same as filing no return at all. On the other hand, these returns alert the Agency to the identity of the resister. Some people have felt that it is far better to submit nothing whatever; then, the IRS will not know what has become of the delinquent (perhaps he has died) and it has no data to feed into its computers. Every individual taxpayer must carefully decide for himself what course of action is best suited to his own needs. It should be noted, however, that though the IRS admits that it has received thousands of Fifth Amendment returns, it has prosecuted only a few of them, and some of the trials have resulted in acquittals.

Some Suggestions for Tax Preparers

One man, who had been preparing tax returns for years and deeply resented the new restrictions placed upon him by the Tax Reform Act of 1976, wondered how he could continue to serve friends and clients without disclosing his activities to the IRS or subjecting himself to possible fines and other sanctions now embodied in the IR Code.

I suggested that since a tax preparer is a person who prepares tax returns for others for a specified fee, he might solve his problem by not establishing definite charges for his work and not actually preparing the documents himself. Instead of asking for specific amounts of money, he could suggest that he would appreciate a free-will gift from friends, who would merely receive some help and direction in making out their own returns. Thus, he would not be working primarily in the preparation of returns. Nor would he inscribe his name or Social Security number on them. All writing would be done by the taxpayer; the IRS would never know that anyone except the taxpayer was involved.

Two years later, this man reported that the system worked very well; very few of his friends had been audited, none of them paid any additional taxes, and their free-will offerings to him were approximately equal to his previous fees.

Therefore, if they wish to avoid IRS rules and regulations, tax preparers can emulate this man's technique: (1) do not charge any specific fee for services; (2) suggest, instead, that a free-will gift will be appreciated; (3) have taxpayers write in their own figures on the forms, or have them typed in so that the "preparer's" handwriting will not appear on the form; (4) do not place your own name or Social Security number on the return; (5) have your "friends" leave statements that they were not required to pay a definite fee; and (6) keep a list of your "friends," using their last names only.

Since any money received in this manner constitutes a gift, it is doubtful that it need be reported as income, especially if some of the "friends" received the same service without making any contribution at all, which would establish the fact that the service was free.

The Perjury Line on the 1040

Everyone should know that the Perjury Line on the 1040 means that every person who signs under it subjects himself to the penalties of a felony if the return is not, to his best belief and knowledge, "true, correct, and complete" in every respect.

I once asked the IRS how perjury could be committed when the statement was not attested before a notary public or other official empowered to administer oaths. The reply was somewhat startling: that perjury was in no way involved; therefore, the punishment for a misstatement was three years imprisonment instead of five (which can be imposed for perjury).

Thus, a misstatement does not constitute perjury unless given before a notary public, even though the penalties are those for perjury. Nevertheless, a misstatement is a felony, punishable by three years in the slammer!

More confused than ever, I inquired what punishment could be inflicted on a taxpayer if he made full disclosure in his return, paid all taxes on time, but deleted the perjury line. Believe it or not, a high-placed IRS official replied that in such case, the taxpayer would be deemed to have made no return at all, and the statute of limitations for auditing (three years) and for criminal prosecution (six years) would never begin to run; therefore, the return could be audited, say, fifty years after the taxpayer's death. Or he could be sent to prison for failure to file under Section 7203 of the IR Code as long as he remained among the living.

But the IRS knows there are difficulties: First, if it audits and finds no reason for making an additional assessment, no further tax can be levied; and, second, if it brings a criminal action for non-filing, it must haul the accused before a jury. I happen to know that many people have been deleting the perjury line for years, and the IRS has not brought any criminal action against any of them—at least to my knowledge.

In the course of my correspondence with the IRS on this subject, I became aware of the real reason for the perjury line. Without it, the IRS would be unable to bring criminal charges against any person who is knowingly guilty of an omission from, or a false statement in, his return. The IRS would therefore be compelled to do its own research to uncover any such failure, and could, upon discovery thereof, bring only a civil procedure to collect, or attempt to collect, any taxes due.

Taxpayer Rights

Over the years, Congress has passed some laws that benefit taxpayers. Also, the courts have established considerable case law, clipping some of the claws of the IRS. According to the 1977 edition of the *Handbook for Intelligence Agents*, the following guidelines must be observed.

1. "Federal courts must take judicial notice of such matters as the Constitution, statutes of the United States (including legislative history), treaties, and contents of the Federal Register, in which the Internal Revenue and other administrative regulations are published" (Section 223.4(3)). The Fourth and Fifth and Sixth amendments to the Constitution are quoted (Sec. 241.2). Thus, while U.S. District Courts ignore the Constitution unless forced to observe it, they can be compelled to recognize it.
2. "The defendant [in a criminal case] may show his misconception of the Internal Revenue law as evidence of his lack of willfulness." (Sec. 223.5(d)) Thus, if a person is criminally charged, he can win an acquittal by showing that his understanding of some IR Code provision differs from that of the Agency or the courts.
3. A safety deposit box may be opened and examined only with the consent of the owner; and, if items therein are examined, an inventory of these "shall be prepared in the presence of the taxpayer and, if possible, in the presence of another agent." There are further restrictions on the IRS—everything must be replaced and returned to the depository. (Section 233.12(12))
4. The mere failure to report a felony is no offense; to be such, there must be an overt act of concealment or an attempt to abet in the offence. (Sec. 241.32)
5. Only one inspection of a taxpayer's records is permitted for any one year. (Sec. 241.34)
6. "Evidence obtained by federal officers in violation of constitutional provisions (such as the Fourth and Fifth Amendments) at any stage of an investigation or proceeding, will be excluded at the instance of the defendant in the trial of a criminal case." (Sec. 241.41) There are strict rules for obtaining valid evidence; for example, any

statement not preceded by the Miranda Warning is inadmissible in court, as is evidence obtained by various kinds of surveillance, entrapment, bugging, etc.

7. The use of electronic devices is severely restricted for surveillance. (Sec. 241.43.)

8. Concerning the recording of conversations at a conference. "If the witness [the taxpayer] elects to mechanically record the conversation, the Service should give serious consideration to making its own recording." (Sec. 241.5)

9. The Fifth Amendment absolutely protects the taxpayer against giving any evidence or answering any question that might incriminate him or tend to do so. (Sec. 242.11)

10. If a taxpayer is ordered by a U.S. District Court to appear and answer questions, though he may not make a blanket denial, he may take the Fifth in answer to each specific question.

The Fifth does not empower the taxpayer to refuse to bring records into court or to an IRS office when ordered to do so by a U.S. District Court judge, "but he may decline to submit them for inspection on constitutional grounds" when he appears there. (Sec. 242.12)

Furthermore, since only the taxpayer himself can know whether such records could, or tend to, incriminate he alone is the ultimate judge in this situation. There can be no criminal punishment for taking the Fifth, for refusing to answer questions or declining to exhibit books and records. This right is stated repeatedly. (Cf. Sec. 267.41)

11. In any non-custodial interrogation by an intelligence agent, the Miranda Warning must be read. (Sec. 242.132) This requirement is even more stringent in all custodial interrogations. (Sec. 242.133) Without such warning, no statement made to an IRS agent may ever be used in a court proceeding.

12. A corporation officer may legally refuse to give information concerning the corporation if it could tend to incriminate him personally. He also has the absolute right not to "testify regarding the whereabouts of corporate records not in his possession." (Sec. 242.32) Furthermore, he can take the Fifth Amendment in reply to any other question pertaining to such records if the answer could tend to incriminate him personally.

13. The *Handbook* tacitly admits that the administrative summons, 2039 or 1039A, is legally unenforceable; that only a U.S. District Court order need be obeyed; and it warns against its use in cases where knowledgable taxpayers are involved. (Secs. 263, 264, 265)

14. Examination of taxpayer records will, "if possible, be at the place that will best suit his [the taxpayer's] convenience." This is a right the taxpayer should always insist upon. (Sec. 266)

15. There is virtually no situation in which a "search and seizure operation" without a warrant is permitted. Should one take place without proper and valid authority, any evidence obtained thereby will be inadmissible in court. (Sec. 283.3) A valid warrant must include: (1) exact description and location of premises; (b) name of owner and person in occupancy; (c) description of property to be seized; (d) Internal Revenue Code sections under which operation is carried out; and (e, f, g) various other restrictions and requirements. (Sec. 283.4(6))

16. "Avoidance of taxes is not a criminal offense. Any attempt to reduce, avoid, minimize, or alleviate taxes by legitimate means is permissible." (Sec. 312)

17. In using the Net-Worth Method to establish taxable income, the government must be careful to exclude all non-taxable items of income; furthermore, it must prove pertinent income derives from taxable sources. (Sec. 324.5(1)) In such procedures, the "burden of proof is on the government." And it must either "prove a likely source of income or negate all non-taxable sources of income." (Sec. 324.5(3))

18. The government must establish, in a Net-Worth investigation, "that the [bank] deposits reflect income which is current." (Sec. 346.4(1)) And it must prove by documentary evidence that such deposits did not derive from previous savings, gifts, return of loans, transfer of funds from one account to another, or from exempt securities, etc.

19. The government must prove, in a Net-Worth computation, that income or bank deposits are not attributable to other years, or a duplicate of current income items already accounted for by the taxpayer. (Sec. 326.5(1))

20. In conducting undercover activities, agents must avoid any appearance of entrapment. That is, if a taxpayer commits an offense suggested by the agent or if the agent in any way counsels, causes, or initiates such offense, there can be no valid charges against the citizen-taxpayer. (Intelligence Division Guidance for Undercover Operations, Feb. 5, 1977, Sec. 4.10.)

Exemptions for Capital Gains

IRS *Publication* 544 discusses in great detail the questions of taxation of capital gains from the sale of property; however, it does not explain all the facts, nor does the Code itself anywhere explicitly state that no capital-gains tax is due until the basis has been recovered.

The fact is that such immunity to capital-gains taxation exists primarily through interpretation of Section 453 and is stated only in certain Regulations. When I asked the IRS for clarification, I was told that since there is case law on both sides of this question, it was uncertain whether or not a tax could be imposed on capital gains before complete recovery of basis. But the Agency was unable to cite any unfavorable case law; I know now that no such law exists.

From Section 988 of the 1981 edition of the *Master Tax Guide*, published by the Commerce Clearing House, 4025 W. Peterson Avenue, Chicago, 60646, we learn that there is no recapture of accelerated depreciation after ten years of operation.

Section 667 states that the contract price to a seller of real estate or other property is what he actually receives—not the amount paid by the purchaser, from which realtor's commissions, escrow fees, title insurance charges, etc. are subtracted.

Section 999 declares: "A cash basis seller who does not receive the purchase price in the year of sale, either in cash, notes, or other negotiable obligations which are the same as cash, does not report any gain until he has fully recovered his adjusted basis for the property sold." The authority on which this is based is not contained in the Code itself, but is spelled out in the 1978 Standard Federal Tax Records (available in any good law library) in Sections 2831.063 and 2874.01.

Preserving your Privacy

The Tax Reform Act of 1976 established certain procedures that the IRS must follow before it can obtain records held by any third party; however, with considerable maneuvering and delaying tactics the IRS can usually gain access to bank records and other documents in the hands of lawyers, accountants, etc. However, the law contained in Section 7609(c) of the IR Code is a big help toward maintaining privacy.

(One couple we know achieved complete privacy by having only self-employed income, living in furnished apartments with no tenant-rosters, moving two or three times a year, maintaining no bank accounts in their own names, and having their mail sent to a maildrop. They have paid no income taxes nor made any returns for years; and they feel sure of lifetime immunity and privacy, though some people may consider their methods too heavy a price.)

Let us summarize some of the techniques an increasing number of people use to insure privacy. Many carry no substantial bank balances, and, if they have checking accounts, keep them at very small amounts, using the money only to pay for such items that are of no interest to the IRS anyway—such as utility bills. When such people receive checks, they cash them at the issuing banks or use them to pay obligations by endorsing them over to third parties so there is no trail at the bank for the IRS to follow. If substantial sums are owed, especially to people in other cities, they purchase travelers' checks, postal money orders, or drafts from banks other than those with which they keep their own checking or savings accounts.

Some people simply buy travelers' checks in large quantities and use them to pay everything. As Mark Skousen notes in an article dealing with this subject, Swiss Bankers Travellers Checks are particularly desirable, not only for the anonymity they confer, but they increase in value if the American dollar declines. For information, write Thomas Cook, 587 Fifth Avenue, New York, N.Y. 10017, which also offers travelers' checks in other currencies.

Another method to prevent IRS intrusion is to use non-reproducible checks made of dark red paper. These can be obtained from Liberty Graphics, P. O. Box 3614, Charlotte, N.C. 28203. Another ploy is to write checks in a certain kind of ink that will not photograph under microfilming.

Still another method to achieve privacy is the use of a foreign checking account, for example in Canada or certain European countries. However, care should be used in establishing such accounts, as U.S. law requires that their existence be divulged.

One favorite means of securing privacy is the purchase of gold bullion or coins (preferably Krugerrands) and keeping them in a safe place.

There are other types of investments that not only assure privacy, but that also enable one to avoid taxation with complete legality; among them, tax-exempt bonds are perhaps the most important. Before July 1, 1983, there was no official record of transactions involving their transfer, no rosters of owners, and no reports were made of payments to anyone. Holders of such unregistered securities simply clipped the coupons, cashed or deposited them at any bank or savings and loan association, and did whatever they wished with the proceeds. Had any IRS agent asked whether you had such assets, it was your privilege to inform him that this was a purely private matter, since the revenue from them was excludable from gross (i.e., reportable) income, under Section 115 of the Internal Revenue Code.

However, as of July 1, 1983, all bonds—federal, municipal, and other—were required to be registered; they carry no coupons, and payments are made to the owners directly by the issuers. Still, there will always be some of the older bonds available from brokers, which people can obtain—perhaps at somewhat higher prices—into the foreseeable future.

11

Why the Income Tax Should be Abolished: The Indictment and the Alternative

Origin and History

In order to get the Sixteenth Amendment ratified, its proponents declared in 1909–13 that no tax would ever be imposed on any portion of income necessary to sustain a decent, contemporary standard of living; in fact, only large, unearned incomes were to be taxed, except perhaps during a national emergency, such as a war. Exemptions of $3,000 for single people and $4,000 for families were established—comparable to $20,000 and $30,000 in 1983–84. In 1916, the levy was one percent on incomes up to $50,000, when it rose to two percent. The highest rate of six percent took effect at $500,000. Had federal income taxation continued on this basis, there would never have been any reason for a tax rebellion.

However, at the same time the system was growing to onerous proportions under Franklin Delano Roosevelt, it was developing into a monstrosity costing the people perhaps three times as much as the Treasury collects. Since taxes are imposed on production and service, they become, like expenditures for material and labor, a built-in element of cost. Furthermore, as products proceed through the steps of manufacture and distribution, all basic costs escalate before reaching the product's ultimate destination—the consumers. If labor and other costs total $6 and taxes $2 before the goods reach the consumer, a 50 percent mark-up at retail will mean an additional increase of $1 in the price because of the taxes. The final price will therefore be $12.00 instead of $9.00.

In fiscal 1980, the federal income tax produced $359.9 billion, of which $287.5 billion was personal; however, since the great bulk of this was levied upon production or service, we must conclude that prices to consumers were increased by approximately $750 billion. The doctor, lawyer, barber, etc., all add their income taxes to the fees they charge; the restaurant proprietor increases prices for the same reason; the corporation executive who earns $100,000 could, without the income tax, have the same living standard with a compensation of $50,000.

Its True Cost and Complexity

Let us see how burdens affect an independent carpenter or painter who has one helper and who contracts to perform a service for a homeowner. (Computation for the year 1982.)

Contract price for labor			$1,000.00
For Contractor		$600.00	
For Helper		400.00	
Income tax for Contractor (30%)	$180.00		
Contractor's SS tax (9.35%)	56.00		
Helper's income tax (25%)	100.00		
Helper's SS tax (6.65%)	26.80		
Contractor's share of helper's SS tax	26.80		
TOTAL FEDERAL TAXES	389.70		
Remaining for workers			610.30
For Contractor		$337.10	
For Helper		273.20	

Thus, nearly 40 percent of the entire contract price is taken by the federal government in income and SS taxes!

However, this is by no means the whole story, as all living costs are increased at least 30 percent because of these levies alone. Furthermore, most states also levy income taxes. If these levies were abolished, only $400 instead of $1,000 would be necessary to supply the same actual income or purchasing power.

We have concluded that the income tax should be repealed entirely, or, at the very least, removed from all productive activity and earned income. Any such tax should be levied only on large, unearned revenues and on unproductive corporations, such as foundations—which now remain virtually untaxed. Any estate tax should have an exemption of at least $600,000, exacted across the board without allowances, deductions, or preferences of any kind. A levy of 25 percent would yield far more than the present tax, which rises to 77 percent, but which is so generously supplied with loopholes that large estates escape nearly all taxation.

The Internal Revenue Code is an elaborate and esoteric conglomeration of confusion and contradictions; many of its provisions are total perversions of logic, reason, and common sense. The Code contains a bewildering mass of references and cross-references; sections that could be written so that an average high school graduate could understand them are coiled in spirals of obscurity and mystery which frustrate even the most superior intelligence. Too often, only those provisions that threaten taxpayers with fines and imprisonment are so written that they cannot be misunderstood.

Is it any wonder, then, that a tax-resistance movement has spread to every corner of the United States and is involving taxpayers on all economic levels?

Illegal Practices of the IRS

The IR Code not only violates certain provisions of the Bill of Rights, it also, in the administration of the Code, breaks its own "laws." The IRS is known to: monitor the telephones and open the mail of private citizens, burglarize people's homes and offices, subject citizens to electronic and other types of surveillance, make extensive use of undercover agents, conduct schools of spying, and use secret manuals to instruct its operatives in various kinds of illegal activities.

In addition, the IRS:

1. Uses various methods to force its victims to give testimony against themselves.
2. Requires its victims to prove their innocence on pain of severe punishment.
3. Employs deceit and concealment on a colossal scale.
4. Demands full disclosure from taxpayers, but withholds information from them.
5. Requires taxpayers to confer the power-of-attorney on anyone representing them.
6. Uses testimony of unknown informers, who may not be questioned or cross-examined.
7. Has power to seize property without due process of law; even when there is no proof of fraud or of obligation.
8. Arrogates to itself legislative, judicial, and executive powers, the perfect definition of despotism.
9. Is primarily interested in confiscating property.
10. Seizes property or money due taxpayers but held by others.
11. Pays bribes to spies, informers, betrayers, and undercover agents.
12. Is immune to prosecution.
13. Invents devious snares to entrap its victims.
14. Has laws with esoteric and contradictory provisions which almost no one can understand and which can be used to bluff taxpayers into making payments beyond what are due.

Corruption, Scandals, and Immunity

It is not difficult to understand why the IRS goes to great lengths to conceal its operations. Although open bribes are not now often solicited—so far as we know—, during the Truman Administration bribe extortion was so common that the Service was finally forced to admit to it, although it was subsequently swept under the rug. Of the three Commissioners of Internal Revenue during this period Joseph D. Noonan went to prison and George Schoeneman resigned under fire for failing to report their bribes as income. The third, T. Coleman Andrews, left the Service in disgust, declaring that, to stop such practices, the Sixteenth Amendment should be repealed.

In their book, *The Green Felt Jungle,* Ed Reid and Ovid Demaris describe a situation typical of that era. Patrick Mooney, Chief Field Deputy of the Office of Collections of Internal Revenue for Nevada, together with another official in the Service, organized a corporation known as the Mountain City Consolidated Copper Company with total assets of less than $15,000. They sold 2,254,000 shares of stock at up to $.40 each, mostly to owners of gambling casinos, bars, nightclubs, etc. No one who purchased such stock was ever indicted for tax evasion; one man, however, who refused to buy, was convicted and sent to prison. Although Mooney collected hundreds of thousands of dollars in bribes, he was exonerated by his employers and retired with all his loot intact.

However, as a result of the stench reeking from such scandals, Section 7214 was added to the IR Code, which declares in subsection (a):

> Any officer or employee of the United States acting in connection with any revenue law of the United States (1) who is guilty of any extortion of wilful oppression under color of law, or (2) who knowingly demands other or greater sums than are authorized by law . . . shall be dismissed from office or discharged from employment, and, upon conviction thereof, shall be fined not more than $10,000, or imprisoned not more than 5 years, or both. . . .
>
> The court shall also render judgment against the said officer or employee for the amount of damages sustained, in favor of the injured, to be collected by summary execution.

Unless words have ceased to possess meaning, this declares that if any agent or officer of the IRS demands money not due or more than is due, he is subject to a fine of $10,000 and a prison sentence of five years, and must make restitution by summary judgment.

Since illegal assessments—i.e., demands which cannot be sustained—have been made millions of times, it is doubtful that any agent, auditor, or officer could escape heavy fines and prison sentences if this were properly enforced.

But wait! In the wording of the law the redemptory term *knowingly* is inserted before "demands other or greater sums than are authorized by law. . . ." Thus, the plea of ignorance enables the agent or officer to escape punishment for demanding sums not due or greater than are due.

Unless the Constitution has been fully abrogated, the IRS is an illegal operation and its agents should be subject to indictment and conviction. Yet they are protected by Section 7421(c), which states that: "A suit against any officer or employee of the United States . . . for the recovery of any internal revenue tax alleged to have been erroneously or illegally assessed or collected, or of any penalty claimed to have been excessive or in any manner wrongfully collected, shall be treated as if the United States were a party to such suit in applying the doctrine of res judicata . . . in respect to any internal revenue tax. . . ."

This means that no matter what wrongs an IRS agent or officer may have committed, any suit against him will be treated as if it had already been settled. Nor is this all: under Section 7401, the IRS invokes immunity under the doctrine of Sovereign Immunity: "No civil action for the collection or recovery of taxes, or of any fine, penalty, or forfeiture, shall be commenced unless the Secretary or his delegate authorizes or sanctions the proceeding and the Attorney General or his delegate directs that the action be commenced." In short, no IRS agent or officer may be sued, nor is the Agency itself subject to court action, *except by its own consent!*

The doctrines of *res judicata* and Sovereign Immunity are both totally repugnant to the common law and our own Constitution. If agents were held personally responsible for their actions, no doubt IRS depredations would be drastically reduced. Furthermore, when a taxpayer is injured, he should have the same recourse as anyone against whom a wrong has been perpetrated; that is, he should be allowed to file charges in a criminal court, and the prosecuting attorney should be required to seek a conviction precisely as he does upon competent evidence against a burglar or a murderer.

How the IRS Drives Capital into Exile

When I toured Europe in 1951, the streets were filled with American-made automobiles. Today, the situation is reversed. German, French, Italian, English, Japanese, and Swedish cars are everywhere in the United States. And this is true of almost every kind of merchandise: cameras, watches, shoes, printing presses, electrical machinery, and a host of other items. Is it not ironic that the most advanced industrial nation in the world should find its products excluded, not only from foreign markets, but even from its own?

This situation is explained only in part by the lower wages paid to foreign labor, which, in fact, is counterbalanced by the more advanced techniques of American mass production. The real reason for the dichoctomy is the federal income and SS taxes which, by increasing all prices by at least 30 percent, make selling U.S. products difficult or impossible in most parts of the world. How can Germany, which pays high wages to its workers, flood this country with cars and other products? Very simply: Though much of its revenue derives from the value-added tax, this is not imposed on goods for export. Thus, an American can buy a Volkswagen after it crosses the Atlantic for several hundred dollars less than the man who worked on its production must pay for it.

As a result of our senseless system untold billions of American capital have fled abroad, where it is invested in plants that disgorge Niagaras of goods for the American market. As a result, millions of American jobs have been lost and a disastrous imbalance of international payments has ensued.

The Real Purpose of the IRS

Taxes fall most heavily upon the middle, or producing, classes. Levies on corporations are simply passed on to consumers in the form of higher prices. Unearned billions in the form of interest, annuities, rentals, royalties, capital gains, trust distributions and other forms of income accruing mostly to the rich are immune from SS taxation, as well as, in many cases, income levies.

Most churches, colleges, universities, schools, and charities enjoy various advantages from the government—including subsidies. Even a college that refuses to accept a grant from the federal government may still find itself subject to control and supervision. Hillsdale College in Michigan eschews any financial aid from the government; nevertheless, because some of its students receive private loans guaranteed by a federal agency, it has been declared a "recipient institution," subject to the sort of regimentation it could escape only by expelling these students or providing them with other financing.

With the freedom to exercise such powers, it is obvious that the ultimate purpose of the IRS is not primarily to collect taxes, but to create an authoritarian collectivist and conforming society. It is indeed ironic that the implementation of such a sinister goal is financed by the very people the IRS has reduced to economic and political servitude.

The Limits of a Constitutional Government

We advocate a limited government as set forth in the Constitution, one which would reduce its budget by at least 50 percent, and one which could meet its expenses without either a corporate or an individual income tax. We advocate the replacement of the present Social Security System with one consisting of mandatory trusts. We hold that the federal government should carry on only those activities, specifically enumerated in Art. I, Sec. 8, of the Constitution, which are:

1. to lay and collect taxes in the form of duties, imposts, and excises, to pay debts and provide for the common defense, and the General Welfare of the United States;
2. to borrow money on the credit of the United States;
3. to regulate foreign and interstate commerce;
4. to establish rules for naturalization and bankruptcies;
5. to coin money, regulate the value thereof, and of foreign coin, and to fix the standards of weights and measures;
6. to provide for the punishment of counterfeiting;
7. to establish post offices and post roads;
8. to provide for copyrights and patents;
9. to constitute tribunals inferior to the Supreme Court;
10. to define and punish piracies and felonies on the high seas;
11. to declare war and make rules concerning captures on land and water;
12. to raise and support armies;
13. to provide and maintain a navy;
14. to make rules governing the land and naval forces;
15. to provide for a militia and execute the laws of the nation, suppress insurrection, and repel invasion;
16. to provide for state militias, operating under the control of the states;
17. to provide a seat for the national government;
18. to make all laws necessary for carrying into execution the foregoing powers and functions.

That is all; as Jefferson declared, Congress is not empowered under the Constitution to appropriate money for purposes other than those here specifically enumerated.

The federal government, as it operates today, though, maintains that the Welfare Clause in Number 1 (above) gives the general government implied powers to expand its sphere of interest into almost every field of public and private endeavor. Our Founding Fathers meant Welfare as those things that would be equally available to all citizens, such as roads, not subsidies that would be taken from producers and given to non-producers. The current interpretation is a complete perversion of the Constitution.

12

What Could and Should be Done

One of the most frequent questions asked when we appear on radio or TV programs is what support would be available to the federal government should the income tax be abolished. We have no hesitation in replying that other sources of revenue could be obtained to meet federal needs, even if it continued to operate with a budget comparable to that of 1984–85, or larger, as is now contemplated. One obvious alternative, should it be necessary, is a general transactions tax levied on personal services, the sale of consumer goods, and the exchange of all capital assets, including securities. Such levies are non-discriminatory and infinitely more fair, economical, and productive than the existing system.

In 1980, state sales and use taxes, which averaged four percent in forty-four states, produced $79,027,000,000. A national five percent tax would therefore have produced at least $110 billion; had this been extended to the sales of property, securities, and professional and other services, the sum probably would have been around $150 billion. By 1984–85, it might conceivably have exceeded $200 billion. Thus, together with the termination of certain unconstitutional programs, a general transactions tax of five percent would be ample for all legitimate activities carried on by the government in Washington. Both the personal and the corporations tax could be eliminated.

If a general transactions tax were to replace the present income tax, every person would pay his fair share and the Treasury would obtain the same income at perhaps one-third of the present cost to the people. However, great as the resulting economic benefits would be, these would be overshadowed by other advantages. At a single stroke, the uncertainty, the terror, the discrimination, the invasion of privacy, the unconstitutional administration of the income tax, the universal imperative to cheat and lie, could all be terminated.

The proponents of federal income taxation declare that since sales taxes fall most heavily on the poor, only levies on large incomes can force the rich to pay their fair share. No greater deception, however, has ever been concocted: The fact is that the rich become the super-rich because of the loopholes in the IR Code—which they dearly love—for this very purpose, and which allows them at present to avoid at least $100 billion in federal taxation. Since taxes on production increase all costs to consumers by at least 30 percent, they fall most heavily on those whose incomes must be expended largely on food, clothing, housing, and other basic necessities. Without personal and corporate income taxation, the car that now sells for $10,000 would cost only $7,000; the house now priced at $100,000, would be available for about $65,000; the loaf of bread that now costs $1 would be priced at 65 cents. And so on throughout the economic spectrum.

At the same time, as we have noted, income taxation now falls very lightly on large unearned incomes and upon vast accumulations of wealth, because of exempt securities, other forms of untaxed income, and a galaxy of other loopholes.

In 1968, we proposed (1) that everyone be granted automatic exemptions equal to the cost of maintaining a decent, contemporary standard of living—at that time, $8,000 for single persons and $15,000 for families; (2) that all other exemptions, allowances, deductions, and preferences be terminated, except for large medical expenditures, plus a five percent deduction for investment in a retirement fund or trust; (3) that all other income be taxed across the board; (4) that taxable income up to $50,000 be subject to a 25 percent levy and that amounts above this to 50 percent; (5) that all estates above $250,000 be subject to a tax of 25 percent without any deductions; and (6) that capital gains, above statutory exemptions, be taxed at the same rate.

We demonstrated that this reconstruction would relieve 80 percent of the American people of income taxation and still yield at least as much revenue to the Treasury.

Though in 1968 we did not recommend the repeal of the Sixteenth Amendment, we are now convinced that because as long as Congress retains its power to inflict an income tax, it will continue to exercise this tyranny by making it more cumbersome, unjust, complicated, and discriminatory year after year, we are today unalterably committed to repeal.

Nevertheless, until repeal is accomplished we suggest some drastic reform along the lines indicated above. Levels of exemption would need to be adjusted proportionately with inflation. Single people should have automatic exemptions of $15,000, and families, from $25,000 to $30,000—with no other deductions except for large medical expenses and the investment in a retirement plan. Immunity to estates should be at least $600,000, with an across-the-board tax of 25 percent on all amounts in excess thereof. A 50 percent income tax levy would be imposed only on unearned incomes exceeding $100,000.

It is indeed interesting that Congress is now seriously considering proposals to overhaul the tax structure along the lines I proposed in 1968 in my book *The Great Tax Fraud* (Devin-Adair; no longer in print).

Addendum

Before constitutional government can be restored in the United States, we believe that it will be necessary:

1. To abolish the personal and corporation income tax, or, alternatively, to replace it with a five percent general transactions tax, which would be fair, equitable, and easy and inexpensive to administer, and would cost the people only one-third as much for each dollar received by the government as it does under the present system of income taxation.

2. To replace the Federal Reserve with a constitutional monetary system which would make continued deficit spending by the Federal government impossible, and would insure a stable money unit and the integrity of contracts for years to come. It would also preserve the value of such investments as stocks, bonds, securities of all kinds, bank deposits, insurance policies, etc., all of which drop in value with rising inflation.

3. To replace the Social Security system with a Universal Trust Plan, which would create estates for every person receiving an income. These estates would remain intact for heirs and devisees, no matter when death occurs; they would provide retirement incomes several times as large as those now received under Social Security.

The implementation of these proposals would constitute one of the greatest, most beneficent, and far-reaching socio-economic revolutions in the history of mankind and would create a society in which the old would no longer be a burden upon the young and in which tens of millions would enjoy comfortable retirements entirely on their own savings.

It is generally observed that the United States is today in a state of crisis and stands at the crossroads of history, just as Athens did in 596 B.C. when Solon reorganized its economy, its currency, and its social system, and, by so doing, put it on the path to unparalleled greatness and glory. Without such reforms, the spectacular achievements of this City State would have been impossible.

America hovers today on the threshold either of infinite greatness or rapid decline and degeneration. It is as simple as that, and as terrifying. And if our nation falls into such a condition, it will drag the civilization of the entire Western world with it into a new Dark Age, in which all of freedom and self-reliance will be lost.

However, we still have an alternative. Even those judges and politicians who daily betray our Constitution still pay lip service to it. If our Congress, our courts, and our government agencies can be made to follow that incomparable document in letter, spirit, and in truth, then our nation will experience a renascence, like the Phoenix rising from its ashes into renewed and glorious life.

Appendix I

Additional Freedom Fighters

The following are only a few of the host of patriots outstanding in the battle to restore the Constitution. Since it is impossible to include them all, some of the most representative are listed here.

Howard Jarvis and Paul Gann. These were the sparkplugs who brought victory for the taxpayers in California when Proposition #13 was adopted by an overwhelming majority on June 2, 1978. The Proposition reduced the taxes on real estate from about three percent to one percent of market value—a tax cut of about $7 billion. In spite of ominous forebodings to the contrary, the State seems to have ample revenue for carrying on all necessary services.

Anita and Jim (Ajay) Lowery. I first met Anita Kerns about 12 years ago when she was publishing *The Taxpayer's Forum,* which dealt with local problems and advocated an amendment to the California Constitution similar to Proposition #13. Because she was deeply interested in the general tax movement, Liberty Lobby helped her establish *The Tax Strike News,* an immediate success. Soon afterward, she met and teamed up with Jim Lowery; subsequently, they changed the name of the publication to *The Justice Times* and moved from California to Arkansas, where they are now firmly established. Their publication probably covers the news of the tax movement in greater detail and more efficiently than any other. Its distribution and influence have grown enormously during recent years.

Robert Lyons. Bob Lyons has for years conducted seminars at which outstanding Freedom Fighters address interested audiences. He has also published *T.R.U.E.* (Taxpayer's Reform United Endeavor) *News,* as well as other material useful in the tax resistance movement.

Dr. Edward A. Cupp. Dr. Edward Cupp of Hopwood, Pennsylvania, was for years one of our foremost freedom fighters. His refusal to pay income taxes was based on the fact that Federal Reserve notes are neither dollars nor constitutional money. He so arranged his affairs that none of his personal income could be documented and, therefore, the government would have nothing to seize. Although he lost in the Tax Court, the judge's decision stated that, while Article I, Section 10, of the Constitution does not apply to the federal government, *it does apply to the states,* a tremendous concession. Having divested himself of all personal assets, Dr. Cupp continued his medical practice until his death in 1982. The IRS never collected one penny from him or his estate.

Walt Mann III. Walt Mann of St. George, Utah, lectures at patriot rallies throughout the country and conducts regular seminars in law procedures. He is co-author of a Jurisdictional Law Document, which states that with the government's first demand for money from a citizen, his trial has begun; in order to protect himself, that citizen must challenge the government's jurisdiction in order to establish a record of defense. Because no lawyer dares to make such a challenge—since he is himself a part of the court system—the citizen must make the challenge. Mann's Administrative Law Demand demands that court jurisdiction be proved at the beginning, and failing that, the government and the court must leave you alone.

Claire Kelley. I met Claire Kelley more than 12 years ago when she was already involved in the Freedom Movement. A few years ago, she moved from California to Ohio, where she has organized her own church. She regularly conducts specialized seminars on criminal law, constitutional rights, legal procedures, and problems dealing with the income tax. She is a columnist for *The Justice Times* and *The National Educator.*

Dr. Austin B. Tibbets. After several years of intensive activity in the Freedom Movement in Texas, during which he conducted many seminars on how to defeat the IRS, the government finally indicted Dr. Tibbets on three counts of tax evasion and three for filing improper returns. At his trial, on June 16–18, 1980, in Amarillo, the judge charged the jury so that it had little choice except to convict. He was given three one-year and three five-year terms, to be served concurrently, together with a fine of $2,000 and five years of probation. After serving 18 months, he was paroled for three-and-a-half years, followed by supervised probation for five more.

Dr. Tibbets is no ordinary criminal. He served with the highest distinction in the armed forces during WW II; furthermore, even the IRS claimed that no more than a few hundred dollars of taxes would have been due had he made conventional returns.

Pastor James Love. The Reverend James Love of the American Bible Church of College Park, Georgia, is another who, together with his church, was a target of IRS investigation and persecution for at least six years. Finally, however, after a battle in the Tax Court, he won a complete victory.

Norman Crowhurst. Norman Crowhurst of Dallas, Oregon, an English-American engineer, tells a harrowing tale of IRS persecution. He was indicted in a U.S. District Court on five counts of having made "improper" returns; at his trial on July 27–29, 1977, he was convicted on what he describes as perjured testimony. The following November, he was given five years of probation, but no prison term or fine. He declared that the IRS pressured all his potential employers to prevent him from obtaining employment in his field of expertise. But he remained busy gathering information, addressing seminars, and producing and publishing his *Samaritan News*, which had a strong religious flavor and which seems to have attained considerable popularity.

Frank McNulty. In 1973, Frank McNulty won $128,000 in the Irish Sweepstakes and deposited the money in a foreign bank. When he refused to pay the American income tax on it, he was charged with and convicted of tax evasion. He spent two years at Terminal Island in California followed by 18 months in the Springfield Medical Center in Missouri. After he was released, he still refused to pay; and has been constantly harassed for the sum allegedly due, which rose from $75,000 in 1975 to $160,000 in 1979.

He still swears that he will never pay the IRS one penny.

Walter H. Pusch. Walter H. Pusch of Houston, Texas, organized his Church of the Tolerants some years ago; ever since he has been fighting bigotry in organized religion and the Internal Revenue Service. His Appeal from an adverse decision in the Tax Court to the United States Circuit Court of Appeals for the Fifth District, a document of 24 pages, includes almost every argument a non-traditional church could make in demanding the same rights and immunities enjoyed by the traditonals.

In spite of harassment, Pusch continues to operate his Church, which promotes an ideal in which all those with different religious beliefs will regard each other with friendship and esteem, instead of suspicion and hatred.

William A. Drexler. This man, who has had one of the most meteoric careers in the tax movement, first achieved attention in 1972, when he won acquittal in a dramatic trial in Minnesota—in which the jury took only fifteen minutes to reach a verdict. He was later indicted for his involvement in the trial of Jim Scott in Fresno, California, but was again acquitted. However, as time went on, he became so prominent that the government went to extreme lengths to obtain a conviction, which it did in another trial in 1981, after which he was placed under bond of $750,000. He left the country for a while, but later returned and is now serving a term at the Terminal Island federal penitentiary.

Bill Kaysing. Bill Kaysing, who calls himself the Fastest Pen in the West, has written more than 20 books, among which the most popular are *Tax Wars, Privacy, How to Get it and Enjoy It,* and *We Never Went to the Moon,* all published by the Eden Press of Fountain Valley, California. He explains in detail how he has lived for many years in complete privacy without paying taxes. His latest book is *Tax Relief* (1981).

Earll Schooff. A few years ago, Earll Schoof of Aloha, Oregon, organized the American Constitutional and Civil Rights Union, which undertakes the enormous task of defending trusts established by various promoters, and which are challenged or invalidated by the IRS. He has scored a number of definite victories in this very important area of litigation.

Dave Wilber. David Wilber, a disciple of the late Merrill Jenkins of St. Louis, Missouri, who established the Monetary Realist Society, is now the head of that organization. He lectures nation-wide on the money issues, and distributes related tapes and other materials.

Bill "Tycoon" Greene. The author of two best-sellers, *Think Like a Tycoon* and *Win Your Personal Tax-Revolt*, Bill Greene appeared at various seminars and published various other materials, including a newsletter, *A Complete Study Course, The Tax Fighters' Guide*, and in 1982, *101 New Loopholes: the 1982 Reagan Tax Package*. Because of paying no income taxes, the IRS finally indicted, tried, and convicted him. He was given an 8-year sentence and sent to Lompoc Penetentiary. He was released after serving little more than a year.

Ken Causey. For several years, Kenneth Causey of Las Vegas led a tax resistance movement in that city, where he conducted meetings and seminars at which he expounded his views and philosopy. He was indicted in 1982 and convicted in 1983.

Byron Foote. One of the most persistent soldiers in the battle to restore the Constitution is Byron Foote of Pasadena, California. He first ran afoul of the tax authorities in 1971, when they discovered that he had not enrolled the employees of his water bed company in the State Unemployment Program; they also found that he had not withheld or transmitted Social Security or income tax payments to either the State or federal government. Lured away from his place of business, State agents entered it, and seized all the movable property.

Foote is the author of a book called *The Happy Taxpayer*, in which he tells people to create happiness for themselves and the tax collectors by not bothering them by sending them forms or in any way imposing on their time. He keeps audiences at seminars in stiches, laughing at his irony and sarcasm at the expense of the bureaucrats.

Appendix II

Publications Dedicated to the Freedom Movement

I regularly receive at least 40 or 50 publications, of which I consider the following representative.

The Constitutional Patriots' Action News. The first issue, September–October 1981, contains an enormous amount of information. Covering all the States in alphabetical order, it lists 246 names, addresses, and sometimes detailed descriptions, of organizations and individuals prominent in the Freedom Movement. The publication's slogan is: "We must labor to restore and perpetuate a truly constitutional government as laid down by our Founding Fathers, in order to stop the erosion thereof, and then regain our Liberty, Rights, Freedom, and Property for ourselves and our children." Write or phone Freedom Publication Center, 1332 N. Lake Avenue, Pasadena, California 91104, (213) 798-5242.

The Spotlight, a weekly, published by Liberty Lobby, is the largest, most influential publication featuring news and articles on the tax resistence movement, the battle against the Federal Reserve System, and the encroachment of the General Government upon the powers of the States. Over 300,000 circulation. Address: 300 Independence Avenue, S.E., Washington, D.C. 20003.

The Justice Times, a monthly, edited and published by Anita and Jim (Ajay) Lowery, devoted exclusively to the tax movement. Features news stories and information of every kind related to the battle to restore the Constitution. Address: P.O. Box 562, Clinton, Arkansas 70031.

The National Educator, a monthly, edited and published by Jim Townsend, features stories and educational articles dealing wih the Freedom Movement, especially material calling for repeal of the Federal Reserve Act. Address: P.O. Box 333, 1110 South Pomona Avenue, Fullerton, California 92632.

Your Heritage News, founded by Armen Condo, edited by Sandy Mitchum, and published by Your Heritage Protection Association.

Usually 24–36 pages, it featured news stories and educational material concerning the constitutional movement. It always included a complete listing of meetings and seminars sponsored by the Association. It lost many subscribers after Armen Condo's conviction, and was forced to cease publication in November 1984.

The Ruff Times, edited by Howard Ruff. Address: P.O. Box 2000, San Ramon, California 94583.

The Freedom League, published by the Irwin Schiff organization. Address: 2140 W. Chapman, Suite 223, Orange, California 92668.

My Informer. Address: Box 70224, Seattle, Washington 98107.

The Correspondent, a monthly, edited by Peggy Christensen. Address: P.O. Box 8508, Missoula, Montana 59807.

A *Newsletter*, edited by Earl Schoof, published by the Constitutional and Civil Rights Union. Address: 18055 S.W. Jay Street, Aloha, Oregon 97006.

The Good Samaritan, a monthly, edited and published by Norman Crowhurst. Address: P.O. Box 63, Dallas, Oregon 97338.

World Economic Review, edited by Dan Raines. Address: P.O. Box 507, Chalmette, Louisiana 70044.

The American Way, edited by the Reverend James Love, published by the American Bible Church. Address: 3100 Godby Road, 11-F, College Park, Georgia 30349.

The Northern Lights Glimmer, a newsletter published by the Alaskan Patriots in Action. Address: Box 8853, Anchorage, Alaska 99508.

Freedom, published by the Church of Scientology. Address: North Berendo Street, Los Angeles, California 90027.

The World Peace News, edited by William Conklin, published by the Church of World Peace. Address: 3296 Raleigh, Denver, Colorado 80212.

Men and Money, published by the Committee for Monetary Research and Education. Address: P.O. Box 1630, Greenwood, Connecticut 06836.

Research Reports, published by the American Institute for Economic Research, Great Barrington, Massachusetts 02130.

Pro Se Litigants. Address: 807 Carlisle, Independence, Missouri 64054.

The Upright Ostrich. Address: P.O. Box 100787, Fort Lauderdale, Florida 23110.

The Arizona Patriot, edited by Ty Hardin. Address: P.O. Box 2281, Prescott, Arizona 86302.

The American Patriot and *The Fact Finder*, edited and produced by Harry Everingham, published by the Arizona Breakfast Club. Addresses: P.O. Drawer A, Scottsdale, Arizona 85252 and P.O. Box 10555, Phoenix, Arizona 85065.

The Liberty Amendment News, edited by Armen Moths. Address: Box 2388, El Cajon, California 92021.

Tough Talk, a monthly newsletter, edited by Marvin Cooley. Address: 525 E. Baseline Road, Mesa, Arizona 85204.

Lyke Publications, Inc., Economic News Review and Economic Digest. Address: P.O. Box 94425, Schaumburg, Illinois 60194.

The Bulletin, edited and produced by Archibald E. Roberts, published by the Committee to Restore the Constitution. Address: P.O. Box 986, Fort Collins, Colorado 80522.

The Financial and Security Digest and *The Financial Professional*, edited and published by Robert White. Address: P.O. Box 1928, Cocoa, Florida 32922.

Educational Research Report, prepared and issued by Dr. George Arlen. Covers such issues as trusts and various types of litigation involving the IRS. Published by the American Patriots Association. Address: 122 Spanish Village, #637, Dallas, Texas 75248.

The Journal of Freedom, edited by D. L. Kimball. Address: P.O. Box 158, Fayette, Iowa 52142.

The Freeman, a monthly journal of Ideas on Liberty, edited by Paul L. Poirot. Address: 30 South Broadway, Irvington-on-Hudson, New York 10553.

Index